Crisis Intervention Training
For Disaster Workers

An Introduction

GEORGE W. DOHERTY

Rocky Mountain
Disaster Mental Health Institute Press

Learning from the Past and Planning For the Future

Rocky Mountain DMH Institute Press is an Imprint of Loving Healing Press

Rocky Mountain Disaster Mental Health Institute, Inc.
PO Box 786
Laramie, WY 82073-0786

http://www.rmrinstitute.org
email: rockymountain@mail2emergency.com
Phone: 307-399-4818

Library of Congress Cataloging-in-Publication Data

Doherty, George W. (George William)
 Crisis intervention training for disaster workers : an introduction / by George W. Doherty.
     p. cm.
 Includes bibliographical references and index.
 ISBN-13: 978-1-932690-42-2 (pbk. : alk. paper)
 ISBN-10: 1-932690-42-5 (pbk. : alk. paper)
 1. Crisis intervention (Mental health services)--Handbooks, manuals, etc. I. Title.
 RC480.6.D64 2007
 362.2'04251--dc22

                                        2007028458

Rocky Mountain DMH Institute Press is an Imprint of:

Loving Healing Press   http://www.LovingHealing.com
5145 Pontiac Trail   info@LovingHealing.com
Ann Arbor, MI 48105   Fax +1 734 663 6861
USA

Contents and Course Outline

Table of Figures

About the Cover – Medicine Bow Peak

The Medicine Bow Mountains are a mountain range in the Rocky Mountains in southern Wyoming and in northern Colorado. From the northern end of the Front Range, the range extends north from Cameron Pass along the border between Larimer and Jackson counties in Colorado northward into south central Wyoming west of Laramie, in Albany and Carbon counties to the route of the Union Pacific Railroad. The highest peak in the range is Medicine Bow Peak (12,013 ft), located in the northern end of the range in southwestern Albany County, Wyoming. Much of the range is located within the Medicine Bow National Forest. The range runs northward from the Never Summer Mountains on the continental divide. On its eastern flank it is drained by the Laramie River, another tributary of the North Platte. In Wyoming this range is known as the Snowy Range.

United Airlines Flight 409 was a scheduled flight departing from Denver, Colorado to Salt Lake City, Utah on October 6, 1955. The DC-4 aircraft crashed into Medicine Bow Peak, near Centennial, Wyoming killing all 66 people on board (63 passengers, 3 crew members.) Passengers included members of the Mormon Tabernacle Choir, and military personnel. At the time, this was the worst crash in U.S. commercial aviation history.

Flight 409 left Denver, Colorado at 6:33 AM that morning, some 83 minutes after its scheduled departure time. The flight path 409 was expected to take was north of Laramie, Wyoming, then over the town of Rock River, Wyoming, and onward to Salt Lake City.

The plane did not report in over the town of Rock Springs at 8:11 AM as expected. With the plane's status unknown, the Civil Aeronautics Authority was notified of the missing craft. No radar was in place for civil aviation in this region in 1955. With no radar traces, manual searches were required to find the aircraft.

The Wyoming Air National Guard dispatched two planes, one of which found the aircraft's wreckage atop Medicine Bow Peak. The pilot of the search plane, Mel Conine, speculated that the plane may have been taking an unauthorized shortcut away from its specified flight plan in an effort to make up for its 83 minute delay out of Denver.

Recovery of passenger and crew remains were extremely difficult and took a full five days to complete. Small fragments of flight 409's airframe still exist on this mountaintop. Flight 409's crash, and other crashes which occurred shortly after convinced the U.S. Congress to improve airline safety procedures, and increase the use of radar for civil aviation.

Goals and Objectives

GOALS: This course will introduce you to disasters, the community response, the role of first responders, and the role of Disaster Mental Health Services and Critical Incident Stress management responders and teams. It will provide a brief overview of Disaster Mental Health Services and Critical Incident Stress Management and their roles in responding to the needs of both victims and disaster workers. The role of critical incident stress management will be presented and discussed both for disasters and for critical incidents. This includes discussion about war, terrorism and the follow-up responses by mental health professionals.

Objectives

Following completion of this course, you should be able to:

- Describe what disasters are and how they affect people and their communities.

- Identify how the community, including voluntary and community organizations, government, business, and labor, work together to prepare for, respond to, and recover from disasters.

- Identify activities in preparing for, responding to, and recovering from disasters.

- Describe the mental health services provided to people affected by disaster.

- Identify how disaster mental health professionals provide these services.

- Describe the roles mental health professionals play in Disaster Services and Critical Incident Stress Management.

- Identify the skills and abilities you have that you would like to apply as a volunteer with Disaster Services and Critical Incident Stress Management as a team member.

- Define 'crisis intervention" as it relates to disaster situations and critical incidents.

- Identify the stages of disaster recovery and problems associated with each stage.

- Identify the signs and symptoms of disaster induced stress and emotional trauma.

- Discuss and be able to recognize disaster's and critical incident's effects and impacts on victims and workers, including posttraumatic stress.

- Identify common strategies for coping with disaster and critical incident related stress.

- Demonstrate basic disaster mental health professional responses to disaster related crisis situations/scenarios.

Course Content

The content of this course includes general theory and models of Disaster Mental Health, Critical Incident Stress Management, crisis intervention techniques commonly used in these situations, supportive research, and practice of approaches used in responding to the victims, workers and communities affected by disasters, critical incidents and terrorism threats.

1 Introduction

Working with survivors following the loss of loved ones, homes, property or community is one role of disaster mental health professionals. Besides meeting their basic physical needs, clients will need to understand the grieving process, which may extend for a prolonged period of time. Disaster mental health professionals also work with first responders and other responders to disasters and critical incidents. Their role here is to assist in keeping responders on the job and to help mitigate post-traumatic stress.

Throughout this course, you will learn why Critical Incident Stress Management, Defusing, Debriefing and other forms of crisis intervention have important roles in alleviating disaster induced stress and in preventing further psychological complications among victims and first responders.

Definitions

A crisis is defined in terms of an individual's response to a situation rather than in terms of the situation itself. The same situation may produce a crisis in one person, but not in another. A crisis exists when a person feels so threatened in a situation that he/she cannot cope with it. Their normal resources for dealing with an emergency break down and the individual becomes immobilized. Thus, a crisis exists IN a person. The individual may become confused and overwhelmed by the situation and unable to meet the demands placed upon him/her. It is therefore understandable that a disaster may produce a crisis reaction in an individual, whether they are a survivor or a responder.

A crisis may also be an important learning experience for an individual. Normal patterns of behavior have fallen apart, leaving defenses down. The individual is open and accepting of help in problem solving in order to restore his/her equilibrium. New coping skills and strategies may be developed to assist with this as well as future crises which may occur.

Following are some of the definitions of major techniques which are commonly used by disaster mental health professionals to assist responders and victims who may have experienced a disaster related crisis.

Crisis Intervention: Focuses on providing immediate emotional support (psychological first aid) at times when a person's own resources appear to have failed to adequately cope with a problem.

Critical Incident Stress: The reactions that occur during or immediately after the actual incident, disaster or stressor.

Defusing: An on-scene opportunity for responders involved in a stressful incident to vent their feelings, and institute coping strategies which can reduce stress while they are still working in the assignment setting.

Debriefing: An organized approach to supporting disaster responders who have been involved in emergency operations under conditions of extreme stress in order to assist in mitigating long-term emotional trauma. Usually done at the end of an assignment as part of exiting procedure to assist the responder in putting closure on the experience.

Critical Incident: Any situation faced by emergency responders or survivors that causes them to experience unusually strong emotional reactions which have the potential to interfere with their ability to function, either on the scene or later.

<table>
<tr><td>

2

</td><td>

Fundamentals

</td><td>

</td></tr>
</table>

Fundamentals of Victims' Responses to Disasters

In order to fully understand the necessity for and functions of a *Crisis Intervention Team*, it is important to have a basic understanding of the psychological factors which influence the emotional responses of disaster victims and responders. This section presents and discusses the basics of those factors and the resulting commonly observed responses of survivors and responders.

Loss, Mourning, and Grief

All survivors of disaster suffer loss. They suffer loss of safety and security, loss of property, loss of community, loss of status, loss of beauty, loss of health, or loss of a loved one. Following a disaster, all individuals begin a natural and normal recovery process through mourning and grief.

In our western culture, we put emphasis on life and youth. We often refuse to think about death. It is normal to be upset by a major loss—and then to suffer because of it. Bereavement is always deeply painful when the connection that has been broken is of any importance. The loss which is the reason for our mourning most often involves a person close to us. However, it can also be a familiar animal, an object to which we are very attached, or a value we have held dear. In mourning, the connection with what we have lost is more important than the nature of the lost object itself.

Grief is the process of working through all the thoughts, memories and emotions associated with that loss, until an acceptance is reached which allows the person to place the event in proper perspective. Theories of stages of grief resolution provide general guidelines about possible sequential steps a person *may* go through prior to reaching acceptance of the event. These stages include: Denial, Anger, Bargaining, Depression, and Acceptance (see Fig. 2-1). Whereas these theories provide general guidelines, each person must grieve according to his or her own values and time line. However, some persons will have trouble recovering emotionally and may not begin the process of mourning effectively. This may result in troubling and painful emotional side effects. Sometimes these side effects may not appear immediately. They may remain beneath the surface until another crisis brings the emotions out into the open. Hence, many individuals may be surprised by an increase in emotionality around the third month, sixth month, and one year anniversaries of the event. Crisis intervention can assist victims and facilitate their progress in proceeding through the predictable phases of mourning, thus avoiding surprise reactions or emotional paralysis later.

• Denial
• Anger
• Bargaining
• Depression
• Acceptance

Fig. 2–1 Stages of Grieving (Kübler–Ross)

Grief is the process of working through all the thoughts, memories, and emotions associated with a loss, until an acceptance is reached that allows the person to place the event into the proper perspective. Some typical reactions to grief might include:

- People who say they are drained of energy, purpose and faith. They feel like they are dead.

- Victims who insist they do not have time to work through the grief with "all the other things that have to be done", and ignore their grief.

- People who insist they have "recovered" in only a few weeks after the disaster, and who are probably mistaking denial for recovery.

- Victims who focus only on the loss and are unable to take any action toward their own recovery.

- Each of these extreme emotional states is very common, very counter-productive, and requires active crisis intervention.

Stages of Grieving

Denial: At the news of a misfortune, tragedy or disaster, our first reaction is not to accept it, but to refuse it ("No, it's not true! No! It's not possible!"). The opposite would be abnormal. This is a sign that it is essential for our psychological organization to avoid pain without ignoring reality. This refusal is, at the same time, the beginning of an awareness of the horrible reality and is aimed at protecting us from the violence of the shock.

Anger: A feeling of anger is experienced at the fact of our powerlessness in the face of something imposed on us arbitrarily. This anger is inevitable and it must be permitted. It allows the expression of our helplessness at the situation. Therefore, it isn't surprising that survivors (and sometimes responders) take out their anger on the people around them (government and municipal officials, rescue personnel, insurance companies, their families and friends, etc.). Hence, there is the need to be able to verbalize and vent this anger in post-traumatic sessions with a counselor.

Depression: The path toward the acceptance of bereavement passes through the stage of depression. At the beginning of mourning, and for a long time after during this stage of depression, the lost being is omnipresent. Of course, he or she is lost to us in reality we agree and we are trying to accept it. However, inside, we reinforce our connection to him or her, because we no longer have it in objective reality. This process of intense re-appropriation allows us, at the same time, both to lessen our pain and to console ourselves in a way by means of the temporary survival of the loved being within us. At the same time, this movement enables the work of detachment to be carried out little by little.

Generally, slowly over time, these movements of detachment become less frequent, the pain subsides, the sadness lessens, the lost being seems less present and his or her importance tends to decrease. The end of mourning is approaching.

Acceptance: This stage is neither happy nor unhappy. Mourning leaves a scar as does any wound. But the self once again becomes free to live, love and create. One is surprised to find oneself looking toward the future, making plans. It is the end of mourning.

The normal process of mourning takes place over a period of several months.

Returning To Equilibrium

Mental health is described by Antoine Parot as "a psychic ability to function in a harmonious, agreeable, effective manner when circumstances allow, to cope flexibly with difficult situations and to reestablish one's dynamic equilibrium after a test."

Every time a *stressful event* happens, there are certain recognized compensating factors which can help promote a *return to equilibrium.* These include:

- Perception of the event by the individual

- The situational reports which are available

- Mechanisms of adaptation

The presence or absence of such factors will make all the difference in one's return to a state of equilibrium. The strength or weakness of one or more of these factors may be directly related to the initiation or resolution of a crisis.

Why Do Some People Reach A State Of Crisis?

When stress originates externally, *internal changes* occur. This is why certain events can cause a strong emotional reaction in one person and leave another indifferent. There are a number of factors that contribute to how one reacts to an event. These include the following:

Perception of the event

- **When the event is perceived realistically**: There is an awareness of the relationship between the event and the sensations of stress, which in itself will reduce the tension. It is likely that the state of stress will be resolved effectively.

- **When the perception of the event is distorted:** There is no awareness of the connection between the event and the feeling of stress. Any attempt to resolve the problem will be affected accordingly.

- **Hypotheses to verify concerning the individual's perception of the event:**
    - What meaning does the event have in the person's eyes?
    - How will it affect his/her future?
    - Is he/she able to look at it realistically? Or does he/she misinterpret its meaning?

Support by the Natural Network

Support by the natural network means the support given by people in the individual's immediate circle who are accessible and who can be relied on to help at that time. In a stressful situation, the lack or inadequacy of resources can leave an individual in a vulnerable position conducive to a state of disequilibrium or crisis.

Mechanisms of Adaptation

These mechanisms reduce the tension and help promote adaptation to stressful situations. They can be activated consciously or *unconsciously*. Throughout life, individuals learn to use various methods to adapt to anxiety and reduce tension. These mechanisms aim at maintaining and protecting their equilibrium. When an event happens which causes stress,

Phase	Time Frame of Phase	Emotions	Behaviors	Most Important Resources
Heroic	Occurs at time of impact and period immediately afterward.	Altruism. All emotions are strong and direct at this time.	Use of energy to save their own and others' lives and property.	Family groups, neighbors, and emergency teams.
Honeymoon	From 1 week to 3 to 6 months after the disaster.	Strong sense of having shared a catastrophe experience and lived through it. Expectations of great assistance from official and government resources.	Victims clear out debris and wreckage buoyed by promises of great help in rebuilding their lives.	Pre-existing community groups and emergent community groups which develop from specific needs caused by disaster.
Disillusionment	Lasts from 2 months to 1 or even 2 years.	Strong sense of disappointment, anger, resentment and bitterness appear if there are delays, failures, or unfulfilled hopes or promises of aid.	People concentrate on rebuilding their own lives and solving individual problems. The feeling of "shared community" is lost.	Many outside agencies may now pull out. Indigenous community agencies may weaken. Alternative resources may need to be explored.
Reconstruction	Lasts for several years following the disaster.	Victims realize that they need to solve the problem of rebuilding their lives. Visible recovery efforts serve to reaffirm belief in themselves and the community. If recovery efforts are delayed, emotional problems which appear may be serious and intense.	People have assumed the responsibility for their own recovery. New construction programs and plans reaffirm belief in capabilities and ability to recover.	Community groups with a long-term investment in the community and its people become key elements in this phase.

Fig. 2-2: Stages of Disaster Recovery

and the learned mechanisms of adaptation are not effective, the discomfort is experienced at a *conscious level.*

Stages of Disaster Recovery

Just as there are stages of individual grieving, there are also stages of disaster in communities. The emotional responses of a community can be very closely tied together with emotional responses of individuals.

Heroic Stage

The Heroic Stage lasts from impact or pre-impact to approximately one week post impact (this will be longer with more severe widespread events. e.g., Hurricane Katrina). People respond to the demands of the situation by performing heroic acts to save lives and property. There is a sense of sharing with others who have been through the same experience. There is almost a feeling of "family", even with strangers. There is immediate support from family members both in and out of the area and by agency and governmental disaster personnel promising assistance. Feelings of euphoria are common. There is strong media support for the plight of the victims and the needs of the community. Activity levels are high. However, efficiency levels are low. Pain and loss, including physical pain, may not be recognized.

The most important resources during the Heroic Stage are family, neighbors, and emergency service responders.

During the immediate post-impact phases, responders react and respond with high levels of energy, and seek information and facts. They develop and coordinate plans, equipment and staff resources. Following the impact, adrenaline levels are high. Responders continue to push themselves through the stress signals and past warnings.

Honeymoon Stage

The Honeymoon Stage follows the Heroic Stage and may last for several weeks following the disaster. In the early parts of this stage, many survivors, even those who have sustained major losses, are feeling a sense of well-being for having survived. Shelters may at first be seen as central meeting places to talk about shared experiences. They are also seen as being a safe place to stay until they can return to their homes. Supported and encouraged by the promises of assistance by disaster relief personnel from voluntary and federal agencies, survivors clear the dirt and debris from their homes in anticipation of the help they believe will restore their lives.

The community as a whole pulls together in initial clean-up and distribution of supplies. Church and civic groups become active in meeting the various needs of the community. "Super Volunteers" who are not ready to deal with their own losses work from dawn until after dark helping their friends and neighbors get back on their feet. In the early parts of this stage, the community's expectations of the various volunteer and governmental agencies are extremely high. Their faith in those organizations' ability to help them recover is frequently unrealistic.

Some of the common emotional reactions during this stage include: adrenaline rush, anxiety, anger and frustration, survival guilt, restlessness, workaholism, risk-taking behaviors and hyperactivity.

Disaster mental health professionals can assist during this stage by educating about common stress reactions and coping techniques, working with distressed clients, advocating for breaks and time off, defusing workers, team building, etc.

Disillusionment Stage

The greatest amount of frustration in the recovery process happens during the time it takes to process relief forms. The disaster event may be 3 or more weeks in the past before a disaster declaration is made. This time can be called a "Second Disaster". It is usually the period when the greatest amount of stress is seen because continual stressors are added to those experienced in the initial event. Victims must be encouraged to ventilate their built-up emotional energy.

The disillusionment Stage lasts from one month to one or even two or more years. As the Honeymoon Stage passes into the Disillusionment Stage, the excitement of the media attention in the earlier stages begins to wane. Rather than feeling supported by the media, victims begin to feel that they are objects of insensitive curiosity. At the same time, they feel let down and isolated when the media no longer covers the story and moves on to other, fresher news. The departure of the media at the same time victims are beginning to dig out can be extremely upsetting.

Victims begin to ask for answers, especially if the disaster could have been avoided, or if negligence of a person or agency was involved. Community support at this stage can be extremely important in determining the course of recovery.

During this stage, disaster mental health professionals work with clients, offer debriefings, defusings, and other crisis interventions for staff, mediate problems between staff and supervisors or clients, advocate for time off, educate about methods to decrease stress, and assist with team building as centers begin to consolidate and/or close down.

Reconstruction Stage

The final stage is the Reconstruction Stage. Victims come to the realization that the rebuilding of homes and businesses is primarily their responsibility. The rebuilding of the community reaffirms the victims' belief in themselves and the community. This stage may take from several years to the rest of their lives, depending on the amount of damage. If the rebuilding is delayed, the recovery process will also be delayed.

Many of the disaster related stress reactions will return when conditions are right for another disaster similar to the one the victims have experienced.

When the emergency response phase of the disaster is over, responders return to business as usual at their routine jobs. They may experience frustration and loss after the intensity of the emergency situation. Local staff may also be victims, thus facing job pressures, as well as feeling overwhelmed by needs to complete their own recovery, feelings of loss, depression, anger, etc. By providing crisis intervention following a disaster it is hoped that both responders and survivors can develop effective coping mechanisms that will assist them through the stages of recovery with less long term emotional impact.

Summary

This section has discussed how all disaster victims proceed through recognized stages of grieving, from denial to acceptance. Also, just as there are recognized stages of grieving, there are recognized stages of disaster and expected individual and community reactions during the different stages. By understanding these stages, it will help you to better understand how disaster victims and responders may react psychologically. As a result, you will be better able to meet the emotional needs that arise due to disaster.

Symptoms of Psychological Trauma

In a person's life when there occur events which threaten his/her biological, physical or social well-being, there is a resulting disequilibrium. When this well-being is threatened, people react with anxiety. When there are a particularly large number of painful or unpleasant stimuli like those associated with a disaster or tragedy, the individual requires a great capacity for adaptation. The mental health literature describes the stress following disaster and tragedy as a precise set of symptoms manifested after an extraordinary traumatic event.

Symptoms of disaster caused stress will vary greatly based on an individual's prior history of personal trauma, age and ethnic background. Some of the typical symptoms experienced by both victims and responders are briefly discussed below.

- Individuals may have an exaggerated startle response or exhibit hyper-vigilance. This is frequently seen after earthquakes, where people are known to jump after loud or sudden noises, such as doors slamming or trucks rumbling by.

- They may experience phobias about weather conditions (e.g., responses to wind noises following a tornado or hurricane) or other reminders that the accident or situation could happen again.

- They may experience difficulty with memory or calculations.

- Suddenly, they cannot balance their checkbook, or remember simple tasks, appointments, or such things as their address or phone number when asked.

- They may exhibit anger or even rage over their lack of control over the occurrence and their impotence at preventing it and protecting their families.

- Many times this may be displaced towards those who are trying to help.

BASIC ID

Typical stress reactions to disaster trauma can be assessed by adapting the multi-modal behavioral approach initially outlined by Lazarus (1976, 1989, 2000). He used the acronym *BASIC ID* to identify areas of concern for assessment (see Fig. 2-3 on next 3 pages).

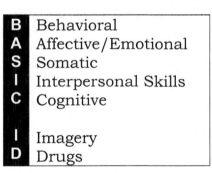

B	Behavioral
A	Affective/Emotional
S	Somatic
I	Interpersonal Skills
C	Cognitive
I	Imagery
D	Drugs

Behavioral Responses	
• Hyper startle response	• Worried, rigid look, nervous activity
• Hyperactivity	• Withdrawal or social isolation
• Workaholism	
• Reckless, risk-taking behaviors	• Inability to express self verbally or in writing
• Carelessness in tasks, leading to an increase in injuries	• Difficulty returning to normal activity
• Excessive use of sick leave	• Avoidance of places or activities that are reminders of the event
	• Sexual problems

Affective/Emotional	
• Initial euphoria and relief	• Shame or anger over vulnerability
• Survival guilt	
• Anxiety, fear, insecurity	• Irritability, restlessness, hyper-excitability, agitation
• Pervasive concern over well being of loved ones	• Anger, rage, blame (often directed at those attempting to help)
• Feelings of helplessness, hopelessness	
• Uncontrolled mood swings, periods of crying	• Frustration, cynicism, negativity
• Apathy, isolation, detachment	• Despair, grief, sadness
	• Depression and withdrawal

Fig. 2-3: continued

Somatic	
• Vague body complaints • Muscle aches and pains • Fatigue or generalized weakness • Sleep disturbances • Increased or decreased heart rate or blood pressure • Feeling of pounding heart or pulse • Increase in allergies, colds, flu, headaches	• Trouble breathing or "getting breath" • Tightness in chest, throat or stomach • Sweating • Feelings of heaviness in arms or legs • Numbness or tingling • Changes in appetite or weight • Nausea or GI upsets • Trembling, dizziness or fainting

Imagery
• Sleep disturbances • Nightmares • Flashbacks and recurrent dreams of event • Intrusive thoughts about event • Ruminations about event

Cognitive	
• Inability to concentrate • Difficulty with calculations • Confusion, slowness of thought • Impaired decision making • Amnesia • Preoccupation with event	• Loss of objectivity • Rigidity • Loss of faith • Increased awareness of one's own and loved ones' vulnerability • Repetitive thoughts, memories, ruminations about event • Loss of judgment

Fig. 2-3: continued

Interpersonal Skills
• Irritability and anger towards others
• Family and relationship problems
• Disruption of work, school or social relationships

Drugs/Alcohol
• Increased use of alcohol
• Increased use of drugs

Fig. 2-3: BASIC ID explained

| **3** | # Children and Disasters |  |

Children's Reactions

Children in crisis present a complex challenge. Children in various age groups have specific needs and respond differently to the same crisis event. A serious problem in working with children in crisis situations is that the responders tend to become emotionally involved with the children they are attempting to help. Emotional involvement frequently interferes with proper crisis management.

Reactions of children to a disaster can have both short term and long term effects. A child's view of his or her world as safe and predictable is temporarily lost. Most children have difficulty understanding the damage, injuries, or death that can result from an unexpected or uncontrollable event.

A basic principle in working with children who have experienced a disaster is relating to them as essentially normal children who have experienced a great deal of stress. Most of the problems that appear are likely to be directly related to the disaster and are transitory in nature. Relief from stress and the passage of time will help re-establish equilibrium and functioning for most children without outside help.

Children will often express anger and fear after a disaster. These will be evidenced through continuing anxieties about recurrence of the event, injury, death, or separation and loss. In dealing with children's fears and anxieties, it is best to accept them as being very real to the child. The reactions of the adults around them can also make a great deal of difference in their recovery from the shock of a disaster.

Preschool Children

Children's perceptions of a disaster are primarily determined by the reactions of their parents. Children of preschool age believe that their parents can protect them from all danger. They believe they cannot survive without them. They fear being injured, lost, or abandoned and these fears increase when they find themselves alone or among strangers.

Adults should be aware that the fertile imagination of preschool children makes them more fearful. Three levels of anxiety in pre-school children in a disaster can be identified:

1. **Contagious Anxiety:** This type of anxiety is transmitted by adults. It can be easily handled in difficult circumstances in a child who is not normally anxious by placing the child in calming surroundings.

2. **True or Objective Anxiety:-** This is related to the child's capacity for understanding the nature of the danger threatening him/her and his/her tendency to create fantasies based on concrete events. The child is really afraid because he/she does not know the causes and dangers felt to be threatening. For example, it is useless to try to convince a child that thunder and lightening present no danger if the child does not understand their causes.

   One can respond to the objective fears of children of this age by taking into account their degree of maturity and type of imagination. Adults should help them live through the event and conquer their fears to help prevent the fears from persisting into adulthood.

3. **Profound Anxiety:** Different from fear, this involves separation anxiety. The child fears losing those close to him/her. Everything seems dangerous. Fear is omnipresent.

Generally, young children express themselves little verbally. It is their behavior that reveals their anxiety and fear.

The intensity and duration of a child's symptoms (Fig. 3-1) decrease more rapidly when his or her family or other significant adults are able to indicate that they understand his or her feelings. Children are most fearful when they do not understand what is going on around them. Every effort should be made to keep them accurately informed, thereby relieving their anxieties. Talking with children, providing simple accurate information about the disaster, and listening to what they have to say are probably the most important things we can do. Sharing the fact that adults were frightened too and that it is normal and natural to be afraid is also reassuring to a child. It is comforting to hear "fear is natural. Everybody is afraid at times."

Sleep disturbances are very common for children following a disaster. Behavior is likely to take the form of resistance to bedtime, wakefulness, unwillingness to sleep in their own rooms or beds, refusal to sleep by themselves, desire to be in a parent's bed or to sleep with a light, and insistence that the parent stay in the room until they fall asleep. These behaviors are disruptive to a child's well being. They also increase stress for parents. Some of the more persistent bedtime problems, like night terrors, nightmares, and refusal to fall asleep may point to deep-seated fears and anxieties which may require professional intervention.

When talking with clients with children, it is helpful to explore the family's sleep arrangements. They may need to develop a familiar bedtime routine. This might include reinstating a specific time for going to bed. The family may find it helpful to plan calming, pre-bedtime activities to help reduce chaos in the evening. Developing a quiet recreation which includes the whole family as participants can also be helpful.

• Crying, depression, withdrawal and isolation • Regressive behaviors including thumb sucking, bedwetting, clinging behaviors • Increased fighting, anger, rages • Nightmares and sleep disturbances, including fear of sleeping alone, night terrors, fear of falling asleep	• Not wanting to attend school or other athletic or social events • Headaches, rashes, GI upsets, nausea • Changes in appetite • Fears of future disasters • Fears about death, injury and loss • Separation anxiety or fear • Loss of interest in school and routine activities s

Fig. 3-1: Children's Reactions to Disaster

Ages 6-12

The attitude of the family and the environment have great influence on the degree of anxiety experienced by the child and on what mechanisms the child uses in both the short and long term to cope with stressful situations or events.

The reaction may be immediate or delayed, brief or prolonged, intense or minimal. The child reacts with his/her present personality at a given level of biological and emotional development. The nature and intensity of the reaction will be determined by the child's temperament as well as past experiences. Faced with the same stressful situation, two children may react in entirely different ways. These reactions suggest the adaptations the child is making to assimilate, cope with, and "accept" the painful situation.

The reactions most often expressed will translate in various ways the child's anxiety and his/her defenses against it. These will vary with the age of the child. They include: fear, sleep disturbances, nightmares, loss of appetite, aggressiveness, anger, refusal to go to school, behavioral problems, lack of interest in school, inability to concentrate in school or at play. Sometimes these difficulties occur only in school. Sometimes they only occur at home with the child functioning adequately in the school environment.

An anxious child needs security and, above all, love. The role of the adult consists of helping the child psychologically and trying to understand him/her.

Children can be spared much anxiety if we try to imagine their reaction to the event. Seeing through the child's eyes helps the adult to prepare the child emotionally to face events calmly and confidently as they occur.

Reactions can be prevented or lessened by clarifying the situation through open communication about the traumatic event or situation by those close to the child.

Fears and Anxieties

Fear is a normal reaction to disaster, frequently expressed through continuing anxieties about recurrence of the disaster, injury, death, separation and loss. Because children's fears and anxieties after a disaster often seem strange and unconnected to anything specific in their lives, their relationship to the disaster may be difficult to determine. In dealing with children's fears and anxieties, it is generally best to accept them as being very real to the children. For example, children's fears of returning to the room or school they were in when the disaster struck should be accepted at face value. Treatment efforts should begin with talking about those experiences and reactions.

Before the family can help, however, the children's needs must be understood. This requires an understanding of the family's needs. Families have their own shared beliefs, values, fears and anxieties. Frequently, the children's malfunctioning is a mirror of something wrong in the family. Dissuading them of their fears will not prove effective if their families have the same fears and continue to reinforce them. A family interview should be conducted in which the interviewer can observe the relationship of the children and their families, conceptualize the dynamics of the child-family interactions, and involve the family in a self-help system.

The parents' or adults' reactions to the children make a great difference in their recovery. The intensity and duration of the children's symptoms decrease more rapidly when the families are able to indicate that they understand their feelings. When the children feel that their parents do not understand their fears, they feel ashamed, rejected, and unloved. Tolerance of temporary regressive behavior allows the children to re-develop anew those coping patterns which had been functioning before. Praise offered for positive behavior produces positive change. Routine rules need to be relaxed to allow time for regressive behaviors to run their course and the re-integration process to take place.

When the children show excessive clinging and unwillingness to let their parents out of their sight, they are actually expressing and handling their fears and anxieties of separation or loss most appropriately. They have detected the harmful effects of being separated from their parents and, in their clinging, are trying to prevent a possible recurrence. Generally, the children's fears dissolve when the threat of danger has dissipated and they feel secure once more under the parents' protection.

Children are most fearful when they do not understand what is happening around them. Every effort should be made to keep them accurately informed, thereby alleviating their anxieties. Adults, frequently failing to realize the capacity of children to absorb factual information, do not share what they know, and children receive only partial or erroneous information. Children are developing storehouses of all kinds of information and respond to scientific facts and figures, new language, technical terms, and predictions. Following the 1971 earthquake, the children in Los Angeles were observed to become instant experts. The language used by them in a daycare setting was enriched by technical terms, such as Richter Scale, aftershock, temblor, etc. The children learned these new words from the media and incorporated them readily, using them in play and in talking with each other.

The family should make an effort to remain together as much as possible, for a disaster is a time when the children need their significant adults around them. In addition, the model the adults present at this time can be growth enhancing. For example, when the parents act with strength and calmness, maintaining control at the same time they share feelings of being afraid, they serve the purpose of letting the children see that it is possible to act courageously even in times of stress and fear.

Sleep Disturbances

Sleep disturbances are among the most common problems for children following a disaster. Their behavior is likely to take the form of resistance to bedtime, wakefulness, unwillingness to sleep in their own rooms or beds, refusal to sleep by themselves, desire to be in a parent's bed or to sleep with a light, insistence that the parent stay in the room until they fall asleep, and excessively early rising. Such behaviors are disruptive to a child's well-being. They also increase stress for the parents, who may themselves be experiencing some adult counterpart of their child's disturbed sleep behavior. More persistent bedtime problems, such as night terrors, nightmares, continued awakening at night, and refusal to fall asleep may point to deep-seated fears and anxieties which may require professional intervention.

It is helpful to explore the family's sleep arrangements. The family may need to develop a familiar bedtime routine, such as reinstating a specific time for going to bed. They may find it helpful to plan calming, pre-bedtime activities to reduce chaos in the evening. Teenagers may need to have special consideration for bedtime privacy. Developing a quiet recreation in which the total family participates is also helpful.

Other bedtime problems of children, such as refusing to go to their rooms or to sleep by themselves, frequent awakening at night, or nightmares can be met by greater understanding and flexibility on the part of the parents. The child may be allowed to sleep in the parents' bedroom on a mattress or in a crib, or may be moved into another child's room. A time limit on how long the change will continue should be agreed upon by both parents and child, and it should be adhered to firmly. Some children are satisfied if the parents spend a little extra time in the bedroom with them. If they come out of bed at night, they should be returned to it gently, with the reassurance of a nearby adult presence. Having a night light or leaving the door ajar are both helpful. Getting angry, punishing, spanking, or shouting at the child rarely helps and more frequently makes the situation worse. Sometimes, it becomes clear that it is actually the parent who is fearful of leaving the child alone.

Parents from middle-class families have been educated to believe that allowing their child to sleep in the parents' room has long-lasting deleterious effects on the child. Families accustomed to overcrowded and shared sleeping space have less trouble in allowing children to be close to them. Closeness between parents and children at bedtime reduces the children's and adults' fears.

Providing families with information on how to handle bedtime fears can best be done in the family setting or with groups of families meeting together. The families feel reassured upon learning that what they are experiencing is a normal, natural response, and that time and comfort are great healers. Learning that the sleep disturbance behavior is a problem shared with other families is reassuring.

School Avoidance and School Phobias

It is important for children and teenagers to attend school since, for the most part, the school is the center of life with peers. The school becomes the major source of activity, guidance, direction, and structure for the child. When a child avoids school, it may generally be assumed that a serious problem exists. One of the reasons for not going to school may be fear of leaving the family and being separated from loved ones. The fear may actually be a reflection of the family's insecurity about the child's absence from the home. Some high achieving children may be afraid of failing and, once they have missed some time at school, may have concern about returning. The low performers may find that the chaos of disaster makes it even more difficult for them to concentrate. School authorities should be flexible in the ways they encourage children to attend school.

Programs designed for schools vary. Some projects involve teachers and school counselors, while others provide trained workers who have direct contact with the children and the teachers. In some instances, management within the school setting is advantageous. Troubled children can be identified by their behavior in both the classroom and on the playground. Some of the signs are fighting and crying in school for no apparent reason, increased motor activity, withdrawal, inattentiveness, marked drop in school performance, school phobia, rapid mood changes, incessant talking about the disaster, and marked sensitivity to weather changes. Puppetry and psychodrama conducted by a counselor or teacher in the classroom or in special groups are helpful in re-enacting the disaster. They may be followed by discussions and reports by the children of their own experiences in the event. Field trips to disaster sites may be arranged, and group meetings with students and parents may be held. Coloring books, word puzzles, connect-the-dot pictures, and arithmetic problems about the disaster build self-confidence. Class projects may be developed in which all the information about the disaster or a previous similar one is collected and made into a book with color drawings. Craft models or replications (such as dams, earthquake geology, volcanoes, rivers, etc.) may be built. Puppets may be made and used to re-enact the disaster.

Children can be encouraged to construct their own games as a way of mastering the feelings associated with the disaster. For example, children play tornado games in which they set up the rules by themselves. In one game, each child is designated as an object, such as a tree, house, car, etc., and one child is the tornado making a noise like a siren and running. The other children begin to run and knock each other over. The "tornado" leaves, and all the children get up and return to their normal activities. Another example has children building a dam in a gutter or ditch and filling it with water. One child then breaks the dam and allows the water to escape harmlessly down the street or into the ditch.

School rap groups are also particularly helpful. Administrative information meetings, teachers' in-service meetings, and parent-teacher meetings can be used for public education. Newsletters and the school newspaper are useful in distributing information among the students. Chat rooms and web-sites on the internet can also be helpful.

Public involvement can be integrated through use of widespread associations, such as Camp Fire Girls, Cub Scouts, Brownies, 4-H, FFA, etc.

Loss, Death and Mourning

It is not unusual for a disaster, particularly a major disaster in which there has been loss of life, to trigger children's questions about death and dying. The fear of the loss of mother or father underlies many of the questions and symptoms a child may develop, such as sleeplessness, night terrors, clinging behavior and others. Often, when loss has occurred, the children's problems are overlooked. No one assists them in handling their reactions to the loss. When a mother or father dies, most children are fearful of what will happen to them if the remaining parent dies as well. Being told that adults will look after them is very reassuring. The children should be encouraged to voice their questions. The adults should be as honest as they can be with their answers. For example, questions about what happens to a person after death can be answered with the statement that the wisest men and women through the ages have tried to answer this question. However, there is no sure answer. Explanations dealing with heaven and hell, or afterlife, or the flat statement that after death there is nothing are confusing to a child.

It is not uncommon for children to make believe that the deceased parent is still alive. They may call the remaining parent or family a liar and deny their parent's death. Some children may go back and forth between believing and not believing that the parent has died and may ask such questions as "When is Daddy coming home from being dead?" or "I know Mommy's dead, but when is she going to make my supper?" Young children may not realize that there is no return from death—not even for a moment.

Many of the same issues that adults struggle with in coming to terms with death are also found in children's struggles. Magical thinking is more prevalent in childhood. Most children, when they are very young, believe that wishing for, or thinking about, something can make it happen. Children who have had angry thoughts or death wishes toward the parent (as most children have at one time or another) need to be reassured that these thoughts did not cause something to happen. Children may believe that fighting with a sibling can cause a parent's death and that ceasing to fight will prevent the other parent from dying. They need reassurance that the parent's or family member's death was not their fault, that it was caused by an accident or illness. It is comforting to be told that there are some things they cannot control, such as parents getting sick or having an accident or dying. These can be contrasted with things they can control, such as the games they play, whether or not they play fairly, whether or not they do their chores and homework.

Both the child and family may suffer loss of pets, property, valuables, and treasured sentimental objects. Such losses may have as much impact on them as the loss of a loved one. A mourning process can be anticipated. When family treasures or sentimental objects are still available, they can be helpful to the mourners. They often provide something tangible as a security object. Families in disaster frequently return to the ruins to retrieve what seem like valueless objects. This is understandable because mourning pertains to the loss of home and objects as well as to loss of loved ones.

Responders need to know that mourning has a purpose and that crying by both a child and an adult is helpful. A child needs to be aware that thoughts about the dead person are likely to come to mind over and over. Forgetting takes time and overt mourning helps them integrate the loss more quickly. The family that expresses concern and annoyance at a child who asks the same questions about death over and over again needs to understand that this is the child's way of adapting to the loss.

Suicidal Ideation

Threats or attempts to injure or kill oneself in latency-age children and younger are rare. However, they are not uncommon among adolescents. Any indication of suicidal feelings must be taken seriously. The most frequent motivation is loss of close family, a sweetheart, and of significant objects such as pets, instruments, or a car. Even loss of the opportunity to participate in team sports for the year may bring on serious depression.

Feelings of helplessness, hopelessness, and worthlessness are strong indicators of suicide potential, expressed verbally or nonverbally through behavioral signs—withdrawal, asocial behavior, loss of interest, apathy, and agitation; physical symptoms—sleep and appetite disturbance; and cognitive process changes—loss of alternatives, poor judgment, and reasoning ability. Evidence of caring and concern are the most immediate, effective elements of help which can be provided by all responders. Generally, however, any person with suicidal ideation should be referred to professional help.

Confusion

A trouble sign that requires immediate attention, confusion implies a deep-seated disturbance which also probably requires referral to a mental health professional. Confusion generally refers to a disorientation in which the young person has lost the ability to sort out incoming stimuli, whether sensory or cognitive. As a result he/she is overwhelmed by a profusion of feelings and thoughts. Associations with familiar objects may be distorted or disappear, regressive behavior may reappear, and feelings displayed may be inappropriate for the occasion. In extreme cases, immobilization or uncontrolled movement may occur. The mental health professional can begin the process of helping to reorient the children by talking to them calmly, by providing them with specific information, and by being caring and understanding.

Antisocial Behavior

Behavior problems—group delinquency, vandalism, stealing, and aggressiveness—have been reported in some communities following a disaster. These behaviors may be a reaction of an adolescent with low self-esteem to community disruption. A major problem for the adolescents is the boredom and isolation from peers which comes from disruption of their usual activities in school and on the playground. One way to counteract this is to involve adolescents and their peers, under adult direction, in clean-up activities which may be therapeutic to the teenagers and beneficial to the community. The adolescents also serve as an excellent resource for helping elderly people and babysitting for families.

It should be remembered, however, that young people of this age have difficulty expressing their fears and anxieties, lest they seem less competent to their peers and themselves. The use of peer rap groups, in which teens can talk about their disaster experiences and ventilate feelings, is helpful in relieving buried anxieties. A "natural" setting for these rap groups, such as school, work or task sites, or wherever teenagers congregate, is desirable. Training teenagers to lead their own rap groups should be considered. Boy Scout and Girl Scout leaders and teachers are natural leaders/trainers.

Children with Special Needs

Two groups of children with special needs are briefly discussed below: those with prior developmental or physical problems; and those who have been injured or become ill as a result of the disaster. Both require more intensive attention in a disaster than normal or less seriously affected children.

The Exceptional Children

Exceptional children are defined as those who have developmental disabilities or physical limitations, such as blindness, hearing impairment, orthopedic handicaps, mental retardation, cerebral palsy, etc. Exceptional children have special needs that require consideration when a disaster occurs. Disasters and their periods of disruption bring additional burdens upon the parents of exceptional children. These parents have problems just in coping with their children's needs on a day-to-day basis. The emotional needs of exceptional children are very likely to be exacerbated by a disaster of any magnitude.

Most exceptional children live in their own homes and receive assistance from community agencies. The agencies, part of the network of human services in the community, may need to be alerted to the special needs of the children in home settings. Exceptional children find it more difficult to function when their usual home environment is damaged or if they are moved to strange surroundings. Helping such children to understand what has occurred requires heightened sensitivity. Generally, it would be desirable to have professionals who normally are in contact with the children assist in providing help. The professionals are able to locate and identify the children in the community and determine what special services they need, such as schooling or medical care.

Exceptional children depend to a greater extent than other children on the consistency and predictability of their environment and the people around them. Familiarity with their surroundings is particularly important to mentally retarded children, who tend to become confused and agitated by traumatic events. One reaction is increased levels of clinging behavior. Parents of these children may need the short-term support of the crisis responder. For example, parents would be helped by learning that their children have greater need for reassurance so that they can anticipate and be tolerant of the increased demands. The parents would also benefit from a crisis group with other parents of exceptional children. Special education teachers can be a source of assistance for the children. In as much as they are persons familiar to the families and children, they can be very effective in assisting both.

Planning in advance for the needs of children in residential settings, such as treatment centers for mentally ill, mentally retarded, or physically handicapped children, and for day programs for children, such as child-care centers and schools, should have high priority. These agencies should all have their own plans that include staff deployment, evacuation to alternate settings, and ways to contact and inform families of the well-being and location of their children.

The Injured or Ill Children

Like any children who undergo medical procedures, children who have been physically injured in a disaster or who have become ill and have been brought to the hospital or the doctor's office will be less traumatized by the injury if the medical procedures that are about to occur are explained to them. In most up-to-date hospitals this is part of the hospital routine. Consultants can inquire about the local hospital and professional associations and involve them in crisis planning. Every effort should be made to have a member of the immediate family remain with the child during hospital stays and to be present when the child receives medical care. This is reassuring to the family and to the child.

Parents should encourage children to return to school. They should talk with their teachers about any problems that are evident either at home or in school. Parent-teacher meetings and programs can assist in integrating school and family efforts at reassurance and can encourage the child to understand his/her feelings and to cope with loss and the need to get on with life.

It is important to be aware that each child may react differently, even within the same family. Each child may need a different type of help to cope with his/her feelings about and reactions to the disaster.

Adolescents

At this age the motor skills of young people are often equal to those of adults. However, it is important for adolescents not to exceed their abilities and to realize that other aspects of their personalities are not as advanced as their physical development. The mental maturity of adolescents has no direct relation to their physical growth. Adults should not allow themselves to be influenced by appearances and expect an adolescent to have an adult mentality.

Adolescents have a great need to appear competent to those around them. They struggle to gain independence from their families and are divided between a desire for increased responsibilities and a wish to return to the dependent role of childhood. Beyond the family and the school, peer groups have a favored place in their concerns and provide them with various means for validating themselves.

A disaster can have many repercussions on adolescents, depending on its impact on family, friends, and the environment. They show physical, emotional, cognitive and behavioral reactions similar to those of adults.

Studies have shown that the difficulties experienced by adolescents after a disaster are boredom and loneliness resulting from isolation from peers due to disturbance of their activities and re-housing of their families.

Finally, following a disaster, an adolescent may suddenly have to assume an adult role and cope with the need to become the head of the family and provide financial and emotional support to the other members of the family. The adolescent's way of envisioning his/her responsibilities depends on a variety of factors, including cultural background, age, religious views, education, personal equilibrium, and conception of life.

Providing Help for Children and Families

General Steps in the Helping Process

A basic principle in working with problems of children in disasters is that they are essentially normal children who have experienced great stress. Most of the problems which appear are likely, therefore, to be directly related to the disaster and transitory in nature.

The process recommended for helping children and families often starts with "crisis intervention", which can be provided by trained and supervised paraprofessionals and volunteers. The primary goal in crisis intervention is to identify, respond to, and relieve the stresses developed as a result of the crisis (disaster) and then to re-establish normal functioning as quickly as possible. Sometimes the reaction is mild. Other times it is severe. Also, the responders must be trained to recognize when the condition is mild and can be handled by the families (with guidance) and when it is severe and needs professional help. The general steps in the helping process include:

1. Establishing Rapport

a) Letting the children know you are interested in them and want to help them.

b) Checking with the children to make sure that they understand what you are saying and that you understand them.

c) Having genuine respect and regard for the children and their families.

d) Communicating trust and promising only what you can do.

e) Communicating acceptance of the children and their families.

f) Communicating to the children and their families that you are an informed authority.

2. Identifying, Defining And Focusing On The Problem

Like adults, children going through a crisis may seem confused and chaotic in their thinking. It is helpful to the children and families to identify a specific problem and to define it and focus on it first. If possible, the problem should be quickly resolved so that the children and families quickly experience a sense of success and control. Evaluating the seriousness of the problem should determine the families' capacity for dealing with it.

3. Understanding Feelings

Empathy is the ability to see and feel as others do. Being empathetic with children requires patience, for children frequently are unable to express their fears and the adults need to appreciate the kind and intensity of the children's feelings. For example, adults may be required to listen to a child's account of a disaster many times while the child "works through" the disaster by talking it out.

4. Listening Carefully

Frequently, the children's experiences of adults listening to them are unsatisfactory. In working with children, effort should be made to respond to them and to comment frequently. Interrupting the children should be avoided for it tends to happen often and the children may be particularly sensitive to being interrupted by adults.

5. Communicating Clearly

It is important to communicate in language the children understand. The presence of the family is useful in interviews with the children for the families will be more familiar with them and their behavior. In addition, families will be able to learn how to communicate with the children better after observing the interviewer. Simple language should be used in speaking with the children so that they are not excluded from the helping process.

The Use of Play

Few children are able to sit and talk directly about their difficulties or to explore the roots that underlie these difficulties. Most of them are not able to talk about their problems even at a superficial level. Involving the children in play is effective in helping them work through their troubled feelings. Play is one of the natural modes of communication. The fantasies that are verbalized while playing often provide much information about the psychological processes that are at the bottom of children's problems. Children's play following disasters will reflect their experiences. Paints, clay, dolls, and water play allow children outlets for their feelings. They will build dams out of blocks, for example, and have them collapse, or they will build towers and pretend the earth is shaking—activities that obviously mirror an earthquake. Children's drawings will depict on a more or less realistic level the feared hurricane winds or tornadoes. Fortunately, children's play discharges feelings that have been bottled up.

Children seem to use play therapeutically. It is best when they are allowed to make their own interpretations. Adult interpretations often dampen this expressive avenue. Any adults who care for children—teachers, counselors, parents—can encourage children to express their feelings in play. The play experience should be a pleasurable one for both adults and children. Adult helpers should get down to the children's level—literally play on the floor with them when necessary. Secondly, the responders must have the capacity to project themselves into the children's situation and to see the world through the children's eyes. The responders must also have the ability to remember their own childhood experiences sufficiently to be able to appreciate the children's situation.

Parents sometimes feel guilty about the fact that their children are having problems and may feel threatened that outsiders are needed to help. Play therapy involves the parents who can be taught to understand how the children express their feelings and fears through play. Under optimal circumstances, parents play with their children. Following a disaster or other family crisis, parental energies are perforce drawn away from the children. Attracting the families back to their ordinary roles with the children is therapeutic to all concerned.

Individual Counseling

Individual counseling may simply be a time for children to "have someone to talk to". As stated earlier, most children find "just talking about feelings" difficult. However, there are times when friendly, supportive adults are just what children need when their own parents are not able to listen to them because they are busy with their own problems. Following a disaster in which there may be a shortage of trained mental health workers, friendly, caring people who have received some crisis training can be helpful to the children. Because disasters arouse natural fears and anxieties in children, responders' reassurances and emotional support are important. Individual therapy by trained, experienced therapists can be used in severe cases to help the families and children understand the underlying roots of the problem.

Group Sessions

a. Children's Groups

The group experience for children of latency age and older is a natural one because of their daily experiences in classroom settings. Children find it easier to relate to each other than to adults. They gain a lot from a group in which they can talk openly and honestly about their feelings after a disaster. Finding peers who are interested encourages even withdrawn children to talk about their feelings. A leader can provide emotional support and needed information to the group. Children frequently distort the information they receive and are afraid of "feeling foolish" about asking questions. A peer group encourages them to ask their questions, foolish or not.

Group intervention with children is especially useful for therapeutic expression, as they are able to express their fears before their peers once they are reassured that having fears and anxieties is acceptable and that other children (even the bravest ones) also have these feelings. Children retell their experiences with great enthusiasm in group discussions with other children of similar age levels.

Groups function well when the leaders are democratic and care about children. If adults run the group in an authoritarian manner, the group will not "work", and the children will not feel free to talk about their feelings. When groups of children talk about disaster, or draw pictures about them, they are helped to dispel their fears about such happenings. he following is one example of a group technique:

Form a group with a maximum of 12 children. Introduce the purpose as a chance for everyone to learn about the experiences of others in the disaster.

1) Ask all the children what happened to them and their families in the disaster.

2) As the stories appear, ask the children to tell about their own fears (perhaps even act them out in dramatic play).

3) In the course of the discussion, provide factual information on the disaster (what happened, why).

4) Ask members of the group to take turns being helpers. The children are paired and then take turns, first asking for help with a problem and then acting as helpers with the others' problems.

5) Assign two children as co-leaders to help control restlessness and distractibility among the children.

6) Provide the children with paper, plastic materials, clay, or paints, and ask them to depict the disaster. The less verbal children will find this helpful.

b. Parents' Groups

Working with parents in a group is an excellent means of helping them understand their children's behavior and providing them with specific advice on how they can deal with problems. In the group, parents have the opportunity to share their concerns with other parents who may be having similar concerns. Advice from other parents is frequently more acceptable than advice from "experts".

A parent group is useful when it is also educational. Parents often want to be informed on techniques for handling specific problems, such as fears and anxieties, sleep problems, school difficulties, and behavior problems.

Often the parents in groups express their own fears. Helping the parents understand their own fears makes them more effective with their children. The groups and group leaders are most supportive to the parents when they reinforce strengths present in the families and help them see how they have been able to deal efficiently with problems in the past. If additional help is needed from other resources in the community, the group leaders should have the information available.

Telephone Crisis Service

A telephone crisis line offering help with problems of children in disasters is effective in reaching the community. Families find it is an acceptable way to ask for help, and it is an efficient way to reach large numbers of families. The crisis line can be publicized on radio and TV as available "to help parents deal with their children's fears and anxieties". The media are usually pleased to announce the availability of the crisis line as a public service. The telephone line should be staffed by professionals and by trained volunteers under supervision. Volunteers can be recruited from local colleges and universities and from the community at large and, prior to receiving calls, should be trained in crisis techniques. Experience has shown that only a small proportion of the families calling need to be seen in person. Most of the callers are able to be helped by telephone advice. When they do need to be seen in the clinic, they often can be helped in group sessions. Specific, directive advice is crucial for the success of the telephone crisis line.

The typical calls will be about bedtime fears, clinging, and other behaviors that seem to reflect separation anxiety. For example:

A mother calls to ask advice about her toddler who will not stay in his crib. The advice might be for the parent to stay in the child's room until he falls asleep or to move the crib into the parents' bedroom for a few days.

Another typical call is from a parent of a 6-year old who states that the child has become fearful of leaving the parent's side. An increase in the amount of time spent with the child, much verbal reassurance, and more holding might be advised.

A mother of an 8-year-old girl reports that her daughter seems "obsessed" with talking about the disaster and is fearful of another one occurring. The responder listens supportively to the mother, asks her to elaborate on the family situation, on what has already been done to comfort the child, and asks which methods she has already tried to deal with the situation. The responder helps the mother understand the behavior by telling her this is the child's method of mastering anxiety. The responder offers reassurance by indicating that this is normal behavior and that the child needs to ventilate her feelings. Ways of handling the problem may include rap groups for the child to share anxieties with peers, and play or school projects which would use the disaster as their subject. If the parent's fears need to be alleviated, some individual counseling or group discussions may be recommended.

In all cases a follow-up is necessary. The mother is asked to call back to report on the success of the suggestions. The responder may also call her to see what has happened since they last talked. If feasible, an outreach visit can be made if the mother is not able to come to the agency to receive counseling.

Arrangements may need to be made through the local disaster coordinator to establish a toll-free number so that callers from outlying areas can easily contact the service.

Role of the Family

A basic principle in working with a child with an emotional problem is that it is a family problem, not just the child's problem, which is presented. The family should be considered the unit to be counseled. Every member should be involved with the process. In addition, one should take advantage of the assistance provided by the concern, interest, and availability of various members of the family. Sometimes adult members of the family may be experiencing emotional distress but hesitate to seek help. The family is frequently more able to seek help on the children's behalf than on that of its adult members. The family may, in fact, use the children's problems as a way of also asking for help for others in the family. This request should be respected not confronted. By having the family involved, others in the family can also be helped. Denial that problems exist may still occur, however, in some cultural and disadvantaged areas.

When the family's equilibrium is upset by stress, it may be pushed off balance temporarily, and the family shows signs of not being able to fulfill its usual functions. Time and informed interventions help in re-establishing the family and its developmental role.

4	# Special Risk Groups	

There are many feelings and reactions people share in common response to the direct and indirect effects of disasters. However, certain groups are more at risk for some reactions than others.

Common Needs and Reactions

1. Concern for basic survival

2. Grief over loss of loved ones or loss of prized possessions

3. Separation anxiety centered on self and also expressed as fear for safety of significant others

4. Regressive behaviors, e.g. reappearance of thumb sucking among children

5. Relocation and isolation anxieties

6. Need to express feelings about experiences during the disaster

7. Need to feel one is a part of the community and its rehabilitation efforts

8. Altruism and desire to help others

Middle–Age, Elderly, and Older Adults

Middle Age

On the face of it, middle-aged persons seem to be an unlikely special group with specific problems. However, they are, and it is helpful to be alert to these, especially for the possibility of emotional problems arising in later, rather than immediate, post-disaster periods. Consider the family which loses its home and most possessions in a flood. Forced to rebuild, they must do so with far more cost and highly inflated financial expenses. Retirement with the mortgage paid off is now out of the question, and prospects of an old age with adequate pension and comfortable living may have vanished. It takes a while for these conditions and the realizations of a reappraised future to sink in. They may and do, however, have any number of effects such as psychosomatic problems, relationship difficulties, and occupational dissatisfactions.

Feeling and Behavior Symptoms

- Psychosomatic problems, ulcers, diabetes, heart trouble
- Withdrawal, anger, suspicion, irritability, apathy
- Loss of appetite, sleep problems, loss of interest in everyday activities

Treatment Options

- Arrange for medical care for physical symptoms
- Persuade victims to talk with family physician, clergyman, friends, or to accept professional help
- Help find medical and financial assistance
- Keep channels of communication open with members of the family
- Help family to recognize physical signs of depression and need for professional counseling

Elderly

The elderly represent their family's memories, their special link with culture and religion. They are members of the community who are able to define their own needs and ask for the services needed to meet them. Most elderly people show strength and courage in disasters. Their life experience has enabled them to acquire the ability to recover. Their physical, emotional, cognitive and behavioral reactions are similar to those of younger adults.

The reactions of elderly people to disaster may include expressing their worries about the future and the loss of their physical health, their role in the family, social contacts, and financial security.

With age, we observe greater vulnerability in persons who are alone (unmarried, widows and widowers, divorced) as well as extreme sensitivity to emotional losses and socioeconomic and cultural changes.

Lacking sufficient validation and emotional links with other generations in the community, elderly people become vulnerable to the whole range of physical, psychological and social tensions.

Older Adults

Senior citizens of concern here are non-institutionalized persons whose life sphere has become circumscribed due to aging, primarily, rather than to specific multiple disabilities. These older persons typically do not have highly active schedules during the day. They spend their time mostly with others of similar age and circumstances in daily routines which have become comfortable. Others are confined to house or apartment, frequently alone. When these familiar routines are disrupted by the disaster, and particularly when residential loss and relocation occur, it would be expected that the senior citizen might exhibit some symptoms.

Feeling and Behavior Symptoms

- Depression, Withdrawal
- Apathy
- Agitation, anger
- Irritability, suspicion
- Disorientation
- Confusion
- Memory loss
- Accelerated physical decline
- Increase in number of somatic complaints

Treatment Options

- Provide strong and persistent verbal reassurance
- Assist with recovery of physical possessions; make frequent home visits, arrange for companions
- Give special attention to suitable residential relocation, e.g., familiar surroundings and acquaintances
- Help in re-establishing familial and social contacts
- Assist in obtaining medical and financial assistance
- Help re-establish medication regime
- Provide escort and transportation services

An important issue is the despair accompanying loss of property and objects, which is a loss of ties with the past. Often, because loss of life has occurred among neighbors or friends, mourning the loss of sentimental objects and loss of property seems "inappropriate". However, these can and do constitute significant psychological loss.

Society and Culture

Socioeconomic Classes

Socioeconomic circumstances are important influences on attitudes and reactions of people in stress situations. More importantly, these factors have a strong effect on the readiness with which individuals will seek or accept help voluntarily for emotional distress. For example, persons in lower economic circumstances are generally more inclined to seek medical rather than psychological treatment. This re-emphasizes the importance of "outreach" efforts in disaster relief work. Otherwise, these people will not be reached and may not get the help they need. By contrast, people in intermediate and upper income economic circumstances are more aware of and less likely to resist accepting all kinds of help when needed. These social groups would also be expected to be more likely to understand the possibilities of long-range benefits from early use of the services offered, i.e., heading off future problems by dealing with them now. Upper income people might be less inclined, however, to welcome outreach and "free" services as compared with lower and middle income groups.

Cultural and Racial Differences

Reports from disaster relief workers in recent years have emphasized the importance of social and cultural differences, especially of races, language, economic levels, class, and ethnicity. There are also reports of socially isolated groups who display what amounts to sub-cultural differences of attitudes and daily life patterns as a result of geographical isolation and dependence on a single occupational source, for example, small mining towns. For these groups it is essential that outreach efforts be channeled through representatives or facilities within the subculture area. Differences of language and custom, if ignored, will lead to frustration and failure by those attempting to render services.

Feelings and Behavior Symptoms

- Depression

- Apathy

- Feelings of helplessness and hopelessness

- Resignation (to God's will)

- Suspicious of help offered by "outsiders"

- Ignoring or rejecting available sources of "outside" help

- Tendency to close ranks and accept assistance only from family and close friends

Treatment Options

- Channel all assistance through local religious and community sources

- Place emphasis on informational and educational assistance

- Outreach all services with the exception of those requiring special

- facilities such as hospitals and clinics

Institutionalized Persons

Individuals who are in institutions during a disaster are susceptible to frustration, anxiety, and panic as a consequence of their limited mobility and helpless dependence on their caretakers. The circumstances will vary widely depending on the type of institution. However, there are some common reactions which might be expected to occur in general medical hospitals, mental hospitals, adult and juvenile correctional agencies, and convalescent facilities.

Feelings and Behavior Symptoms

- Fear
- Frustration
- Anxiety
- Helplessness
- Anger
- Panic
- "Escape"

Treatment Options

- Assist in relocation to safe housing

- Provide reassurance and information regarding disaster status

- Assist in making contact with loved ones and friends

- Encourage involvement in housekeeping and rehabilitation duties

- Provide opportunities for group discussions of fears and anxiety

Other Special Risk Groups

People in Emotional Crises

When a person is experiencing an emotional crisis, it is usually apparent even to the casual observer. In a disaster it might be expected that the direct and indirect effects of the catastrophe might produce severe emotional crises for some people. Precipitating causes could be death or separation from loved ones, sudden loss of contact with friends and familiar routines and settings, or simply the physical force of the disaster itself. The last mentioned can in some cases bring about overwhelming feelings of inadequacy in some who are suddenly confronted with their own feelings of helplessness and mortality.

Feelings and Behavior Symptoms

- Emotional shock

- Apathy

- Numbness

- Agitated depression

- Disorientation and confusion

- Preservation behavior

- Hyperactivity

- Minimal emotional control, e.g. explosive anger, uncontrollable crying

- Physical symptoms, e.g., dizziness, nausea, fainting spells, headaches, hyperventilation, rapid heartbeat

Treatment Options

- Give verbal and physical reassurance

- Assist in coping with some specific and tangible problem

- Help in relocating loved ones

- Help in getting care for loved ones who are injured

- Help in locating and making arrangements for loved ones who did not survive

- Give assistance and encouragement in assessing extent of damage to personal property and beginning to repair or rebuild damaged home or business

- Assist in getting medical attention if needed

People Requiring Emergency Medical Care

Those who are in need of immediate and surgical treatment, in addition to suffering from physical shock, may also experience anxiety caused by separation from loved ones or a lack of information about the extent of damage to home, place of business, or the community itself. The degree of anxiety experienced by the injured person may aggravate his/her physical state and affect response to medical treatment. Having mental health services available at medical treatment facilities during and following the disaster has been found useful. The responder may provide invaluable relief and reassurance to the injured person by obtaining information about loved ones or about the status of property and possessions.

Human Service and Disaster Relief Workers

Responders in all phases of disaster relief—whether protective services, nongovernmental shelters, clothing and food services, governmental rehabilitation and reclamation services, or human service workers—expose themselves to unprecedented personal demands in their desire to help meet the needs of the victims. For many the disaster takes precedence over all other responsibilities and activities, and the responders devote all their time to the disaster-created tasks, at least in the immediate post-impact period. As some order returns, many of the responders, especially volunteers, return to their regular jobs, but at the same time attempt to continue with their disaster work. The result of the overwork is the "burn-out" syndrome—a state of exhaustion, irritability, and fatigue which creeps up unrecognized and undetected upon the individual and markedly decreases his/her effectiveness and capability. The best way to forestall the "burn-out" syndrome is to expect it, to be alert to its early signs, and to act authoritatively in relieving the stress. Four primary areas of symptomatology have been identified:

Feelings and Behavior Symptoms

- **Thinking:** Mental confusion, slowness of thought, inability to make judgments and decisions, loss of ability to conceptualize alternatives or to prioritize tasks, loss of objectivity in evaluating own functioning, etc.
- **Psychological:** Depression, irritability, anxiety, hyper-excitability, excessive rage reactions, etc.
- **Somatic:** Physical exhaustion, loss of energy, gastrointestinal distress, appetite disturbances, hypochondria, sleep disorders, tremors, etc.
- **Behavioral:** Hyperactivity, excessive fatigue, inability to express self verbally or in writing, etc.

Management

The first step is to be aware of, to be alert for, and to recognize the symptoms of "burn-out" syndrome when they first appear. The earlier they are recognized the better. All personnel need to be instructed about the early symptoms so that they may recognize it not only in themselves but also in their fellow workers. Any such observations, either about themselves or about others, should be reported to their supervisors. The latter also need to be alert to any early symptoms in their staff so that they can intervene. The supervisor should talk to the individual and try to get him/her to recognize the symptoms in him/herself. The supervisor can then make sure the person is relieved from his/her duties for a short period of time. Guilt over leaving the activity is relieved by giving official permission to stop and by pointing out how the worker is no longer helping because of the loss of his/her effectiveness. The responder can be reassured that he/she can return and that he/she will have improved greatly as a result of the short recuperation. The supervisor should at first attempt to persuade the helper to take the time off, but, if necessary, should order it. The syndrome may appear early or well into the post-disaster period, from 2 weeks to a year. On the average, it seems to take about 4 to 6 weeks for most of the symptoms to appear.

Cultural and Ethnic Minorities

Regardless of how many announcements may be made on radio or TV, this group will not understand what assistance is available if they do not understand the language. Cultural differences, especially of race and language, may be important. For these groups, it is essential that outreach efforts be channeled through representatives or facilities in the area. Differences in language and/or customs, if ignored, will lead to frustration by those attempting to provide services. It is important to provide education about differences in the grieving process, provide handouts on disaster related stress in appropriate languages, assist with referrals to culturally appropriate counseling services, etc.

5 Cultural Aspects of Disasters

Background

Disasters can have profound effects on a community, on families, and, specifically on children and adolescents. Pre-existing health risk factors can affect health care during and after a disaster. Disasters cause disruptions to normal patterns resulting in behavioral reactions to disaster, including posttraumatic stress. The relationship between the disaster experience and the traumatic responses of the individual is not a direct one. It is mediated by the perception of the disaster as a risk and a threat to the community at the individual level. It is also mediated by culture which determines the coping styles in case of loss, the social networks and resources.

The mental health community in the United States was caught unaware after 9/11 with respect to treatment of survivors of terrorist attacks. Because this form of trauma is quite rare in this country, few trauma specialists had extensive experience, or taught regularly on this subject. Because the primary objective of terrorism is the creation of demoralization, fear, and uncertainty in the general population, a focus on mental health from therapeutic and public health perspectives is critically important to successfully resolving such crises.

- Previous history of trauma or stress in country of origin
- Immigration status
- Level of trust or mistrust of government agencies
- Level of acculturation
- Language fluency or literacy
- Social status
- Economic situation and ability to recover financially
- Disaster losses may reawaken prior losses and trauma
- Mistrust of "outsiders"
- Definition of family and individual's role in family
- Support systems
- Role of those perceived as "helpers"
- Belief system regarding disaster (e.g. fate, responsibility, punishment, guilt)
- Religious belief systems
- Values regarding asking for help
- Rituals and traditions, particularly relating to grieving

Fig. 5-1: Ethnic Group Factors

Surveys following 9/11 showed unequivocally that symptomatology related to the attacks were found in hundreds of thousands of people, most of whom were not escapees or the families of the deceased. Soon after 9/11, Marshall & Suh (2003) formed a collaboration with other academic sites in Manhattan to rapidly increase capacity for providing state-of-the-art training and treatment for trauma-related psychiatric problems. Their experience suggests that evidence-based treatments such as Prolonged Exposure Therapy have proven successful in treating 9/11-related PTSD. However, special clinical issues arose, such as the influence of culture on clinical presentation and treatment expectations in a multiethnic community.

Working Outside the Cultural Milieu

Collomb (1973) attempted to answer the question: What impels a mental health professional to offer services outside his or her usual geographic and cultural milieu, and how may these motives interfere with his or her optimal functioning as a therapist? He presented a provisional typology of what might be called the cultural distortions of countertransference. On the basis of his observations, he distinguished three attitudes that could be described as those of universalism, cultural uniqueness, and rejection of one's own culture of origin. One prerequisite with which it is difficult to disagree is that the therapist, as part of his/her expertise and competence, should know the culture within which he/she operates. Devereux (1969), for example, applied himself to a thorough study of the "Plains Indians", preparatory and concurrent to conducting psychotherapy with one of them.

Therapists working in a cross-cultural setting should approach this task with a maximum of self-awareness and be prepared to deal with their own distortions of the therapy experience and relationship. In her work with members of other cultures in Miami, Florida, Weidman (1975) pioneered the concept of culture-broker—a well-informed intermediary whose inputs are brought to bear on the therapy process. The client remains the major source of information about those features of his/her cultural experience which might otherwise baffle the therapist. The limit of this mode of inquiry is that the individual, not the culture, is the focus of all therapy (Draguns, 1981). Sessions should not deteriorate into ethnographic data-gathering in its own right and for its own purpose nor to satisfy the therapist's curiosity. Rather, the referent should be: Is this information needed for therapy, and, if so, how?

In summary, counselors should have knowledge of the culture they work in as part of their expertise and competence. Giordano and Giordano

(1976) provided some very valuable and specific information to keep in mind when initiating and maintaining contact with clients of another culture. The knowledge of the culture of one's clients provides the counselor with an entree and/or point of departure. The experience of the counselor with a cultural group or the information on it in the relevant professional literature serves as a source of hypotheses, to be verified, discarded and/or modified based on acquisition of further information. Working together with a counselor/healer from the culture could vastly improve the probability of success in appropriate interventions. This would be of special concern in a disaster or major crisis situation.

Cross–Cultural Examples in Disasters

Canino, Bravo, Rubio-Stipec, & Woodbury (1990) examined effects of the 1985 floods in Puerto Rico on mental health symptoms and diagnoses to determine the extent to which such effects were influenced by demographics and previous symptoms. They studied 912 people between the ages of 17-68 using a Spanish version of the Diagnostic Interview Schedule. They found that the onset of depression, generalized anxiety and PTSD was significantly more common among those exposed to a disaster than among those not exposed. They suggested that the increase in stress-related disorders in exposed subjects indicated that the stress of disaster increased their mental morbidity.

In another study, Escobar, Canino, Rubio-Stipec & Bravo (1992) interviewed 375 individuals before and after severe floods and mudslides in Puerto Rico. They used a Spanish version of the Diagnostic Interview Schedule to study the prevalence of somatization symptoms. 139 individuals were classified as having been exposed to disaster and 236 as not exposed. They found that exposure to disaster was related to a higher prevalence of medically unexplained physical symptoms. The most prevalent symptoms were gastrointestinal (abdominal pain, vomiting, nausea, excessive gas) and pseudo neurological (amnesia, paralysis, fainting, unusual spells, etc).

Guarnaccia (1993), in the first community based study of *ataques de nervios* (attacks of nerves), discussed the issue of categorizing it as a culture-bound syndrome. He conducted a psychiatric epidemiology survey using 912 subjects between the ages of 17-68 in Puerto Rico. This study was performed in 1987 to measure the psychosocial effects of a disaster which occurred on the island in 1985. He also had access to earlier data from a survey done in 1984. Guarnaccia identified stressful situations surrounding ataques. They were correlated with other psychiatric diagnoses and it was found that subjects who reported ataques de nervios were more likely to meet criteria for depression, dysthymia, generalized anxiety disorder, panic disorder, and PTSD. Guarnaccia suggests that the term "popular illness" is a better descriptive term for the syndrome than is "culture-bound syndrome".

The 1985 floods and mudslides in Puerto Rico caused considerable damage and death. As part of a major study (Guarnaccia, Canino, Rubio-Stipec, & Bravo, 1993) an additional question was added to the Diagnostic Interview Schedule/Disaster Supplement concerning ataques de nervios. Using this, researchers studied the category using a representative, community based sample of 912 people. 145 reported an ataque de nervios. Of these most were female, older, less educated, and formerly married. They were also more likely to meet criteria for anxiety and depressive disorders than those who had not experienced an ataque.

Perilla, Norris & Lavizzo (2002) studied a sample of 404 residents of southern Florida who were interviewed in their own homes six months following Hurricane Andrew. The sample was composed of equal numbers of Hispanics, non-Hispanic blacks, and Caucasians. Ethnic groups differed strongly in the prevalence of posttraumatic stress disorder (PTSD). Caucasian disaster victims showed the lowest rate (15%), Spanish-preferring Latinos showed the highest rate (38%), and African-Americans showed a rate (23%) between these two extremes. Additional analyses attempted to explain these symptom differences in terms of differential exposure and differential vulnerability to trauma. Both explanations had merit but neither completely accounted for observed ethnic differences. Cultural-specific responses to Hurricane Andrew suggested the need to view psychological symptoms in light of the possible adaptive nature of the behaviors due to political, social, economic, and historical perspectives.

Apfelbaum (2000) examined the disturbing conditions of uprootedness which now mark most people's cultural lives, and focused on the extreme case of genocide to emphasize that however inevitable the sense of loss, exile and unfamiliarity, it remains vital at the same time to retain narratives of cultural filiations and affiliation. She argues that genocides go well beyond their primary goal of physically annihilating a social group in its entirety. Ultimately, they also eradicate the very cultural roots by which this group has historically established and maintained its identity. Being a 'survivor' (or child of a survivor) of such a disaster thus means becoming a 'cultural orphan,' violently separated from one culture now gone and silenced, who must attempt an existence and a reconstruction of identity on the sole basis of the 'host' culture. There is often no space in the latter to recapture the 'lost' roots. Social identity is intimately embedded with culture.

In summary, it appears that the most common symptoms displayed across the cultures sampled in the above studies of victims of various disasters were those associated with the diagnoses of depression, anxiety and PTSD. They manifest themselves in different ways within cultures, but the symptoms tend to fit the general diagnostic criteria for depression, anxiety disorders and PTSD. How to approach dealing with these in a culturally relevant counseling context is the task faced by the cross-cultural counselor providing disaster mental health services and psychological first aid.

Culture and PTSD

The diagnostic category of post traumatic stress disorder (PTSD) is relatively new and culture can play a very important role. There is only limited literature addressing the cultural aspects of this disorder unlike schizophrenia and depression, which have been extensively written about from this perspective. However, it is clear that cultural factors have an important role to play in the genesis and presentation of PTSD, and in how it is perceived, responded to and treated. The impact of culture on the incidence and characteristics of PTSD is related to reactions to natural disasters (e.g., floods, earthquakes) and man-made disasters (e.g., industrial accidents, imprisonment, torture). Culture is important in determining an individual's reactions to stressful situations and in influencing recovery from PTSD (de Silva, 1993). Reports of PTSD across different cultures, settings (e.g. war, natural disasters, other disasters, violence, accidents, concentration camp experience, torture, imprisonment during war), PTSD and culture (e.g. perception of trauma and the reactions of society, social support, role of the military culture in war, cultural and national differences in responses to trauma, issues related to therapy) are not very plentiful. However, the literature that is available suggests that the use of the diagnosis of PTSD has not been very useful across cultures as it is based on the western cultural discourse that stress is an outcome of loss of control over nature (deVries, 1996). Trauma is an important dimension because the meaning of trauma is often culturally specific. The social and religious rituals surrounding loss and disaster have an important healing role in both individual and community trauma. Specific functions of social supports help in minimizing the impact of trauma, and the protective role of attachment. For example, Priya (2002) provides a glimpse of suffering and healing among the survivors of an earthquake that occurred in Bhuj in 2001. An ethnographic approach was used for this study. Priya found that the faith of the people that discharging their duties (karma) would lead them to peace and harmony with nature has resulted in better healing among the survivors in rural areas than among those in urban areas where life is guided mainly by materialistic goals. Priya proposes that suffering and healing help to understand earthquake survivors better than PTSD. Chemtob (1996) presents an ecologically centered definition of culture that highlights why it is important to consider the cultural context within which PTSD develops, focusing on cultural variation in the response to trauma. Unfortunately, impediments to the study of culture and trauma have resulted in a paucity of empirical research that bears directly on culture's impact on trauma.

Rabalais, Ruggiero & Scotti (2002) note the lack of attention to issues of cultural diversity in disaster-related research. They provide some interesting and important ideas for incorporating diversity-related concepts (e.g., acculturation stress, cultural beliefs and customs, kin networks) into future research efforts with diverse populations. Given the limitations of the current literature, Rabalais et al outline three goals for study. The first is to provide an overview of socioeconomic status and social support, two factors that may be relevant to ethnically diverse samples. They also propose that culture may serve as either a risk or a protective factor. A second goal they identify is to summarize studies of disasters among ethnically diverse, disaster-exposed, American children to provide a background for how ethnicity might interact with risk and protective factors to affect the development of PTSD in children. Finally, they use the example of American Indian youth to demonstrate the need for further empirical investigation of cultural variables as potential risk and protective factors for PTSD.

Cultural Approaches or Models

Ridha & Orlin (1996) reviewed the effectiveness of seven Kuwaiti institutions created to help Kuwaiti citizens recover from the effects of the Iraqi occupation of 1990-1991. Three charities focused on helping men and four charities focused their efforts on women's problems. Problems suffered by Kuwaiti citizens included disturbed sleep patterns, anxiety, excessive fear of the dark or loud noises, feelings of hopelessness and lack of control, aggressive behavior against other persons, and destruction of property. Ridha & Orlin concluded that the Western model for disaster and catastrophe is incompatible with Kuwaiti culture. An intervention and service delivery model more suitable for an Arabian Islamic sociocultural context was recommended.

Shen (2002) investigated the effectiveness of short-term child-centered group play therapy in elementary school settings with Chinese children in

Taiwan who experienced an earthquake in 1999. 65 children (aged 8-12 yrs) were screened. Children in the experimental group scored significantly lower on anxiety level and suicide risk after play therapy than did children in the control group. The effects of the treatment support previous studies of play therapy with American children. These findings suggest the possibility of using disaster intervention services which adopt Western helping techniques with school children of non-Western cultures.

In assessing children's reactions to the extreme stress of war and disasters, Aptekar & Stoecklin (1997) suggest focusing on three ways in which culture interacts with children's' reactions to extreme stress. These include how culture mediates the possible range of child responses from PTSD to a relatively benign reaction, and finally to actually improved mental health.

Ecevit & Kasapoglu (2002) conducted a survey of 500 male and female survivors (aged 19-80 yrs) of the 1999 earthquake in Turkey to investigate their levels of alienation and forms of preparedness for future disasters. It was found that the level of alienation in general was not very significant and that level of education was the most important influential independent variable. The only alienation component found to have a negative impact on the responsible behavior related to preparedness for earthquakes was the social isolation variable. As level of education increases and social isolation decreases, responsible behavior increases. The existence of little such research in developing societies like Turkey increases the importance of this work and it should have a positive impact on similar future studies.

Grief: A Brief Cross-Cultural Perspective

Cultural beliefs can be both resources and barriers in providing support for grieving families. Across cultures, people differ in what they believe and understand about life and death, what they feel, what elicits those feelings, the perceived implications of those feelings, the ways they express those feelings, the appropriateness of certain feelings, and the techniques for dealing with feelings that cannot be directly expressed (Rosenblatt, 1993). Historical studies have shown how individuals in western culture

have mourned differently over time (Newnes, 1991; Kohn & Levav, 1990). A cross-cultural perspective shows an infinite variety in people's responses to death, in how they mourn, and in the nature of their internalization of the lost object. Rather than being process-oriented, mourning is seen as an adaptive response to specific task demands arising from loss that must be dealt with regardless of individual, culture, or historical era (Hagman, 1995).

Americans report thinking significantly more about grief, religious feelings and death than do Japanese (Asai & Barnlund, 1998). Ancestor worship in Japan is ritual. It is supported by a sophisticated theory through which the living manage their bonds with the dead. It is a process similar to the resolution of grief in the modern west (Klass, 1996). Klass & Heath (1997) explored the grief of Japanese parents after abortion and the ritual by which the grief is resolved. The ritual is Mizuko Ruyo. Mizuko means child of the water. Ruyo is a Buddhist offering. In a ritual drama played out by Jizo, the bodhisattva who suffers for others, the parents' pain and the child's pain are connected. In that connection, the pain of each is resolved. The child is made part of the community and does not become a spirit bringing harm to the family. The parents can fulfill their obligation to care for the child and transform the sense of kurnon, sickness unto death, into a realization of Buddhism's first noble truth, that all life is suffering. In a slightly different cultural context, The Bardo Thodol (Tibetan Book of the Dead) together with its associated ritual provides a way to understand how Buddhism in Tibetan culture manages the issues associated with what is called grief in Western psychology. The resolution of grief in the survivors is intertwined with the journey to rebirth of the deceased (Goss & Klass, 1997).

The primary mental health benefits of ritual are closely tied to the relational aspects of the ritual process. These act to validate and encourage the healthy expression of a wide range of human emotions. Jacobs (1992) concludes that religious ceremony and ritual functions mitigate anxiety and deal effectively with other problematic emotional states. Religious rites have a cathartic effect as emotions are released and expressed through attachment and connection to significant others. Reeves (1989, 1990) suggests that ritual can be used to assist individuals to move from a maladaptive to an adaptive style of grieving.

Rubin (1990) used social network theory to compare mourning behaviors in the United States with those in Israeli kibbutz. He found that, in a dense social network such as a small or medium-sized kibbutz, mourning is part of a wider circle of family, friends, neighbors, and co-workers. He suggests that the funerals in the United States may force loose social networks to generate an image of social support. Rubin suggests using social network theory as a basis for cross-cultural analysis of the range of participation in mourning rituals.

Hagman (1995) reviewed the standard psychoanalytic model of mourning and suggests that the model may not be generally valid. The psychoanalytic literature and data from clinical practice fail to confirm basic components of mourning theory. Stroebe (1992,1993) challenges the belief in the importance of "grief work" for adjustment to bereavement (the grief work hypothesis). She examined claims made in theoretical formulations and principles of grief counseling and therapy concerning the necessity of working through loss. Reviews of empirical evidence and cross-cultural findings document alternative patterns of coping with grief. Stroebe argues that there are grounds for questioning the hypothesis:

- Existing definitions and operationalizations are problematic;
- The few empirical studies that have examined the impact of grief work have yielded equivocal results;
- Grief work is not a universal concept.

She proposes a revision of the definition of grief work, which overcomes the confounding of the process with symptomatology and should facilitate future empirical testing, and suggests a differential approach.

Teams of counselors dispatched to mass casualty disaster sites can at times be an overwhelming presence. Sensitivity to cultural needs and desires are necessary to provide appropriate and desired services. Newell (1998) in a cross-cultural study of privacy found that the majority of students (aged 17-45) from Ireland, Senegal and the United States in their study believed that not being disturbed was the most important element of privacy and grief. Fatigue and need to focus were the main affective sets associated with seeking privacy. The affect associated with a desire for privacy, the definition of privacy as a condition of the person, the duration of the average privacy experience, and the change in affect at the completion of the experience suggested that privacy has a therapeutic effect.

In summary, sensitivity to the culturally appropriate needs for ritual in responding to grief and providing for privacy and personal needs are paramount. Imposing a "one size fits all" grief model on people, however well intentioned, may cause more harm and ill feeling than good. Respect for the beliefs, rituals and desires of those affected can accomplish far more than unwanted attention and interventions.

Cross-Cultural Counseling/Therapy

Responses to disasters (natural and man-made) are handled initially by those in the area immediately affected. When there are insufficient local resources available or the extent of the disaster is overwhelmingly large, outside assistance is usually called for. Developed countries like the United States and Canada have prepared disaster response plans that address the situation and help people affected through a national response (Lystad, 1990). Within countries having pluralistic populations such as Canada and the United States, disaster workers need to be aware of, and sensitive to, cultural mores and differences. When disaster workers from these and/or other countries seek to assist with disasters in another country, it is essential that they have an understanding of the cultural norms and expectations of the population they hope to assist (Marsella, Friedman, & Gerrity, 1996). This is especially true for disaster mental health professionals. How different cultural groups handle stress and deal with stressors, their abilities, needs and desires for certain types of assistance, their motivations, their senses of honor and pride, their religious orientations and beliefs, their political systems and leadership, and their ways of handling and dealing with grief and loss are just some of the variables which are affected by cultural differences (Mak & Nadelson, 1996). Another one is communication—not just language differences, but also the nuances of specific words, phrases, slogans, proverbs, and colloquialisms. Well-intentioned attempts to help can easily be at risk for being misunderstood as meddling, interference or even as political attempts to influence and/or control.

There has been a powerful development of comprehensive mental health services throughout the world. Much of the literature in this field has been devoted to the maladaptation and stress of the culture contact situation (Draguns, 1981; Higginbotham, 1976, 1979a, 1979b); Diop, Collignon and Gueye, 1976; Pedersen, Lonner and Draguns, 1976; Taft, 1977; Pinter, 1969). The problems of people removed from their cultural roots through migration, sojourn or involuntary displacement occupy the work of a great many culturally-oriented mental health professionals.

There is a considerable amount of information available on how to help people who are casualties of intercultural mobility. Some examples include distraught college students, confused immigrants, traumatized expellees and refugees, discouraged and dissatisfied Peace Corps volunteers. Pinter (1969) reported a number of attempts to sketch a composite portrait of an individual who is least or most likely to succumb to such stress. Characteristics of host environments have also been scrutinized in attempts to identify those features which contribute to making such an environment particularly stressful or unusually stress-free for newcomers (Pinter, 1978).

There is a sizeable background of literature which deals with psychotherapy and counseling with individuals who have been transplanted to a new cultural setting (Szapocznik, Scopetta, Arondale & Kurtines, 1978; David, 1976). This body of writing provides practical relevant information for the professional involved in extending services to immigrants, sojourners or returnees from intensive cross-cultural encounters.

All people respond to stimuli and situations by either changing themselves or the environment and by combining these two operations in various proportions. Historically, the implicit goal of counseling and psychotherapy has been to bring about a greater degree of conformity to the norms of the dominant majority group. The contemporary cross-cultural counselor or therapist faces a choice. He/she can prepare the client for changing obstacles in the environment, or he/she can equip the client for a greater degree of accommodation to the social structure in its current state. The increase in the individual's options also involves choices on the extent and nature of one's relationships, reference groups, and identity, especially in relation to one's ethnic or cultural group.

Wrenn (1962) was among the first to sensitize counselors to the problem of cultural encapsulation and warned against the imposition of culturally alien goals, values and practices upon clients across cultural lines. Pedersen (1976) took the position that, at least in a multicultural setting like the United States, crossing the cultural gulf in the mental health field is the rule rather than the exception.

The Vail Conference on Clinical Psychology which was sponsored by the American Psychological Association elevated the knowledge of the cultures of one's clients to an ethical imperative (Korman, 1974). As a result, doing therapy or counseling without cultural sensitivity, knowledge or awareness is not just problematic. It has been declared unethical. The implication of these recommendations is that the knowledge on therapy and culture has ceased to be an esoteric field. Instead, it has become a matter of direct and practical concern for those who provide services across cultures.

What features of a culture are reflected in its therapeutic services? What kinds of models are implicitly emulated in the conduct of psychotherapy? One can only point to statements placing psychotherapy in its respective cultural context and relating it to the needs, expectations, models and opportunities experienced in that culture (Draguns, 1975; Neki, 1973; Wittkower & Warnes, 1974). Does addition of healers of one's own cultural tradition result in the enhancement of effectiveness of mental health services? One area where such an investigation has been made was about the efficacy of Morita Therapy (Miura and Usa, 1970; Reynolds, 1976) and Naikan Therapy (Tanaka-Matsumi, 1979) in Japan. These are two procedures indigenous to their culture, yet developed and practiced by modern mental health professionals.

In Japan, the two indigenously developed therapies, Naikan and Morita, are based on guilt induction and control and on suppression of communication respectively. In the Naikan system, the client is admonished to think of all the ways in which he has wronged his mother (Tanaka-Matsumi, 1979). In the course of Morita therapy, what the client may say and when and how it is said is elaborately restricted and ritualized (Reynolds, 1976). The contrast between Western expectations and Japanese therapy is stark. Documentation on Morita therapy indicates that this therapy works in a substantial proportion of cases on its home grounds. As Sue (1977) has pointed out, therapy and counseling services geared to a culturally distinct group have to be appropriate in process and in goals to be acceptable and effective.

One of the things that therapists of different orientations and cultures share is the ability to generate perceptions of competence and concern in their clients (Torrey, 1972). The role of the therapist, regardless of technique, is catalytic, enabling the client to make use of his/her existing assets and strengths (Prince, 1976, 1980). Non-western cultures have tended to rely to a greater extent than the West upon the induction of altered states of consciousness to bring about these catalytic effects.

Jilek-Aal (1978) noted the effectiveness of the Salish Indian spirit dance in promoting therapeutic change in that cultural group. It induces regression through an altered state of consciousness, promotes the experience of death and rebirth, and provides the participant with a new identity reoriented toward the ideal of the Salish culture. The rationale and the procedure appear to be reminiscent of the fixed-role therapy of George Kelly (1955) with the exception of greater reliance on affective and regressive processes, and on altered states of consciousness.

Cultural Role of Families Following Disasters

Solomon, Bravo, Rubio-Stipec, and Canino (1993) hypothesized that family roles (marital and parental status) would moderate effects of disaster exposure on the mental health of victims. Their study included residents of St. Louis who were exposed to floods and dioxin and Puerto Rican residents exposed to floods and mudslides. Worst outcomes in St. Louis were found for single and married parents who were exposed to disaster. Their symptoms significantly exceeded those of non-exposed, non-victim single parents. Puerto Rican victims without families were reported as having higher levels of alcohol abuse symptoms than any other subgroup. The authors found that perceived emotional support was an important moderator of disaster effect on psychiatric distress in Puerto Rico and generally overrode the effect of family role.

In a related study, Solomon and Canino (1990) looked at the appropriateness of DSM-III-R criteria for PTSD. They examined whether

1) the psychiatric sequelae resulting from exposure to extraordinary traumatic events (stressor criterion A) differed from the sequelae resulting from exposure to more common yet stressful life experiences, and

2) PTSD sequelae (criteria B&D) accurately described the responses of victims even of extreme events fitting the DSM-III-R definition of stressor.

They used data from 452 St. Louis victims exposed to floods and/or unsafe dioxin levels and 912 Puerto Rico victims of mudslides/flooding. Some common stressful events (e.g. moving, money problems) were found to relate more closely to PTSD symptoms than did extraordinary events. They found that exposure to disaster strongly related to symptoms of re-experiencing (criterion B). Reports of symptoms related to avoidance (criterion C) were uncommon.

In a study of acute stress reaction in family members, Ma, Lu, Liu, A-Er-Ken, et al (1995) worked with family members of the victims from a fire disaster in Kelamayi, Xinjiang Province, China which took place on December 8, 1994. Participants included 9 male and 72 female adults (aged 18-61). Those who visited the mental health clinic within one week of the event were identified with acute stress reaction according to the International Classification of Diseases-10 (ICD-10). Participants who visited the clinic within 3-5 weeks of the event were diagnosed with acute stress reaction according to family members' description. Subjects clinical manifestations (e.g. extreme sadness, agitating activity, stuporous state, and loss of consciousness), treatment (supporting or sub-hibernation therapy and the use of benzodiazapines), remission (within 48 hours to 2 weeks), frequency of diagnoses, correlation of stress from the event, and severity of acute stress reaction were the focus of their concerns.

Some cultural/ethnic groups place more value and receive more support from an extended family and/or community structure than others (Doherty, 1987). It is incumbent on the visiting counselor to have an understanding of the roles of these groups in order to provide more adequate and appropriate interventions for families and family members within the context of their own cultures.

Children

In an article about psychosocial intervention in disaster management in the Philippines, Ladrido and Perlas (1996) identify 3 phases of intervention: impact, inventory, and reconstruction/rehabilitation. In this framework, psychosocial processing (PSP) is aimed at helping victims re-establish equilibrium and harmony following a disaster and at regaining personal control. They identified six types of PSP activities: critical incident stress debriefing; multiple group; action-related; activity-based (for special groups such as children and adolescents); team-building; and community organization for crisis management. Ladrido and Perlas contend that delivery of psychosocial intervention to disaster victims in general, and children in particular, has a beneficial filtering effect that can significantly reduce the number of those suffering from incapacitating symptoms.

Children exposed to disasters are at risk for a number of mental health related problems. The type and severity depend on the nature and extent of disaster trauma, the influence of family and community, the resilience or vulnerability of the child, and symptom onset and duration (Aptekar& Boore, 1990). Levels of functioning and cross-cultural differences also play an important part.

Schreiber (1999) described a firestorm which struck Laguna Beach, CA on October 30, 1993 in which 400 homes were lost. He described a FEMA supported program which provided services for affected children and parents over a 17 month period. The results he reported found that levels of PTSD and comorbid depression were significantly higher in children whose homes were destroyed. Current dissatisfactions with living arrangements and perceptions of greater difficulty in school were seen as being strong correlates of distress. He discussed factors related to sustained vulnerability, post disaster stresses, adversities and traumatic reminders. The findings presented were suggested as confirming the need for extended mental health services beyond the initial event as the risk from disaster exposure continued to accrue over time.

It is well established that children and adolescents can manifest adult-like PTSD after experiencing a life-threatening stressor (Yule, 1994). Delamater and Applegate (1999) examined post-traumatic stress disorder (PTSD), behavioral adjustment, and developmental outcomes in preschool children exposed to Hurricane Andrew in 1992. Their study measured mothers' self-reports of their child's symptoms of PTSD. They concluded that many young children can be expected to exhibit PTSD symptoms and other behavioral disruptions for at least 18 months following exposure to a natural disaster. Their study demonstrated that preschool age children exposed to the stress of a major hurricane are more likely to exhibit symptoms of PTSD than a comparison group who are less exposed. Children with PTSD at 12 months were reported as being more likely to be developmentally delayed at 18 months and those with PTSD at 18 months were also likely to be delayed. They suggest the children are at risk for failure to achieve normal development in cognitive, social and emotional skills and conclude that children with PTSD are at risk for developmental delays. This study is one of the first to examine the effects of PTSD on the general development of young children and presents information that will require further study in this important area.

In the light of recent school incidents in the United States, it is of importance to find ways to develop approaches for dealing with some of the psychological, social and educational aspects of the critical challenges faced during severe crises. Stein (1997) offers a blueprint for the school psychology profession to take a leadership role in these areas. Some of the challenges he identifies include preparing communities to cope effectively with crises at the individual, school, community, and national levels; preparing children and adults to deal with potential and actual disasters; intervening on the spot during crises; and treating the psychological problems that may manifest in the aftermath. Using experiences of the past 20 years in Israel, including the relatively recent traumatic events such as the assassination of prime minister Yitzhak Rabin, Stein presents a model in which he describes different stages of reaction. In his model he places emphasis on the role of the schools and of school psychologists in developing and implementing prevention programs which emphasize the fostering of inner strengths and resources in children and teachers and making provision for the professionals helping the community in times of crisis. He also suggests future development of the school psychology profession into a broader community service.

Saylor (1993) provides a valuable resource for disaster planners, crisis interventionists, clinicians, and researchers in a book dealing with the prevention and treatment of children's mental health problems following disasters. Along with other colleagues, Saylor discusses basic theory, assessment and intervention techniques and provides a critical survey of relevant literature. Children's perceptions of disasters and crises are largely determined by the reactions of their parents. Depending on their ages, experiences, cultural teachings, beliefs, etc. they tend to have a number of common physical, emotional, cognitive and behavioral reactions. Younger children may experience different levels of contagious, objective and/or profound anxiety. Older children (adolescents), due to the disaster or crisis, may suddenly have to assume the role as head of the family. How they see these responsibilities depends to a large extent on such factors as cultural background, age, religious views, education, personal equilibrium and how they view life in general.

In summary, children may appear more resilient in their response and recovery from disaster. However, the research and literature suggest they are at risk for PTSD, depression and anxiety disorders as well as possible developmental delays as a result. Children will follow the leads of their parents, cultural/ethnic groups and belief systems. Interventions should involve, wherever possible, collaboration with a "culture-broker" or practitioner from the affected cultural group.

Responders

Those who respond to disasters and crises internationally in another culture, must be cognizant of certain issues in order to be effective in their efforts. Paton (1996) identified several important issues that relief agencies should address prior to deployment. These include:

- Define the problems posed by international disasters for relief workers and their organizations;

- Seek to define the preparatory and support needs of those who will provide relief services overseas;

- Discuss the consequences of disaster work for the families of relief workers;

- Draw upon the experiences of others who have provided search and rescue services and health assistance;

- Discuss organizational and management issues;

- Discuss and outline the current political environment;

- Discuss individual influences on well-being; and,

- Discuss the consequences of disaster work for family members.

Covering these areas in a pre-brief for workers and their families can help prevent and mitigate later problems and difficulties. Follow-up with responders following a deployment is also important. Depression, anxiety and PTSD appear to be the most prevalent results of disasters in those who have been exposed to them. Follow-up with responders after a relief effort is an important disaster mental health function. Mental disorders resulting from intense exposure to disaster incidents are possible even among seasoned veterans (McFarlane, 1990).

Approaches

Managing disaster situations is difficult at best. Strategies for improving international disaster operations can help develop and provide more effective responses. It is important to learn from crisis events, coordinate international disaster assistance, provide adequate and accurate information in disaster environments, learn how to take appropriate actions, and develop trust in disaster operations (Comfort, 1989; Paton, 1996).

The roles of local health and mental health professionals in assisting victims in coping with disasters is outlined in a book published by the World Health Organization (1989). It sets out a clear guide to what should be done by the community and local health personnel at the time of a disaster to organize rescue work and emergency care and to solve the many survival and health problems which can result from the disaster. It describes various emergencies resulting from disasters and steps that communities and local health personnel can take to prepare for the eventuality of a disaster and to prevent and mitigate its consequences. Another good resource in this area are the publications and manuals on psychosocial services in emergency measures situations prepared by the Ministry of Health and Social Services of the Government of Quebec, Canada (Martel, 1999). Health Canada's Emergency Services Division's Disaster Mental Health Manual (1999) is another good resource. In the United States, there are numerous publications available through the American Psychological Association (APA, 1996), American Red Cross (1991, 1998), and the Federal Emergency Management Agency (FEMA, 1994, 1995). Additionally, a comprehensive manual is available through the Department of Social Work at Walter Reed Hospital and the National Center for Posttraumatic Stress Disorders Disaster Mental Health Services (Young, Ford, Ruzek, Friedman, & Gusman, 1999).

In an article on the prevention of the consequences of man-made and natural disasters, de Jong and Joop (1995) reviewed a number of preventive initiatives. They proposed a model that deals with prevention on several levels, going from the International and National levels to communities of displaced persons and refugees, families and individuals. Their model integrates concepts from the fields of public health, psychology, anthropology and psychiatry. Using a matrix structure, they propose multimodal preventive interventions relative to the different societal levels involved, emphasizing prevention of psychosocial and mental health consequences.

Parkes (1997) examined the types of psychosocial problems likely to occur in different types of disasters. Using examples from actual recent disasters, he developed a rather simplified typology which could provide a basis for development of adequate and appropriate psychosocial response plans. He identified nine types of disasters:

- Small local disasters;
- Small national disasters;
- Small international disasters;
- Medium-scale local disasters;
- Medium-scale national disasters;
- Medium-scale international disasters;
- Large-scale local disasters;
- Large-scale national disasters; and,
- Large-scale international disasters.

Within the context of such plans, one way to address identified needs would be through the use of operational definitions for health and culture. Waxler-Morrison, Anderson & Richardson (1990) offer a way to do this by suggesting a number of questions:

- How do those who are affected order their lives and relationships?
- How do they meet their community obligations?
- How can they maximize their mutual satisfactions and well-being?
- How can responders offer the prospect of inducing positive physiological changes that facilitate recovery from illness?

These areas are going to be different for different cultures, making it important to understand prior to offering any psychosocial services. Using this approach along with Maslow's (1987) model for universal human development can provide a more focused and culture-specific approach to providing mental health services in any cross-cultural setting. Taylor (1998) presents an interesting example of how this might be accomplished in an article outlining his approach to providing services following a very destructive cyclone in the Cook Islands in 1997.

Middleton and Raphael (1990) examined consultation in disasters. They looked at major problem areas with respect to psychiatric consultancy in planning responses to disasters. They identified seven major areas of concern:

- Assessment of PTSD and its relationship to character pathology and other diagnoses

- Unique aspects of disasters

- Distinctions between acute effects of disaster and dealing with the long-term effects

- Few psychiatrists working full-time in the area;

- The absence of adequate sanction

- Disasters occurring in overpopulated, Third World countries that do not have at their disposal the resources to cope adequately with immediate rescue and disaster relief operations, let alone to provide mental health intervention

- Responses couched in terms of well-known models.

Fig. 5–2: Major Problem Areas of Psychiatric Consultancy in Planning Responses to Disasters

Some General Conclusions

To successfully accomplish the goals of providing adequate and appropriate cross-cultural disaster mental health services, it is essential for psychologists and other disaster mental health professionals to establish collaborative supportive international relationships (Ring & Vazquez, 1993). The development of a general model of international disaster mental health services with a strong emphasis on cross-cultural factors is needed along with plans for response based on the needs, beliefs, and desires of different countries. Consultation and collaboration with providers and planners in other countries and development of in-country disaster response plans combined with a strong educational component is necessary to help mitigate disaster mental health related responses and problems.

6 | Crises in Rural Areas

Culture and Rurality

Rural psychology has very few major studies concerning practice in rural environments and small communities. Practitioners face some very different problems from their more urban counterparts. Rural practice presents important yet challenging issues for psychology, especially given the North American and international distribution of the population, levels of need for psychological services in rural settings, limited availability of rural services, and migration of rural residents to urban centers. Direct service issues include the need to accommodate a wide variety of mental health difficulties, issues related to client privacy and boundaries, and practical challenges. Indirect service issues include the greater need for diverse professional activities, including collaborative work with professionals having different orientations and beliefs, program development and evaluation, and conducting research with few mentors or peer collaborators. Professional training and development issues include lack of specialized relevant courses and placements, and such personal issues as limited opportunities for recreation and culture, and lack of privacy. Psychology will need to address more fully these complex issues if rural residents are to receive equitable treatment and services (Barbopoulos & Clark, 2003).

Some Cultural Considerations

Beyond the fact that rural culture differs from urban culture, there are also some considerations about ethnic cultural differences that need to be taken into account by practitioners providing services in different rural areas. This is especially important when providing short-term interventions following major disasters, critical incidents and other crises in a culture not one's own. For example, in Puerto Rico, a United States Commonwealth, some background information is very important. The Estado Libre Asociado de Puerto Rico (autonomous commonwealth), established in 1952, redefined the political relationship between the United States and its colony. The ambiguous political status—autonomy without sovereignty, self-government without self-determination—created new social, political, and cultural contradictions. The island's first elected governor, Luis Munoz Marin, was committed to promoting an essentially pure Puerto Rican culture centered around the idealization of traditional rural life, while simultaneously creating a new democratic citizenship, both of which would bolster the new government's legitimacy before its people. Puerto Rican scholar Cati Marsh Kennerley (2003) explores the collective work done by the Division de Educacion de la Comunidad (DivEdCo), the government educational agency charged with promulgating Munoz Marin's ideas about Puerto Rican culture and citizenship. Marsh Kennerley draws from a wide variety of sources to reconstruct an untold history, analyze its contradictions, obtain lessons from DivEdCo's negotiations, and point out its relevance for understanding contemporary Puerto Rican culture. This is important for anyone who will consider providing services in times of need.

In another example, (Gavin,2003) shares her experiences of training and working as a psychoanalytical psychotherapist in the United Kingdom and then in a smaller city in the West of Ireland. The range of people seeking counseling and therapy as well as the social arrangements and their effects of the boundaries of the therapy are discussed. Gavin concludes that it is vital to try to understand the cultural context within which one is working but one has to also be clear about what one considers to be the fundamental of one's particular orientation.

Weyer, Hustey & Rathbun (2003) provide a case study pertaining to the care of a dying 93-yr-old Amish woman with congestive heart failure living in a rural Amish community. They explore the world of the Amish community in some detail. Their overall beliefs, values, and behavior are discussed as well as how their lifestyle affects their health care decisions, access to health care, and reimbursement of services. Weyer et al state that nurse practitioners can offer culturally sensitive and appropriate health care to the Amish population by recognizing important cultural values that have survived for more than 300 years. Such sensitivities are important in understanding and reaching out to other cultural groups effectively.

Phillips, Li & Zhang (2002) present a picture of the current pattern of suicides in China. Suicide rates by sex, 5-yr age-group, and region (urban or rural) reported by the Chinese Ministry of Health were adjusted according to an estimated rate. It was estimated that a mean annual suicide rate of 23 per 100,000 accounted for 3.6% of all deaths in China and was the fifth most important cause of death for rural women, the eighth most important cause for urban women and men, and the fourteenth most important cause for urban men. The toll was particularly high in individuals aged 15-34 yrs, accounting for 18.9% of such deaths. Rural sui-cide rates were three times higher in both sexes, for all age-groups, and over time. Suicide is a major health problem for China; this public-health issue demands intervention development for high risk persons. A number of different explanations are likely plausible for such high rates. Reardon (2002) suggests that the uniquely high rates documented by Phillips et al may be partly explained by the strictly enforced birth quotas in China while Bertolote and Fleischmann (2002) point out the association between suicide and mental disorders.

Rural Problems

Domestic Violence

Wendt, Taylor & Kennedy (2002) provide a critique of the Australian research into rural domestic violence. Research to date has focused on the factors that keep rural women trapped in violent relationships. While this research has been useful in developing policy to address rural domes-tic violence, it has not yet provided information about women's understandings of their rural contexts. Research into domestic violence is moving towards acknowledging and recognizing the complexities and dif-ferences between people's experiences. Wendt et al suggest that it is time to explore the differences between various rural regions and to move away from the assumption that there is one rural culture. They suggest that a move towards feminist post-structural perspectives has strengths in that it enables a focus on the meanings of rural cultures from the perspectives of women who experience, and men who perpetrate, domestic violence. If these meanings become apparent, it may enable local solutions to be im-plemented and contribute knowledge and new ideas.

Although it has been suggested frequently that certain aspects of rural culture present barriers to women escaping domestic violence, research has not yet focused on how rural culture affects women's experiences. Wendt & Cheers (2002) report a study that explored how 14 rural women experiencing domestic violence perceived local cultural beliefs and values, the extent to which they had internalized these, and how they believed ru-ral culture affected them in their situations. Components of their local rural cultures that they identified as impacting on their experiences of domestic violence included: belief in the sanctity and permanence of mar-riage, the importance and privacy of the nuclear family, Christian doctrine, and preservation of intergenerational property transfer. Each woman's story shows that, while rural culture gave them strength to en-dure the violence, it also created internal conflicts between wanting to escape and the cultural beliefs and values that they had internalized. Also, they were afraid of community reactions should they leave. Consequently, they did not disclose their violent situation and had persevered in them far longer than they thought they would have in a different cultural context.

Older People

It has been well documented that people of all ages and cultures reminisce, that is, tell and retell the stories of their lives-whether in the privacy of their own thoughts or in the more public and shared realms of family, friends, community, and media (Campbell, 2002; Webster & McCall, 1999; McAdams, 1993; Bruner, 1990). A consensus on the functions of reminiscing has been more elusive, with thinkers weighing in from a broad range of psychological perspectives (Butler, 1963; Cohler, 1993; Gergen, 1996; Schafer, 1992; Wallace, 1992). Reminiscence generally is considered a narrative activity, in which people conceive and tell stories as a way of making sense of the events that happen to and around them. Narrative is an ongoing process of meaning-making that is both socially-defined and culturally-grounded; that is, people tend to tell different stories at different times and to different audiences. Webster (1993, 1995, 1997, 1999) proposed eight reasons, or factors, for reminiscing and used them in his Reminiscence Functions Scale (RFS, 1993)-Boredom Reduction, Death Preparation, Identity, Problem-Solving, Conversation, Intimacy Maintenance, Bitterness Revival, and Teach/Inform. Campbell (2002) used the RFS to explore the effects on reminiscence functions from clinical depression, specifically in a population of older adults in rural northwestern Illinois. Given that depressed older adults typically experience fatigue/insomnia, anxiety, hopelessness, worthlessness, diminished interest in people and activities, and thoughts of death, Campbell predicted that they would score higher than non-depressed elders on Death Preparation and Bitterness Revival, lower on Conversation and Intimacy Maintenance. Research involving 30 individuals, half of whom had been professionally diagnosed with a significant depressive disorder, demonstrated that the depressed subjects scored significantly higher than their non-depressed peers on Bitterness Revival, with trends toward significance on Boredom Reduction and Identity. No other factor differences were statistically significant. Campbell confirmed that the general tendency within depression to think negatively extends to one's reminiscence. Depressed individuals in this study-more so than their non-depressed peers-identified patterns of reminiscence that frequently focused on painful memories or lost opportunities and served to fill idle, restless time. No difference appeared in the frequency of overall reminiscence.

Rural Practice

Jensen & Royeen (2002) describe the processes and outcomes of an action research project targeted at describing 'best practice' as experienced by interdisciplinary rural health projects funded by the Quentin N. Burdick Program for Rural Interdisciplinary Training, a Federally funded training grant competition in the USA. Each of 15 rural interdisciplinary health training projects across the areas of mental health, chronic disease, diabetes, minority health, and geriatrics was used to build a qualitative case study representing best practice experiences in projects focused on improving rural access to care. Across these programs, best practice is seen in the integrated dimensions of connections, community, and culture. In the USA, academic institutions build meaningful authentic connections with rural communities as they work together in meeting community needs, while demonstrating sensitivity and respect for cultural perspectives. Implications are offered in the context of higher education, health care delivery, and Federal initiatives within the USA.

Children and School Counseling

Early Childhood

Kennedy (2003) investigated the context and causes of global human fertility decline. The global total fertility rate-the average number of children born to women over their lifetimes-has fallen for the past two hundred years. This process, which began in Europe and continues today in the developing world, has been described but not sufficiently explained by demographers. Kennedy's study is directed towards understanding the root causes and context of the trend in falling birth rates for populations around the world. He presents an analysis of this phenomenon with an investigation of Honduras as a case study in fertility decline. He critiques social science theories of fertility decline and argues for a theory that crosses disciplinary boundaries in the social sciences, addresses gender, and includes a component that acknowledges the role of evolutionary forces on human reproductive motivation. He also argues for recognition of the role of culture in human behavior and an understanding of culture as an end product of human evolution. He stresses the need for empirical studies to operationalize and measure cultural variables. Kennedy suggests adapting Warren Miller's Childbearing Questionnaire as a means of operationalizing and measuring natality culture. He describes his data collection technique for adapting and administering this scale using a variety of sampling procedures on 400 people living in and around the city of Catacamas, Olancho, Honduras and presents an analysis of these data and data collected nationally on reproductive attitudes. His analysis demonstrates that there is considerable evidence for cultural agreement about positive and negative motivations for childbearing. However, there is also evidence for important intra-cultural diversity. This diversity is primarily associated with sex and urban or rural location. Kennedy argues that changing evaluations of the appropriate quality and quantity of childbearing drives this cultural diversity of natality culture and that these changing evaluations are related to shifting notions of appropriate masculine and feminine roles. Changing economic opportunities that affect parents' evaluations of their contributions towards their children's futures are suggested as causing these shifting of gender roles.

Research indicates that mothers structure or scaffold children's early play. However, it is unclear whether these findings can be generalized to mothers and children of different cultures. Culture-specific and ecological factors may affect a mother's inclination and motivation to play with her child, her scaffolding behaviors, her involvement in play, and the type and kind of play she engages in. Rajouria (2002) explores and provides preliminary descriptions of how play is defined, perceived, and valued by a sample of fifteen rural Nepali mothers. The study also describes the kind of play interactions Nepali mothers have with their young children who range in age from twelve to thirty-six months. The qualitative method of research was used to address the research questions. Data were collected through participant observation, videotapes of mother-child play in the course of everyday activity in the home, and interviews and discussion with the mothers based on the videotaped activities between them and their children. The results of the study reveal that play appears to be an integral aspect of mother-child interaction in daily care routines and is seen as a valuable means for keeping the child engaged, for managing child behavior, and for encouraging children's co-operation. The mothers in this study have a positive attitude towards play and are aware of the developmental impact it has on children, even though they underestimate their own roles in play interaction with their children. Findings contribute to the field of child development and education by building on existing cross-cultural literature on play. Early childhood educators and practitioners will be able to utilize the results of this study to inform their work in designing and implementing culturally relevant child development and education programs that are meaningful for the target population.

Cultural research on play has been conducted in communities that vary across economic and societal variables, such as subsistence, industry, child integration into adult settings, primary (having contact with few people) and secondary settings, quantity of information to be transmitted, learning style (apprenticeship and instruction), and independence and interdependence. Davis (2002) looks at differences in the local activity settings and interactions surrounding children's play, but across sites that are relatively similar. She studied social play among four to five year olds in three Costa Rican preschools: a rural, public preschool (n = 18), an urban, University Lab preschool (n = 25), and a preschool in an urban, blue-collar neighborhood (n = 29). The data were video tapes of play, ethnographic field notes, a child assessment of friendships, and teacher interviews about their goals for educating preschoolers. Qualitative and quantitative data were integrated. Children's spontaneous play was influenced by the cultural structuring of activity settings and teachers' socialization practices. (20) found significant differences between the rural and Lab preschools. The children in both groups played in dyads. However, the rural children played in large groups and had many friends. The Lab preschool children played in small groups and had fewer friends. The urban, lower-income site was in between. The rural preschool teacher organized the classroom and schedule to support large group interactions. She encouraged inclusion in play, particularly within genders. Children elaborated a few play scripts and invested in a few, established leaders. Children's roles were established by gender and by social knowledge of status relationships. Status rarely changed-leaders stayed leaders, for example. Conversely, the Lab preschool teacher minimized large groups with small, separated work areas. Children were taught to respect individual friendships. They invented many play scripts, and many children were leaders. Roles changed with each play group, and status was based on friendships. Despite relative similarities across sites (ethnicity, nationality), a comparison of activity settings in play revealed diversity in contexts, mechanisms, and outcomes. Diversity, then, is not a function of ethnicity but can be measured in the daily routines and minutiae of everyday life.

In the Hispano homeland of northern New Mexico, children's lives are shaped by land, by family, by culture, and by community. The way these forces work together forms each child's sense of place and place attachments. Using short case examples (3 children, aged 10 and 11 yrs), Derr (2002) presents a brief overview of children's place experiences and preferences and describes some of the factors that contribute to children's sense of place in 3 communities, of northern New Mexico which represent a range from urban to rural. It demonstrates the important role extended family and direct experience play in shaping children's sense of place and understanding of nature.

Derr (2002) documents the cultural, ecological, and individual experiences that compose a sense of place for children in three communities of northern New Mexico-Mora, Dixon, and Santa Fe-which represent a gradient from rural to urban. Through qualitative methods; Derr explored the place experiences of 89 children and generated thematic areas in which twelve case studies were developed. 'Four wheelers, ramps, and rites of passage' and 'the fort-makers' are themes where children's individual preferences and developmental needs figure highly, and 'Learning Care' and 'The Web' are themes where experience is particularly influenced by the guidance of family, adults, community, and culture. When children experienced nature, culture, and family as an interwoven entity, their connections and attachments were indeed strong and meaningful. When sense of place was strong, grandparents and elders were particularly important in passing on their knowledge and sense of the world to their children, and thus in influencing the way children experienced and mediated place. Some cases also illustrate that a sense of place is not the same as a sense of nature. Other children demonstrated weaker or more diffuse sense of place. In these cases, sense of place usually was not well developed in children for one of two reasons: social stability was not present in their home, neighborhood, or community to enable a sense of place to develop, or mobility weakened place connections and attachments. Children can learn about nature and have productive and interesting lives without a sense of place. However, Derr demonstrates a qualitative difference in the way experiences occur for children with a sense of place than for those without. Sense of place is a compelling concept, and its influence can be significant in children's and families' lives. Yet it will be increasingly important to listen to children, to hear their voices, and to allow their involvement in the creation of a sense of place if it is to be relevant, lasting, and meaningful for the children, themselves.

Role of Counseling in Rural Schools

Sutton & Pearson (2002) examined the role of school counseling in a rural small town school environment. 100 school counselors working in small town and rural schools participated in group sessions. From those subjects 19 individual interviews were conducted. The results of the study are presented through a discussion of the data associated with a set of categories and codes focused on the geographic and community contexts. The specific patterns of the "rural" theme that are presented and discussed are: (a) rural/small town communities, (b) rural/small town culture, (c) counselor visibility and accessibility to the community, (d) the counselor as a community mental health resource, (e) quality of life, and (f) students. Interviews with the subjects gave a rich, different view of the benefits and disadvantages, the possibilities and limitations, and the satisfactions and challenges of the settings in which they worked and lived.

Conclusion

Not only does the culture of rurality have differences from urban areas, but rural cross-cultural differences are also important in understanding and providing appropriate responses and services to residents of rural environments. Further attention and study of these areas as well as the awareness of what is already known is needed to inform mental health and other professionals working in these areas.

Farm and Ranch Crises

Background

Recent concerns in agriculture have caused people to take a look at where their food comes from. The crisis in the cattle industry as a result of concerns surrounding Mad Cow Disease and, in the Far East, concerns about "Bird Flu" in chickens contribute to stressors not only in the general public, but also among farmers and ranchers who strive to keep the population fed.

The US farm crisis in the 1980s refocused national attention on the plight of rural areas. Data indicate that, relative to urban areas, rural America suffers from the double burden of
   a) high levels of poverty, disability, and impairment and
   b) inadequate health and human services.
Wagenfeld (1988) introduced a special issue of the Journal of Rural Community Psychology that presented a status report on the mental health problems of rural areas during that period. Topics discussed included the social ecology of inpatient mental health services, the response of community mental health centers to the farm crisis, innovative mental health services, policy approaches to improving mental health services, and a research agenda for rural community psychology.

Ramirez-Ferrero (2002) challenges interpretations of the ongoing restructuring of the American agricultural sector as simply an economic phenomenon with psychological consequences. Ramirez-Ferrero argues that male farmers' responses to the farm financial crisis are not strictly psychological, individual or idiosyncratic, but cultural. Subjects' actions and beliefs are a consequence of a multiplicity of cultural discourses. It is their socially-constructed sense of self or subjectivity (mediated by cultural processes of power) that determines which ones they internalize, consider and act upon. Rural northwest Oklahoma served as the locus of this study. Research was conducted with farm families and included the collection of life histories from 13 couples, periodic participant-observation on a farm, unstructured and structured interviews with health professionals and focus group research. This study incorporated farmers' life stories, particularly those of crisis, to understand local notions of gender, kinship, land, farming styles, familial and farm goals, and community. Informants' life stories are presented in the context of broader discussions of the history of northwest Oklahoma, agricultural economics, corporate and capitalist processes, and Christianity to understand the social construction of the emotion of pride, an emotion that is critical in understanding men's responses to the farm crisis. Ramirez-Ferrero suggests that emotions are culturally mediated, embodied thoughts that are necessarily evaluative, and therefore challenges the common understanding of emotions as biological and psychological phenomena. Because the patriarchal foundation of farming communities is being eroded by industrial values, men experience the devaluation of cultural ideas that supported their subjectivity, specifically, the emotion of pride. This devaluation, in turn, leads men to actions and inactions that are often negative, destructive and tragic.

Stein (1984) explored the cultural ethos and psychodynamics underlying a duality in the Midwestern/Southwestern US male character, which is encapsulated in the image of the steadfastly sedentary farmer and that of the adventuresome vagabond cowboy—both at war with one another in the same person. This duality is considered primarily within the context of Oklahoma wheat-farming and cattle-ranching families, but it is in fact a variation upon a regional Midwestern/Southwestern US identity. Stein argues that the psychologically primitive qualities attributed and allocated to the Midwest/Southwest by the larger national group keep the unstable regional masculine character "stirred up" and thereby available to the rest of the nation as both negative example and positive source for the current national nostalgia and as support for political "conservatism" and international militarism.

As things change in rural areas, the need for appropriate social services also changes. Martinez-Brawley & Blundall (1991) interviewed 44 farm families in Iowa and Pennsylvania concerning beliefs and attitudes about need and social services. Families in Iowa had been severely affected by an agricultural crisis and were more likely to have had contact with organized social services. Seeking assistance appeared more acceptable in Iowa than in Pennsylvania. Among the families, there was a sense that success and failure had little to do with deservingness. The perception that the world is unfair was overwhelming in Iowa. Families did not view themselves as needing special help as a class of people, yet they did voice concerns about not being understood by outside systems. Services that were found to be the least acceptable in both Iowa and Pennsylvania were those closely associated with depression indicators (e.g., problems with spouse, increased dependency on school, feelings of anxiety or isolation).

Schulman & Armstrong (1990) analyzed interview data from statewide surveys of 670 farm operators collected during a period of economic and ecological crisis to examine relationships among perceived stress, social support, and survival in agriculture. While the level of perceived stress had no relationship with survival, social support had a significant impact on both social psychological and behavioral dimensions of survival in agriculture. Perceived social support increased plans to remain in agriculture and increased the probability of a person continuing farming.

Using data from a statewide survey of 725 North Carolina farm operators collected during a period of economic and ecological crisis in 1986, Schulman & Armstrong (1989) analyzed the relationships between perceived social psychological distress, social support, and demographic, farm structure, and socioeconomic characteristics. Younger operators showed higher distress levels, and age and social support interacted so that social support lowered distress levels more for younger than for older operators. Results also suggested that total family income had a curvilinear relationship with perceived distress. Low and high income farm operators manifested higher levels of distress than middle income operators. Results have implications for policy intervention and farm crisis support programs.

Cook, John R. & Tyler (1989) examined the attitudes of 34 North Dakota farm couples toward receiving help for a personal problem. subjects were assigned to groups according to level of financial coping with respect to the possible loss of their farm (stable, declining, and out of business). subjects who were out of business or declining were more open to receiving help from educational sources than subjects whose farms were stable. Female subjects were open to receiving help regardless of their level of financial coping while their husbands were as receptive to help only at times of financial crisis. subjects showed reluctance to make use of outside resources of any kind.

Leaving the Farm

Early on, Lamarche (1960) suggested that rural crises are created by the movement to the city, especially on the part of the young, and abandonment of the land. Rapid social evolution without any preparation can have undesirable psychological effects.

In the 1980s there was a high level of interest in retirement of farmers because of an aging farm population and concern that the "farm crisis' may have disrupted succession patterns. Keating & Munro (1989) described the process of exit from farm businesses of a group of older farmers and determined the relationship between goals of family succession and behaviors in the exit phase. A sequence of exit from work, management, and ownership was found. Farmers (aged 50+ yrs) who value continuity were most likely to involve sons in management of the operation. Keating & Munro suggested that programs for two-generation farm families may be useful in the early part of the exit phase while estate planning information and programs may be more appropriate to those in the latter part of the process.

Stress on the Farm and Range

Carson; Araquistain & Ide (1994) examined the relationship between potential family vulnerability factors (stressors and strains), manifestations of maladaptation (family discord and distress), family strengths (hardiness), and measures of bonadaptation (quality of life) as reported by 188 men and women representing 100 Idaho farm and ranch families. subjects completed a battery of tests, including the Farm/Ranch Stress Scale, a demographic questionnaire, and four measures from the Family Invulnerability Test. Family strains and stressors unique to farming and ranching were positively associated with family discord and distress but negatively associated with hardiness and quality of life. Greater family hardiness as reported by both wives and husbands was positively correlated with their perceptions of family quality of life.

Plunkett; Henry & Knaub (1999) studied 77 adolescents in farm and ranch families to examine the relationship of demographic variables, family stressor events, and family coping strategies to adolescent adaptation. Results indicated that adolescent age and family transitions were positively related to individual stress. Males reported less family stress than did females. Seeking spiritual support was negatively related to family stress, while the perceived impact of the farm crisis was positively related to family stress. Family support was positively related, and family substance use issues were negatively related, to adolescent satisfaction with family life.

Swisher; Elder & Lorenz (1998) examined how the occupation of farming structures the stress experiences of individuals through the timing and placement of actions. They showed how occupations have effects that spillover into family and friendship relationships. The sample came from the Iowa Youth and Families Project, a longitudinal study of siblings and parents in the aftermath of the farm crisis of the 1980s, and included 424 married couples who had one child in the 7th grade and another child within four years of age of the 1st child. Results show that farming affects both exposure and vulnerability to stressors. Specifically, farm men are more exposed to financial and job-related stressors, while less prone to marital conflict, than non-farmers. Given the importance of cohesion in farm family operations, farm men are more vulnerable to such conflict when it occurs. However, farm men are unaffected, if not consoled, by knowledge of undesirable events in the lives of their friends. It was concluded that farm men use downward social comparisons to cope with the high levels of uncertainty characteristic of farming in the aftermath of the 1980s farm crisis. The lives of rural families who suffered economic hardship and economic pressure caused many to face difficult choices in response to hardship. Multiple adjustments created significant pain for many of these families. This was evidenced by the extreme emotional distress among families who lost a farm as a result of the crisis.

Rettig; Danes & Bauer (1991) describes a resource exchange theory that outlines the dimensions of life quality and presents a multidimensional scale measure of personal evaluations of family life quality based on this theory. The scale includes items representing love, status, services, information, goods, and money resources received from the family. It is suggested that receipt of these resources satisfied personal needs for (1) love and affection, (2) respect and esteem, (3) comfort and assistance, (4) shared meaning, (5) personal things, and (6) money for personal use.

Van Hook (1990) Interviewed 49 adolescents (mean age 16.8 yrs) during the farm crisis. In 66% of the families, there was an increase in parental work responsibilities outside the family farm or business. Family tensions increased in response to the economic uncertainties and change in family roles. The farm crisis was an anxious time for subjects, who described major gaps in family and community information systems. Feelings of personal responsibility for family economic problems were found in 63% of the subjects. The determination of subjects to prepare to cope with an uncertain and unfair world may involve the shift from farming to other occupations. Increased levels of anxiety, depression, and suicide attempts make this a high-risk population during difficult times.

Cecil (1998) describes the development and implementation of Stress: Country Style, an Illinois program designed as a response to stress problems among farm families created by an economic downturn. The program involved a crisis line, outreach counseling, and community education about stress. The relationship between the program and community mental health centers is also addressed. Successes and failures of the program are considered.

Walker & Walker (1998) studied the self-reported incidence of stress-related symptoms in 476 male and 341 female farmers and 70 male and 39 female urban residents. Close to 50% of the farmers reported the frequent to constant occurrence of the symptoms of trouble relaxing, loss of temper, and fatigue; over 30% reported similar occurrence rates for 6 additional symptoms. Self-reported symptom rates were significantly higher in farm women than in farm men, higher in younger farmers, higher in mixed farming operations, and higher in farmers who were holding off-farm employment. Symptom scores were significantly higher in the farmers compared with the urban subjects. Scores on five symptoms distinguished farm and urban subjects. Walker & Walker suggest that the chronic stress associated with the farm financial crisis may have caused a high self-reported incidence of symptoms among farmers.

Loeb & Dvorak (1987) discuss the high level of stress experienced by many of today's farm families. They suggest that health professionals should be aware of the current situation to deal effectively with the farm family as a unit. Therapists must be well versed in farm family dynamics before they can understand the impact of external factors. The following topics are of importance:

- the economics of farming;

- the farm family (husband, wife, in-laws, adult children);

- communication in farm families; and

- health issues.

Loeb & Dvorak conclude that there is no end in sight to the farm crisis and that many more families will need support from trained experts in the future.

Hargrove (1986) examined the myth of rural communities uniting under stress and suggests clinical and community activities for mental health workers during farm crises. A model for understanding human response to natural disasters is useful for understanding response to such crises. Hargrove suggests that the clinical/advocate model developed by G. B. Melton (1983; see also PA, Vol 61:9256) provides a useful perspective from which to operate.

Olson & Schellenberg (1986) examined stressors in farm environments, using data from questionnaire surveys of general, familial, and extra-familial farm stressors. General stressors include problems such as machinery breakdown and harvests, while familial stressors involve role incongruence and conflict. The discussion of extra-familial stressors emphasizes financial stressors and farm financial crises. Olson & Schellenberg suggest that financial stressors are becoming more intense relative to familial factors because of farm crises. They consider directions for community psychology in terms of four types of programs aimed at preventing or alleviating farm financial stress:

1) general education/socialization,

2) individual skill training,

3) development of supportive social agencies, and

4) political action.

They also note the importance of a multiple program approach emphasizing early detection of farm financial stress.

Farmer (1986) suggests that farmers who have failed in the farm crisis of the 1980s blame themselves, although even top producers and managers had been affected. The prevalence of depression is not surprising considering the severity of the losses, the prolonged nature of the stress, and the minimal control farmers have in overcoming their problems. Participation in farm support groups may be effective for families working through a fairly predictable grief cycle involving denial, anxiety, guilt, anger, hostility, confusion, and depression.

Internal and external threats could soon squeeze some ranch and farm families out of business. To assist ranch families with these threats and with amiably transferring the operation to the next generation, Zimmerman (1984) offers a six-step Consensus Management Model that combines strategic planning with psycho-education/family therapy. A pilot test with an intergenerational ranch family indicated improvements in family functioning, including reduced stress and depression and improved self-esteem and family coping levels.

Suicide

Ragland, John D. & Berman (1990-1991) examined the relationship between the farm economic crisis and farmer suicide rates, using data from 15 states in the US from 1980 to 1985. Suicide frequencies for farmers and two control occupations (forestry and transportation workers) were obtained. The 1980 US Census occupational population data were used to convert these frequencies into suicide rates. Suicide rates for farmers were greater than rates for transportation workers (truck drivers), but no different from rates for forestry workers. A significant positive correlation between the declining farm economy and increasing state suicide rates was also found.

Changing Roles

In a longitudinal study using preferences for living near family and in the local community obtained in the 8th and 11th grades, Elder; King & Conger (1996) modeled the social and developmental pathways by which adolescents approach decisions to leave home and settle in other parts of the country. Data come from 351 two-parent families in the Iowa Youth and Family Project, launched in 1989 to investigate the economic stresses and family consequences of the farm crisis. Lack of socioeconomic opportunity; relatively weak and declining ties to parents, kin, and the religious community; and strong educational prospects emerged as strong sources of a declining preference for living near family and in the local community among boys and girls. Whether coupled with family attachments or not, plans to settle elsewhere after education were linked to more elevated feelings of depression and unhappiness about life.

Conger; Elder & Lorenz (1994) examined the plight of several hundred rural families who lived through the years of economic hardship in the mid-1980s. The participants in the Iowa Youth and Families Project included farmers, people from small towns, and those who lost farms and other businesses as a result of the "farm crisis." Conger et al traced the influence of economic hardship on the emotions, behavior, and relationships of parents, children, siblings, husbands, and wives. They interviewed four members in each of 451 rural families. All of the families in the study included a seventh-grade adolescent when they were interviewed in 1989. In addition to this target adolescent, both parents of the seventh-grader and a sibling within four years of age participated in the study. They were particularly concerned with the quality of social relationships both within and outside the family that might affect the various linkages in their theoretical model of family economic stress.

Cook & Heppner (1997) investigated the role of coping strategies, perceived control, and problem-solving appraisal in farmers' career transition processes. The sample, examined previously by P. P. Heppner et al (1991), included 79 male and female farmers (aged 39.2 and 41.6, respectively) who were participating in career transition workshops. Relationships among the three variables and an outcome variable, depressive symptomatology, were examined. Significant correlations were found between problem-solving appraisal and all other variables in this study. Coping strategies were found to be related to depressive symptomatology. In a regression equation, only coping strategies contributed significantly, and no significant interaction was found between coping strategies and perceived control as hypothesized.

McInnes (2000) focused on the complex dynamics related to the family farm and their effect on the rural couple's relationship. The typical relationship examined was where the man is from a farming background and the woman from the city, or, if originally from the land, has lived or studied away from the district and been independent. The challenge for the counselor is to work with the two levels the couple bring:

1) the couple's 'individual' story and

2) the larger context, including the man's family of origin, the family farm, the rural community, and the rural crisis nationally.

A case study of the typical couple's process and outcome in counseling was provided. It was concluded that the traditional stories about men, women and relationships that once ordered the lives of couples on the land are no longer valid in times of enormous social and political change.

In life course theory, the principle of human agency states that "individuals construct their own life course through the choices and actions they take within the constraints and opportunities of history and social circumstances." Elder & Russell (2000) explore the implications of this principle, drawing upon three other principles of life course study:

• The location of individual lives in historical time and place.

• The differential timing of lives through events and experiences.

• Linked lives.

They focus on two historical periods in which adolescence was shaped by the agency of young people and their opportunities and constraints: the Great Depression of the 1930s, and the Great Farm Crisis and rural decline of the 1980s and 1990s. The resulting portrait is documented by research on lives in changing times over three decades. Within these historical eras, Elder & Russell view the agency of youth in terms defined by specific historical times and places. World War II played a major role in structuring pathways out of Depression disadvantage. Fifty years later, migration to urban areas of economic prosperity provided a general escape route for youth in the disadvantaged rural Midwest of the US. In each era, societal changes left their mark on the expression of human agency in youth's "negotiation of adolescence."

Conger; Rueter & Conger (2000) presents research from the Iowa Youth and Families Project (IYFP), a longitudinal study of Iowa families who were living in small towns and on farms during the farm crisis of the 1980s. The research was designed to assess how the macrosocial change and economic upheaval that occurred across the US during the 1980s influenced family functioning and the well-being of parents and their children. (4) describes the empirical and theoretical foundations for the Family Stress Model. The sections that follow summarize findings from the IYFP and other studies relevant to the various processes and mechanisms proposed in the Family Stress Model. (4) also consider research on hypothesized protective mechanisms or dimensions of vulnerability that may moderate the causal linkages proposed in the theoretical model. After reviewing the possible applied significance of this work, they close with a discussion of conclusions that can be drawn from the research conducted thus far and the implications of these findings for future investigations of family economic stress.

In another example, the crisis in the farming industry in the Netherlands has had far-reaching negative consequences for the well-being of farm-families. Based on identity-theory, Gorgievski-Duijvesteijn (1999) hypothesized that job-involvement (the psychological importance of the professional role) would intensify the negative relationship between role-relevant stressors and well-being. Specifically, 107 Dutch, self-employed dairy farm-couples (mean age 52 yrs for husbands and 49 yrs for wives) participated in a study that examined whether job-involvement exacerbates the negative effect of three role-relevant stressors (potential threats to business continuity, restrictions on autonomy as a self-employed person, and financial problems) on two indicators of well-being (job-related worrying and mental health complaints). Gender differences were also explored. Results show partial support for the hypotheses derived from identity-theory in that job-involvement only exacerbates the positive relationship between financial problems and job-related worrying for both spouses. No other moderating effects of job-involvement were found. Although husbands were more involved in farming than wives, the direct effect of the three role-relevant stressors on the two indicators of well-being were similar for both spouses.

During economic downturns, traditional gender allocations of labor have been considered to vary more than in prosperous times. While most studies have examined the division of labor in the household or in paid employment, Lobao & Meyer (1995) examined it where both intersect, in family-owned and family-operated enterprises in the farm sector of the 1980s. This context, combining crisis conditions and the agency of economic actors, should be related to greater flexibility in labor allocations, leading to the feminization of farming. However, a contrasting perspective argues for rigidity of gender roles in farming. Lobao & Meyer use data from a twelve-state midwestern sample and a more detailed Ohio study. The results failed to support the flexibility thesis. The rigidity of production roles was further translated into different factors related to women's and men's stress.

DeFrain & Schroff (1991) examined how city life and country life differences influence parents in their efforts to rear children as well as endeavor to paint a more realistic picture of rural life. They begin with a section on the impact of urbanization on fathers and mothers in the United States, discusses the pluralistic nature of the city, the increased leisure of urban youth as compared to rural youth, the power of the youth peer group in urban areas, the impersonality and anonymity of the city, the pervasive nature of the urban mass media, and the urban ghetto. They focus on the positive aspects of urbanization: the advantages urban organization offers families and the relative affluence of the city compared to the country. They discuss special problems of rural fathers and mothers in the United States, including the dramatic decline in the farm population, the most recent wave of the continuing farm crisis, agricultural fundamentalism, resettlement, the impact of urbanization on farm parents and their children, the fact that the farm parents often find themselves preparing their children for an urban-industrial world they themselves do not fully understand, the difficult realities of the rural economy today, and rural social class barriers farm families face.

Willson (1928) deals with the education of farm children and the relation of education to the migration to non-farming occupations. It is based upon original research of the author for Western North Dakota (N. Dak. Agr. Exper. Sta. Bull. 214, 1928) during the agricultural depression of 1920-1926. The data show that improved agricultural conditions and better financial returns from farming result in improved educational facilities and increased grade and high school attendance by farm children. A decrease in the number of farms did not operate to deprive the children of grade school education. The amount of high school education is decreased as distance from secondary schools and the proportion of foreign-born—especially the Russians—within the community are increased. The percentage of farm children in high schools is increasing. The percentage of farm children entering non-farming occupations increased directly with the amount of education they received. A point demonstrated in this study is the relationship between ability to survive the agricultural crisis and type of family organization. The married individuals who had children survived the depression best of all.

Different Approaches

Peeks (1989) posits that school counselors must be ready to work with children of farm families in crisis to direct solutions to the presenting problems and provide the family with hope for the future. She notes that the problem of the student from a farm family can be viewed as a metaphor (mirroring the parents' own fears about the future and feelings of hopelessness) and a form of protection (diverting parental attention toward a solvable problem).

Mermelstein & Sundet (1998) focused on the decision criteria that influenced 118 directors of rural community mental health centers (CMHCs) as to whether to adopt innovative programming with regard to the crisis among farmers. Five criteria were postulated as independent variables:

- compatibility with the director's values and

- relative advantage,

- observability,

- feasibility, and

- trial-ability of the innovation.

The dependent variables were the amount and type of farm crisis programming and the date of introduction into the CMHC. Findings demonstrate the widespread failure of CMHCs to respond effectively to mental health concerns arising from massive environmental stress. Impediments to innovation appear to be a real or perceived paucity of resources and a mentality favoring existing programs.

Peeks (1989) reviewed the transitions faced by adults from farm families whose farms have failed in the agriculture crisis, including career transition, relocating, a redefined lifestyle, and refocusing on future goals. Students' school problems are discussed as behavioral metaphors for the family's crisis, and a school-based strategy for counselors to help students whose problems are related to the family transitions is described. Six strategic interventions for solving student problems by inviting the parents to school and focusing on positive problem-solving solutions are presented.

Paulsen (1988) asserts that the rural crisis is creating new numbers of rural individuals who are in need of assistance as they cope with the

stress of economic dislocation and the overwhelming difficulties that occur after the loss of a farm or business. Individual, family, and
community treatment aspects are discussed within the thematic context
of a culture in crisis. An urban-based regional family service agency,
Farmers Helping Farmers, is presented as an example of a systems response to the rural crisis. The proposed treatment involves a multilevel
community response that includes self-help support groups, instruction
of adaptive coping skills, and sharing information in rural communities.
Mental health professionals are challenged to further their understanding
of the rural crisis and to adopt more flexible treatment strategies to encompass a multilevel systems response.

Jurich & Russell (1987) evaluated 15 farm families who underwent
therapy at the Kansas State University Family Center, using a model of
family adaptation to stress by H. I. McCubbin et al (see record 1981-
30250-001). Major interventions included reframing, mobilizing resources, and utilizing less indirect means of intervention. subjects showed
a greater increase in well-being at three months than did a general sample of clients. However, stress levels were not lowered as much as the
general sample and life satisfaction was lower at follow-up than the general population.

Davis-Brown & Salamon (1987) argues that families' responses to the
loss of their farm due to the agricultural crisis depend on whether shared
agricultural goals originate primarily from financial or familial motivations. S. Salamon's (1985) farm management style types are combined
with a family stress model by H. I. McCubbin and J. Patterson (1983) to
develop a framework for identifying contrasting capabilities and definitions possessed by families holding divergent agricultural goals. An
instrument based on the application of stress concepts to farm family research is presented for use in counseling families who lose their farms.

Rosenblatt (1990) offers testimony from 42 adults in 24 Minnesota
farm couples who were caught in the farm crisis. They speak of how they
struggled economically, what they understood and felt about their economic situation, and how their relationships within the family and
outside of it were affected by the economic difficulties. The purpose was to
go beneath the statistics, to record people's experiences, feelings, and reflections in their own words, and to understand what happened to them
as individuals and families. That understanding has implications for policy, service delivery, and community action. Extensive face-to-face
interviews were carried out in 1986 by three graduate students in the Department of Family Social Science at the University of Minnesota.
Telephone follow-up interviews were carried out in the latter half of 1987

and early part of 1988 with adults in 23 of the 24 households. Interviews were wide-ranging but focused mainly on the history of the farm operation, what happened in family and community relationships as economic difficulties developed, problems with lenders and creditors, and personal feelings and reflections as things happened. People were also asked to fill out a checklist of feelings, personal reactions and aspects of family relationships that might be influenced by the crisis.

Ferguson & Engels (1989) discussed the 1980s farm crisis that had large numbers of farmers and their families abandoning farming due to new and frequently unmanageable economic realities. Selected issues were discussed with regard to farmers who

1) were then working and living on family farms and

2) were being or had been forced to pursue other occupations.

Ferguson & Engels note that farmers are at a geographical disadvantage for receiving mental health and career counseling services, and most traditional support services are centered in keeping the farmer in agriculture. Counselors and state national counseling organizations need to consider pro bono and sponsored approaches to working with farm families; farmers might benefit from modification of programs aimed at adult education, career development, retirement, and separation and grief.

Van Hook (1987) used the ABCX family-crisis model developed by R. Hill (1949) to identify needs and design intervention strategies while long-term solutions to the crisis are being developed. Basic to the model is the concept that each event has not only an external reality but an internally experienced reality as well. Van Hook suggested that focusing on the family unit strengthens both individual and family resources. Because many farm families have considerable strengths, relatively small intervention efforts may be needed to enable them to mobilize for survival.

To summarize, it is important that the mental health profession be aware of the factors involved in rural crises, socially, economically, community wide and other related variables. Providing appropriate responses, approaches, methods and programs that are individualized for communities and individuals are important in these times of change and increased levels of stress.

Rural Trauma

Background and the Problems

Within one year, in the early 1990s, a small rural American town experienced a series of traumatic events. A number of individuals put in much time and effort toward a crisis plan, known as the Trauma Intervention Plan, which ultimately failed. Taplitz-Levy (2002) explored the factors that added to and detracted from the success of the specific school-based collaborative intervention and research project. The attitudes of crisis team members toward the crisis plans, collaborative work, and research were examined using a series of qualitative research methods. Through qualitative analysis of the data, results show that the Trauma Intervention Plan was hindered by poor communication, a lack of trust, and poor historical relationships between the school team and the out of school consultants. Taplitz-Levy's study gives compelling reasons for school personnel and local community mental health staff to develop positive relationships.

In June 1981, south-eastern Kentucky experienced serious and widespread flooding. In May 1984 a storm system brought tornadoes, strong winds, and severe, extensive flooding to this same area. Norris, Phifer & Kaniasty (1994) studied the psychosocial impact of these events. Their study had three features that hold particular promise for increasing what we know about the effects of disaster:

1) the study's prospective and longitudinal design;

2) its consideration of both individual and collective aspects of disaster exposure; and,

3) its focus on older people (age 55 or older).

This study addressed the following questions:

1) What impact did these two floods have upon the mental, physical, and social functioning of the rural Appalachian victims?

2) Were these individuals able to take these events "in stride" or did they present a serious challenge to their ability to cope?

3) Did these floods leave a lasting impact upon the mental and physical well-being of these individuals or did they only result in relatively minor and short-lived emotional upset?

4) Were some people more affected than others?

5) Were these communities able to "rally around" their members or were they shattered and split apart?

In September 1991, in the small rural town of Hamlet, NC, the fryer exploded at a chicken processing plant killing 25 employees and injuring many more. This disaster stirred national attention, influenced state law and inspection policies, and profoundly affected the entire community.

Derosa (1995) examined the relationship between PTSD and the survivors' subjective experiences of the trauma, their search for meaning and their perceptions of self, of others and of the world around them. They attempted to capture the survivor's experiences of themes such as rage, grief, and a belief in a benevolent world, in conjunction with clinical diagnosis of PTSD (using the Structured Clinical Interview for DSM-IV Axis interview) in order to assess the buffering or exacerbating influence of the subjective experience. Seventy-eight subjects included plant employees, relatives of employees, rescue personnel, and relatives of fire/rescue personnel. They examined several categories of variables:

- Unresolved trauma themes,
- 'Pre-fire' variables including neuroticism
- History of traumatic experiences
- Previous psychiatric treatment,
- "Peri-traumatic" variables including dissociation, fear of injury and level of exposure to the fire,
- Types of social support
- Demographics.

The most robust variables contributing to lifetime diagnosis of PTSD after the fire were having lower socio-economic status, being female, feeling little social support, fearing death/injury and dissociating during the fire. The only significant contribution to the model for chronic PTSD was number of unresolved trauma themes. The degree to which the trauma themes remained maladaptive varied by severity of diagnosis. Exploratory cluster analyses of patterns of unresolved themes among survivors and their families suggested that in addition to the number of unresolved themes, the pattern of thematic resolution is associated with diagnosis.

In 1992, El Salvador ended a twelve-year civil war which caused tremendous social upheaval. Approximately 50,000 civilians were killed, 500,000 displaced, and 750,000 to one million left the country (Lundgren, and Lang, 1994). The impact of the violence left many survivors with traumatic emotional problems. Oakes (1998) studied three rural communities in El Salvador. She examined the emotional reactions to war of eighty respondents analyzing the data from the point of view of respondents. Respondents included those who had only indirect war experiences, those who experienced occasional traumatic events during the war, and those who lived in a war zone and had continuous and extreme experiences during the war. Respondents reacted to everyday events, violence, and war with an escalating pattern of emotions. This pattern began with worries often connected to everyday events, then fears often related to violence, and then to emotional states including "nervios" and affliction, and finally to sadness caused by loss. Some physical reactions related specifically to war, such as jumping at noise, while others, such as headaches, were experienced by all, regardless of amount or type of war experience. Past war experiences often affected how respondents reacted emotionally to everyday events in the present, especially when those events were linked to danger or violence. Respondents who had only indirect exposure to war reacted to present and future events only occasionally and mildly through the standpoint of past events in war, while individuals who had prolonged and extreme war experiences reacted to present and future events much more intensely and regularly through the viewpoint of war. In an additional analysis of a small group of respondents who had lived through extreme warfare, Oakes reported that they had few emotional reactions to normal events that they did not relate to war. She suggested that the sum of many people's emotional reactions, therefore, may cause such configurations of people to have reactions to events that are not based on present reality.

Since 1994, lethal violence toward people suspected of witchcraft has escalated in rural communities in South Africa. Hundreds of older people believed to be witches have been burned to death and thousands who have escaped death have taken refuge in government established camps. Hill (2000) examined a group counseling approach that promotes "sustainable reconciliation" with traumatized individuals in communities divided by violence due to witchcraft persecution. Specifically, Hill examined a single case sample of a group counseling session aimed at reconciliation. Fifteen group members included individuals from conflicting parties from geographic areas in South Africa where there are witch burnings. Beyond the 15 group members, 11 other participants rated the group session and its potential for fostering sustainable reconciliation. These 11 individuals were divided into two groups:

 a) American student raters (N = 3) and

 b) South African observers (N = 8).

This study was constructed as a 10 step process of data gathering and a "constant comparison" (Strauss & Corbin, 1994) of data categorized by all participants. As defined by Glaser and Strauss (1967), the Grounded Theory methodology allowed for an emergence of common themes across raters that could be related to theories for sustainable reconciliation, trauma counseling, group process, and witchcraft persecution. The results of this study suggest that sustainable peace is possible using the "reconciliation group counseling" approach. With these specific types of groups, special consideration must be given to leadership style, building safety, and including the entire community that has been effected by witch persecution. However, according to participants, reconciliation groups will fail if the fundamental reasons for the violence continue to go unattended (e.g., poverty, unemployment). Such fundamental issues perpetuate feelings of fear and hopelessness in community members which fosters an unstable environment. These results suggest that therapists must understand the context of such violence, attend to the trauma symptoms of individuals, and perhaps play a supportive role in the group. The South African observers suggested that successive counseling groups, with public admittance of behavior and retribution for losses would be necessary before sustainable peace could be possible.

The above studies have identified variables, approaches, interventions and make suggestions for a variety of events that produced trauma in rural areas. The following section presents results of studies involving the effects of various trauma-producing events on children, parents and families.

Children, Parents and Families

Youth Violence

Slovak (2000) addressed gaps in the youth violence literature by exploring the types and levels of children's violence exposure in a rural setting. He/she also examined the psychological trauma associated with violence exposure. This study was a secondary data analysis which utilized the rural sample (N = 549) from a larger study. The larger study had conducted a 45 minute questionnaire with students in grades 3 through 8. The questionnaire was designed to tap into children's present and past violence exposure as a victim and witness across the home, school, and neighborhood. This questionnaire also assessed children's trauma symptoms. Slovak found that children in the rural sample were exposed to high amounts of violence as both a victim and witness within and prior to the past year. In general, more boys reported being victims or witnesses to an at least sometimes violent event within the past year compared to girls except for the act of being touched in a private place. In addition more students in the lower grades reported being the victims and witnesses of violent acts compared to students in upper grades. Students reported that home was the place where they were most likely to be victims of violence, with the school being the next most likely place to be victimized at least sometimes. The neighborhood was reported as the least likely place for students to be victims of violence at least sometimes within the past year. Students reported a different trend for witnessing violence. They reported that school was the most likely place to witness violence, with the neighborhood being second. The home was the site reported as the least likely place to witness violence at least sometimes within the past year. Slovak also found that violence exposure variables explained a significant amount of variance in anxiety, anger, dissociation, depression, PTSD and total trauma score above demographic variables. This is consistent with the literature examining the association of trauma and violence exposure. These findings can be utilized to inform policy, practice, and research conducted in rural areas. In addition, the documentation of children's exposure to violence in a rural setting can help banish the stereotype that rural communities are safe havens from violence.

Peltzer (1999) identified exposure to experiences such as violence and the consequences for health in children in a rural South African community. The stratified random sample included 68 (46%) boys and 80 (54%) girls in the age range of 6-16 yrs. Their ethnicity was Northern Sotho. The interviews included the Children's Posttraumatic Stress Disorder Inventory and the Reporting Questionnaire for Children. They grouped experiences into either traumatic or other events. 99 (67%) had directly or vicariously experienced a traumatic event which included witnessing someone killed or seriously injured, serious accident, violent or very unexpected death or suicide of loved one, sexual abuse or rape of relative or friend, violent crime, child abuse, and other life-threatening situations. Scores on the Children's Posttraumatic Stress Disorder Inventory of 17 (8.4%) fulfilled the criterion for posttraumatic stress disorder (PTSD). 71% had more than one score and 53% had more than four scores on the Reporting Questionnaire for Children. Posttraumatic stress symptoms were significantly related to age and experiences such as those mentioned above.

Gun Violence

Slovak & Singer (2001) compared rural youth (Grades 3-8) exposed to gun violence and rural youth not exposed to gun violence on a number of variables: anger, anxiety, dissociation, depression, posttraumatic stress, total trauma, violent behavior, parental monitoring, and levels of violence in the home, school, and community. One-fourth (25%) of the 549 subjects reported having been exposed to gun violence at least once. Youth exposed to gun violence reported significantly more anger, dissociation, posttraumatic stress, and total trauma. In addition, youth exposed to the violence of guns reported significantly higher levels of violent behaviors and exposure to violence in other settings and also reported lower levels of

parental monitoring. This study contributes to the growing body of literature addressing the stereotype that rural communities are not immune to
the violence of firearms. This stereotype can act as a barrier to mental
health practice, research, and policy issues in rural communities.

Slovak (2002) investigated the relationship between access to firearms
and parental monitoring on rural youths' exposure to gun violence and
examined the effect of gun violence exposure on the mental health of
these youths. She administered a survey to 162 students (mean age 14.3
yrs) who participated in a student assistance program that provided in-
school support groups for students in grades 6 through 12. Her results
show that a substantial number of students were exposed to gun violence
and exposure was significantly related to firearm access and parental
monitoring. Furthermore, gun violence exposure was significantly associated with trauma among the youths. Implications for mental health
workers include advising high-risk clients and their families on gun re-
moval and safe storage practices.

Abuse

While recent research has focused on the impact of abuse and other
interpersonal traumas in childhood, little attention has been given to the
experiences of children who have been removed from their homes. In addition to trauma, these children are likely to have had a number of
experiences that may impact their current functioning. Brady & Caraway
(2002) provide descriptive information pertaining to the unique characteristics of children in residential treatment centers, and examines
preliminary factors believed to be associated with current functioning.
Participants included 41 children, aged 7-12 yrs old, recruited from two
treatment centers in the rural Midwest. Children were administered the
Trauma Symptom Checklist for Children and participated in a brief interview. Each child's primary caregiver at the facility completed the Child
Behavior Checklist. Results of the descriptive analyses painted a picture
of chaotic childhood marked by significant stress and trauma. Gender,
child's satisfaction with current discharge plan, and multiple traumatic
experiences were found to be associated with variations in symptomatology. Brady & Caraway's findings may assist service providers and
caregivers in understanding the unique experiences of this population.

Miller & Veltkamp (1988) provide a clinical perspective on the accounts
of sexual abuse of children allegedly occurring in a small, rural community. Variables that are related to the degree of psychological trauma
experienced by the child include types of sexual abuse (such as incest),
age of the child, duration of sexual abuse, degree of coercion or aggression and threat, the adult (known or unknown), the degree of activity, and

the adult/parent response. Miller & Veltkamp address 8 characteristics of the family constellation in abusing families, the multigenerational pattern, specific behavioral indicators of sexual abuse and stages of experiencing sexual abuse and emotional trauma in children, treatment of the sexually abused child and abusive family, and guidelines from the American Academy of Child Psychiatry (1986) for use by clinicians and legal experts in evaluating sexual abuse.

Partner Violence

Partner violence is a serious mental and physical health concern leading to debilitating physical injury in women. Significant psychological sequelae are associated with battering. However, only recent investigations have begun to delineate the different types of psychological distress. The diagnosis of Posttraumatic Stress Disorder (PTSD) has been useful in characterizing the symptoms associated with victims of severe trauma. The DSM-IV criteria for PTSD include re-experiencing trauma, avoidance responses, and heightened arousal. Given the characteristics shared between battered women and other victims of violent crime, Presty (1996) predicted that battered women develop primary features of PTSD. The second hypothesis was that other women would meet DSM-IV criteria for Acute Stress Disorder (ASD). She also performed exploratory analyses to examine relationships between the frequency and severity of abuse and diagnostic categories. The results confirmed the two hypotheses. First, 65.6% of the sample was PTSD-positive, with 5% meeting criteria for ASD. Other anxiety disorders accounted for 13.1%. The prevalence rate of Major Depressive Disorder (MDD) was 70.5%. The comorbidity of depression with PTSD was 84.6%. Physical abuse significantly predicted PTSD development, explaining 11.4% of the total variance. Verbal abuse significantly predicted MDD. Dissociation was predicted by both verbal and physical abuse. Exploratory cluster analysis revealed three typologies of battered women:

Cluster 1 reflected young, poorly educated women, who experienced the greatest physical and sexual abuse. They had the highest levels of PTSD, moderate depression, and the poorest level of functioning.

Cluster 2 women were the oldest, had the most children, and had the longest relationship duration. They experienced more verbal than physical abuse, and had the highest degree of depression, with modest PTSD severity.

Cluster 3 reflected the youngest, most educated group, with the least number of children, and shortest relationship duration.

Murder/Suicide

Following a murder/suicide at the Red Lion Junior High School in Red Lion, Pennsylvania, (the second critical incident in two years for this school district), a crisis response team provided critical incident stress management (CISM) services, response coordination and ongoing support to the students, teachers, parents and community of this small town (Seebold, 2003). Their response team was a diverse blend of professionals from the school district, Pennsylvania State Education Association, school psychologists, and the local employee assistance program (EAP). Within eight days, the school population had moved beyond a horrifying critical incident to begin the process of recovery. This suggests that CISM teams can facilitate recovery following such incidents.

Vicarious Trauma

Connery (2003) examined acute symptoms and functional impairment related to September 11 terrorist attacks among rural community outpatients with severe mental illness. Connery conducted a retrospective chart review for 133 community patients with severe mental illness for the time interval between September 11 and December 31, 2001. This chart review revealed that patients with severe mental illness, even if they are located far from the primary site, can experience vicarious trauma reactions in association with terrorist events. This is consistent with the results of a national study of immediate stress reactions to September 11 among the general population. In summary, this retrospective chart review showed that 18 of a sample of 133 patients with severe mental illness receiving assertive community treatment experienced significant acute stress reactions to the threats of terrorism during the 3 months following September 11, 2001.

Cultural Considerations

Grief Reactions

Fabrega & Nutini (1994) examined the psychological and behavioral concomitants of grief among parents in rural Mexico who experienced sudden and unexpected death of infants and young children. Particular focus was given to the local concept of malevolent witchcraft as an explanation for the deaths. Data on 47 cases of witchcraft-explained deaths were collected as part of a longitudinal study in the early 1960s. Parents constructed a social and psychological picture of the death of their infants that had naturalistic elements (i.e., parental culpability, how the death occurred) that were given a supernatural interpretation. The tragedy was socially shared, and commonality was forged in the ordeal of coping with the trauma. A case illustration was included to illustrate the contrast between social and psychological constructions of reality. The use of symbols to construct meaningful accounts of tragedies and to regulate and restore social relations was described.

Benswanger, Baider & Cornely (1980) present a profile of seven families from rural communities in Pennsylvania Appalachia, each of whom had experienced the death or grave illness of an infant. Geographic, cultural, psychological, and demographic factors were examined to evaluate in its entire context the impact of infant death/illness in this area. Benswanger, Baider & Cornely suggested that such an ecological outlook will allow research to develop effective interventions that will decrease the rural incidence and trauma of infant death.

Dislocation

Mandic & Mihaljevic (1993) reported results of a three month group and individual study with 593 displaced persons of different sexes, ages, marital status, and education. subjects were observed for 12 wks from the moment when they had to leave their homes in the rural parts of East Croatia, their arrival to Osijek and accommodation in social centers. Having been forced to leave their homes and villages, it was an extremely stressful event exceeding the usual life experience and resulting in psychosocial, physiologic, and psycho-behavioral disorders. Only 6.5% of men and 2.4% of women behaved rationally. Psychosocial disorders occurring immediately after leaving their homes were ranked as follows: fear (24.7%), anger and fury (23%), distrust (16.1%), anxiety (12.9%), and despair (7.5%) in men, and fear (34.2%), anxiety (14.8%), panic (15.9%), despair (14.8%), distrust (9%) and fury (8.8%) in women. Concern about the future, own life, parents, property and siblings occurred more often among women. After a 22-wk treatment period, 30% of men and 40% of women reported disorders which were grouped as insomnia, loss of appetite, functional disturbances, increased irritability and depressive mood.

Civil Rights

Rogers (1994) examined the oral narratives of five African-American women and men who were active in the civil rights movement in the deep south in the 1960s. At various times in their five years with the movement in New Orleans and rural Louisiana and Mississippi, these individuals experienced terrorism and violence from segregationist Whites. Some suffered from battle fatigue due to continual exposures to danger and loss. Mid-life interviews with seven former members of New Orleans' chapter of the pacifist, interracial Congress of Racial Equality (CORE) and two of their lawyers—known collectively in New Orleans as the CORE family—

illustrate the incorporation of collective and individual trauma into mature personal narratives. Rogers argues that activists have developed two narrative forms to encapsulate their complex experiences within the civil rights movement—trauma narratives and narratives of redemption. She further argues that mid-life narratives indicate that activists have used these episodes of trauma and redemption to frame and contextualize their life trajectories as consistent with their youthful politics.

It is important to include individual and community level interventions as well as collaborations with relief agencies in addressing crises in culturally different rural environments. Mental health responders are encouraged to broaden their skills to include training in disaster, critical incident and crisis interventions as global awareness of the need for such responses increases.

Responses

Smith, Thompson & Shields (1997) evaluated the effectiveness of a rural emergency medical and trauma services project in increasing the knowledge and confidence of emergency personnel (pre-hospital and hospital) in assessment and management of acutely ill and injured children. Providers from an intervention county who were compared with control providers demonstrated a significantly greater increase in test scores that measured knowledge of pediatric emergencies. Intervention field and hospital personnel also demonstrated significantly greater improvement. Intervention county providers had a significantly greater decrease in anxiety when confronting a scenario of a child with respiratory arrest. They also had a greater increase in confidence about management of the pediatric airway and a greater increase in the adequacy of their pediatric training. Smith, Thompson & Shields concluded that this project offers a model that can be replicated in other rural areas.

Teletherapy/Telemedicine

Patients injured in rural areas die at roughly twice the rate of those patients with similar injuries in urban areas (2). A multitude of explanations have been suggested for higher mortality rates from trauma in the rural areas of the United States. Since rural emergency room (ER) staff see far fewer traumas than ER staff at large metropolitan trauma centers, their lack of exposure to this low-volume problem certainly contributes to the problem. To address discrepancies in trauma education and the delivery of care in rural regions. Ricci, Caputo & Amour (2003) report on a telemedicine system that was utilized to provide rapid consultation from surgeons at the level 1 trauma center and to provide enhanced educational opportunities for rural ambulance emergency first responders.

Forty-one "tele-trauma consults" were performed over the first 30 months of the project, all for major, multi-system trauma. Though many clinical recommendations were made, the system was judged to be life saving in three instances, and both rural and trauma center providers felt the system enhanced clinical care. Early results of a telemedicine system provide encouragement as a means to address discrepancies in the outcomes after major trauma in rural areas, although more work needs to be completed and evaluated.

Although access to health care for rural patients remains a critical challenge, teletherapy may represent a viable means for the delivery of therapeutic services to them. Teletherapy represents an effective and efficient means for providing rehabilitation services for patients in rural communities, and for facilitating mentoring relationships between seasoned professionals and trainees located in rural areas.

7 | Crises and Crisis Interventions

Crises can affect people on many different levels, including psychological wellbeing. In order for an event to qualify as a "crisis," there must be some sense of disruption to one's sense of balance in life; a failure of one's usual coping mechanisms to re-establish equilibrium; and some evidence of functional impairment, such as an inability to concentrate; memory difficulties; sleep disturbances, etc. In a crisis, coping skills fail to re-establish a sense of balance and control in life. People can be at a loss as to where to turn for help.

Although the terms "crisis" and "emergency" may be used interchangeably in the context of counseling, it is useful to distinguish between the two (Chrzanowski, 1977). In psychodynamic theory, "crisis" refers to a turning point or a period when new demands on the ego can't be met successfully by the usual coping mechanisms. At these times, powerful emotions, such as anxiety and guilt, are intense, and cannot continue for long. The possible outcomes of a crisis can be formulated in general terms as:

- Return to the previous state

- Growth process, with an increase in ego strength

- Destructive process (i.e. suicide, homicide, assault) or the emergence of new psychopathology

To complicate matters, crises may resolve into some combination of the above. Erikson (1959) referred to the universal developmental phases of life as "developmental crises", and to individual traumatic events as "accidental crises". Caplan (1964) provided examples of the latter, such as "the death of a loved person; loss or change of a job; a threat to bodily integrity by illness, accident, or surgical operation; or change of role due to developmental or sociocultural transitions, such as going to college, getting married, and becoming a parent." In psychotherapy, acting out and transference and countertransference distortions are additional common sources of crises.

Dealing with Crises

Formulating the Problem

An effective response to a crisis depends in part on the characteristics of the crisis and in part on the therapist's comprehensive understanding of the client. Perry, Cooper and Michels (1987) describe the elements that make up a workable formulation:

1) A summary...that describes the patient's current problems and places them in the context of the patient's current life situation and developmental history;

2) a description of nondynamic factors that may have contributed to the psychiatric disorder;

3) a psychodynamic explanation of the central conflicts, describing their role in the current situation and their genetic origins in the developmental history; and

4) a prediction of how these conflicts are likely to affect treatment and the therapeutic relationship.

Among non-dynamic factors they include such issues as genetic predisposition, mental retardation, overwhelming trauma, and drugs or any physical illness affecting the brain. In assessing current life problems it is important to be on the lookout for changes in biological (including physical illness), psychological and social circumstances of the client's life. Chrzanowski (1977) defined several common categories of crisis:

- The emergence of an acute psychosis, which may or may not require hospitalization.

- Self-destructive acting out often associated with alcohol or drug abuse, promiscuity, or delinquency.

- Major illnesses or serious accidents involving the patient or people close to him or her.

- Family disturbances, including separation and divorce.

- Economic crisis.

- Severe transference distortions (i.e. psychotic transference).

- Serious countertransference distortions.

- The paradoxical upsurge of disturbed and disturbing emotion and behavior when the patient is threatened by success in the therapy, including the prospect of termination, as cause of crisis.

- The response of a significant other who perceives the patient's improvement as a threat.

Whether these types of circumstances lead to an emergency depends on the interactions among the severity of the stress, the strength of the client's ego and support network, and the therapist's skill. Some clients (schizophrenics, chronically depressed, narcissistic, and borderline personalities, substance abusers, and some adolescents) are especially prone to developing crises that become emergencies. In treating vulnerable people, therapists need to be vigilant for personality and behavioral changes that indicate increasing tension or problems in adjusting to routines of daily living. When problems are anticipated, especially early in the course of treatment, the therapist is well advised to meet with the family and lay the groundwork for working together if the need arises.

Crisis Adaptation

The client's adaptive mechanisms function so as to maintain overall physical and psychological equilibrium. However, in a crisis situation, the capacity of the client's (and clinician's!) coping mechanisms may be exceeded, resulting in erratic and impulsive behavior. Although there are no pathognomic signs of impending violence, precipitous assault is quite rare, if indeed it exists at all (of course, warning signs may be subtle). Typically, the crisis process entails:

1) a prodrome,

2) an identified "incident", and

3) a reintegration/restabilization period.

The clinician can optimize crisis outcome through early identification and intervention (depending in clinician sensitivity and judgment), and by adopting the therapeutic stance of collaborating with the client in working through the various stages of crisis adaptation. The clinician must participate in rather than attempt to short-circuit this process.

Aggressive behavior results from the client's experience of fear or anger. Both affects are meaningful and potentially understandable reactions (defensive and offensive, respectively) to the client's (perhaps accurate, perhaps inaccurate) perception of threat. While most clinicians seem to assume that aggressive client behavior is indicative of anger, most aggressive behavior in the clinical setting may instead be a reflection of fear. A fearful client must be approached differently than an angry client. However, this crucial distinction is frequently overlooked. All people direct their behavior according to the channels or alternatives that they perceive. Even a gentle person may fight when feeling cornered without alternatives. in working through the crisis process with any client, the clinician must take great care not to inadvertently structure a situation so that the client's only perceived option to meet essential needs is through dysfunctional means. An acceptable alternative must be allowed to any inappropriate behavior.

Assessment and Intervention

In response to the fearful aggressive client, the clinician may attempt to reduce the degree of threat that the client perceives, verbally (e.g., "It's safe here now") or nonverbally (e.g., allowing plenty of interpersonal distance). Alternatively, the clinician may attempt to help the client feel able to cope with the perceived threat (e.g., "I am on your side, and I will help"). Just as one fearful client may respond better to yielding threat reduction, another may respond better to firm support and enhancement of perceived coping capacity. Similarly, in response to the angry client, the clinician may employ a yielding strategy in order to appease the client and so defuse aggressive potential (e.g., "I am sorry that I hurt your feelings"), or alternatively may respond firmly and inhibit aggressive expression through limit setting.

Good judgment is required for the clinician to choose between the yielding and the firm approach to the angry client. The practical test of the chosen approach lies in the resulting behavior of the client. One angry client may only attempt further to "push around" the yielding clinician. Another angry client may be "pushed over the edge" into violence by the firm clinician. Although appeasement is not synonymous with inappropriately pacifying a bully (it is indeed possible to defuse anger through appeasement without sacrificing the essential interests of both client and clinician), many clinicians seem loath to react gently in the face of anger. It seems likely that the most common precipitant of unnecessary client violence is clinician counter-hostility.

What Is Crisis Intervention?

Everly & Mitchell (1999) define crisis intervention as "the provision of emergency psychological care to victims as to assist those victims in returning to an adaptive level of functioning and to prevent or mitigate the potential negative impact of psychological trauma." Procedures for crisis intervention have evolved from the work of people such as Erich Lindemann (1944), who conducted studies on grieving in the aftermath of a major conflagration at a nightclub. Kardiner and Spiegel (1947) devised three basic principles in crisis work:

1) immediacy of interventions;

2) proximity to the occurrence of the event; and

3) the expectancy that the victim will return to adequate functioning.

Gerald Caplan (1964) concentrated on community mental health programs that emphasized both primary and secondary prevention. While there are many models of crisis intervention, there is general agreement about the principles of crisis intervention that are employed by emergency mental health professionals. These principles are:

1) to alleviate the acute distress of victims;

2) to restore independent functioning; and

3) to prevent or mitigate the aftermath of psychological trauma and post-traumatic stress disorder (PTSD)

(Butcher, 1980; Everly & Mitchell, 1999; Flannery, 1998; Sandoval, 1985).

Factors identified by those who have studied crisis intervention as important agents of change in crisis procedures are: ventilation and abreaction, social support and adaptive coping (Flannery, 1998; Raphael, 1986; Tehrani &Westlake, 1994; Wollmann, 1993).

Techniques

Setting Limits

The ultimate goal in external limit setting is for the client to develop internal controls. However limit setting may be instrumental in the course of the client's development of autonomous self-regulation. Limit setting can be a positive technique inasmuch as it allows the client understand which behaviors are prescribed and which are proscribed. It also gives the client realistic expectations about the behavior of others, thus allowing the client to gain approval rather than disapproval. Furthermore, limit setting may prevent the client from doing something humiliating or harmful, and it can convey clinician concern and competence. Some degree of client resistance to limit setting is a positive sign. Generalized, docile acceptance of the clinician's will is dysfunctional. Whenever any of the client's intention is blocked, an acceptable alternative must be allowed.

Limit setting should be presented to the client as a statement of fact, never as a request, as a bribe, as advice, as punishment, or as a challenge or threat. Reality-based, natural consequences of behavior are a more productive focus than are consequences contrived and maintained by the clinician. Fairness and consistency in limit setting are absolutely essential. Expected and prohibited behaviors must be described concretely in terms of actions that can be performed immediately. The clinician must know the actual enforceable limit, and must never describe either positive or negative consequences that he or she is unable or unwilling to deliver. Generally, limit setting is often utilized too late rather than too early by well-meaning but inexperienced clinicians. Timely implementation can prevent undue deterioration of the client and the therapeutic milieu. Once the need for a behavioral limit has been established, the clinician may briefly explain the limit and its rationale but must avoid being drawn into superfluous discussion or argument.

There are two major methods of limit setting: direct and indirect. The former involves presenting the client with one specific directive. The latter involves presenting the client with choices among acceptable alternatives.

Direct Technique

Essentially, the direct technique of limit setting consists of stating clearly and specifically the required or prohibited behavior. Though the clinician may describe additional consequences of violating the limit, such a statement is not a defining aspect of this method. Whenever possible, a directive should be expressed in a positive format ("do this", which describes acceptable behavior), rather than in the negative ("do not do that", which does not describe acceptable behavior). The direct method is often preferable for the confused or emotionally overwhelmed client.

Indirect Technique

The indirect method of limit setting consists of keeping the client in a state of choosing among acceptable behaviors, thus dividing the client's will to resist. Though it may be easy for the client to oppose a single directive, attention cannot be focused simultaneously on two or more alternatives and so resistance to any one is diminished. The clinician subtly maintains control by limiting the choices while giving the client the opportunity to choose among them ("you can sit down and we can talk about how you are feeling, or you can leave"). Should the client refuse to make any choice, the clinician can then make a time-bound conditional choice on behalf of the client ("if you do not choose to sit down in 10 seconds, I will take that to mean that you choose to leave and I will have the security guards escort you out"). Even when the situation develops in this way, any resistance demonstrated is typically far less than had the client not been given a choice.

The clinician must exercise sound judgment in deciding which limit-setting technique to employ. Some clients will be angered by and vigorously resist directives. Others will be]confused or disorganized by choices. At an appropriate time after such an intervention, the meaning of the limit setting within the context of the therapeutic relationship must be addressed with the client. Ultimately, clinician actions with the client's best interests at heart are likely to be understood and appreciated.

Physical Intervention

Not every episode of potential or actual aggressive behavior can be resolved without physical intervention (e.g., an individual who is so afraid or angry that sustained, meaningful interaction is not possible and with whom an attempt at nonphysical intervention might be dangerous to client and clinician alike). Even in those episodes in which nonphysical intervention might have been possible, less than optimal clinical technique may fail to prevent (or may even precipitate) a physical attack. Just as cardiopulmonary resuscitation (CPR) training is preparation for an emergency situation that may occur only infrequently, brief training may be adequate for the relatively rare event of overt physical aggression and be of critical therapeutic benefit. An in-depth presentation of proper clinical techniques for humane, safe, and effective physical management of the aggressive client is beyond the scope of this article and is available elsewhere (Thackrey, 1987), a few comments are in order.

Physical intervention principles are a conceptual subset of psychological intervention principles. Applied physical techniques are effective only insofar as they utilize psychological as well as mechanical/kinesiological principles. Aggressive behavior is a psychologically meaningful event for both the client and the clinician. Just as sound clinical judgment is required of the clinician in implementing the proper physical intervention, sound judgment is also required of the clinician in implementing the proper physical intervention. There is no single physical response for every possible situation. Instead, the clinician must apply principles to the situation at hand. Effective physical intervention is possible because the clinician is mentally prepared, anticipates the actions and reactions of the client, and optimizes mechanical/kinesiological factors (e.g., leverage, torque).

Applied physical intervention techniques must facilitate therapeutic psychological intervention while protecting both clinician and client. They are treatment procedures, and must meet essential criteria. Primarily, they must be effective. Secondly, they must be safe for both the clinician and the client. Thirdly, they must be absolutely nonabusive, inflicting neither injury nor pain, and preserving the humanity and dignity of the client. Finally, they must require a minimum of clinician training for motor-skill acquisition and retention. Just as principles of psychological intervention are continuously evolving, so also are the principles and techniques of physical intervention technology. Innovations in physical techniques should be evaluated by the practitioner according to the four criteria presented above.

Although some have expressed concern that the inclusion of physical management techniques in the context of training to prevent and manage client aggression might lead to overutilization of these methods, such a concern may be allayed by the substantial research evidence (Thackrey, 1987) demonstrating that appropriate training actually decreases the incidence of assaults and the utilization of restraint, seclusion, etc. High quality training that presents physical management methods within their proper clinical and legal context can serve as one means of helping to preserve the client's rights, consistent with the values traditionally associated with mental health services.

Crisis Intervention and CISM

The crisis intervention model Critical Incident Stress Management (CISM) has evolved to become one of the leading crisis intervention models used in the world. CISM is a comprehensive, multicomponent crisis intervention model. It is a psycho-educational model whose interventions range from the pre-crisis phase through the acute crisis phase and into the post-crisis phase (Flannery & Everly, 2000). CISM employs strategies such as one-on-one interventions, critical incident stress defusings, debriefings and demobilizations. It is important to point out that CISM is not therapy, nor is it designed to replace formal therapy. To keep CISM in its proper perspective, the following analogy may be useful:

> CISM is to formal therapy what emergency medical services are to formal surgery.

In the medical world, prompt treatment by trained personnel of certain physical injuries may preclude the need for formal surgery later on. The same argument is used for CISM. When CISM interventions are promptly delivered by trained personnel, the need to seek formal therapy later on may be alleviated. In addition, as in emergency medical services, CISM can also help facilitate the individual to the next level of care when needed. To understand CISM it may be helpful to look at it from the larger context of crisis intervention.

Both the client and the clinician have rights and responsibilities in the therapeutic setting. The client has the right to be free from harm and to be treated appropriately by the least restrictive methods. The clinician has the right to self-protection and to intervene in an emergency. Both the client and the clinician may be criminally liable for their actions. Judgment is central to the evaluation of the actions of both clients and clinicians.

The clinician must know the general principles that relate to the legal aspects of professional mental health practice. Ultimately, however, the clinician's decisions about the client's treatment should be made on clinical grounds. Actions that make the most clinical sense will typically be best for both client and clinician.

Psychological First Aid

One form of major crisis is critical incidents. Critical incidents are recognized disasters or other crisis situations that evoke unusually strong emotions. Appropriate critical incident crisis-care can provide needed emergency mental health services, prevent the formation of some types of posttraumatic stress disorder (PTSD), and therapeutically modulate the long-term effects of calamity for victims and emergency-care providers. Effective provision of mental health services includes pre-incident preparedness, early intervention with psychological first aid, and postdisaster treatment using critical incident stress debriefing (CISD), grief counseling, brief multimodal therapy, referral to traditional therapy or counseling if necessary, and follow-up.

Crisis intervention is commonly thought of as acute psychological first-aid applied within close temporal proximity to the precipitating event. While all disaster workers should have familiarity with the common patterns of reaction to unusual emotional stress and strain, relatively few are versed in the principles of care for the psychological or emotional casualty. In the aftermath of the Pacific Southwest Airlines Flight 182 disaster, many disaster assistance, public safety, and emergency workers developed a variety of psychological problems and emotional or behavioral symptoms when returning to work or their families after the intensive week-long clean up effort. Acute crisis reaction, intense stress, and job-related impairment were found to be quite common (Davis and Stewart, 1999). Post-traumatic stress reactions and critical incident stress debriefing and defusing were found to be effective methods in decreasing the severity of the effects. Davis and Stewart (1999) suggest some key points to incorporate into the debriefing process used when providing assistance to a traumatized community, victim, first-aid responder, or deployed disaster emergency rescue worker. They recommend a community-wide outreach critical incident stress intervention program and referral network for ongoing continued care and support for all disaster response workers during the immediate aftermath.

The concept of debriefing has been popularized as a mental health intervention in the early phases of response to disaster. Raphael (2003) addresses several issues about psychological debriefing techniques and their place as mental health interventions in the immediate post-disaster or post-trauma phase. Special issues in early intervention and debriefing include physical needs; separation; loss of loved ones; dislocation, loss of home, and destruction of community; human malevolence; making meaning; personality and individual coping styles; timing; and culture. Any intervention should encompass principles such as psychological first aid, ensuring safety, security, survival, shelter, and other basics. For those at high risk following trauma and loss, specialized counseling may be beneficial. It is important to distinguish between immediate post-disaster interventions and those that may be applied appropriately weeks or months after the disaster. With respect to the former, the job of psychologists is not to provide therapy. Rather, it is to administer "psychological first-aid." Rather than intervening with exposure and cognitive restructuring techniques, the task is to offer comfort and support, to depathologize people's reactions to severe stress, to listen empathically, to encourage people to talk to family and friends, and to provide triage.

Leach (1995) describes a psychological first aid system based on the debriefings of survivors of life-threatening situations. Survivors were drawn from both civilian and military personnel who had been involved in shipwrecks, airplane crashes, aircrew ejections, major fires, shootings, mountain and caving accidents, floods, combat, and prisoners-of-war situations. The behaviors of survivors who coped well during such a threat to life were compared with behaviors of those who did not and distilled into a set of principles for psychological first aid. This resulted in a series of simple actions for use within a disaster to return victims to functional behavior as quickly as possible, thus increasing their chance for survival. This model of behavior in disaster is restricted to three phases describing the behavioral natural history of a disaster, namely, period of impact, period of recoil, and period of post-trauma.

Singer (1982)reviews literature dealing with the psychological reactions of individuals and groups to disaster. He looked at characteristic stages of human response to disaster situations as well as the specific immediate reactions of individuals and groups. He examined phenomena such as "scapegoating," long-term reactions, reactions of rescue and relief personnel, psychological first aid, and disaster planning. Singer concludes that the compassionate handling of disaster victims by psychologically informed rescue workers, and the development of intervention programs that facilitate and maintain rather than disband pre-disaster social support systems, can prevent more cases of subsequent physical and emotional problems than physicians, counselors, and psychiatric professionals can ever treat later. This suggests that some form of early intervention can be helpful in preventing some longer term effects.

La Greca and Silverman (2002 review the current state of empirically informed interventions for children and adolescents. They use a chronological system to describe interventions offered pre-disaster (i.e., preparation activities), while disasters are in progress, and during the short- and long-term aftermath. They found that preparatory and early interventions focus primarily on crisis management and enhancing coping skills. In contrast, children and adolescents with persistent and long-term difficulties are likely to need formal treatments for trauma symptoms and bereavement. Interventions for the phases should focus primarily on prompting safety and coping skills and providing crisis management. Interventions appropriate for the first few weeks after the initial phases of disasters (i.e., the post-impact, or short-term adaptation, phase) should focus on immediate physical and psychological needs. Brief, present-focused interventions, such as instrumental aid, information giving, and trauma interviews or debriefings, should feature prominently in this phase. Difficulties persisting months or even years after the impact phase has ended will require more in-depth counseling and/or therapy.

The terrorist attacks in New York on September 11, 2001, and the widespread fears of anthrax poisoning and spreading of smallpox that followed, raised the question of how health and mental health professionals might respond to casualties were similar events to occur elsewhere. International expertise and local experience are instructive in helping to outline the kind of psychological first-aid service that should be made available to disaster casualties. Some of the particular topics about which interveners should be informed, essentials of their involvement, and conditions requiring specialist treatment should all be areas of major concern. Implementation of proposals for action requires discussion with the relevant professional societies, voluntary agencies, and the statutory bureaucracies that have responsibility for dealing with other aspects of trauma and social disruption.

Selecting and Training Disaster Mental Health Staff

Skills and competencies that are required of disaster mental health workers are enough different from the typical inpatient/outpatient clinical practice to require more specialized selection and training. When a disaster strikes a community, having a cadre of specially trained mental health professionals who can be quickly mobilized, oriented, and deployed is critical. If the impacted area does not have this capacity, mutual aid agreements with those communities that have trained and experienced disaster mental health workers will be helpful in the chaotic times immediately following impact.

Predisaster Planning

Much of the confusion and stress present at the time of disaster impact can be eliminated when a mental health agency has a core staff predesignated and trained as a disaster response team. Regular in-service training and participation in disaster exercises in the local jurisdiction can help maintain and fine tune skills. If the resources permit, the team can respond to smaller crises which occur in the jurisdiction. This will provide staff with some first-hand experience they can use when a larger disaster strikes.

Funds for training are hard to come by and sometimes non-existent. Training is considered a necessary and appropriate aspect of the Federal Emergency Management Agency (FEMA) Crisis Counseling programs, both in the Immediate and Regular Programs. Mental health planners and administrators should include realistic training budgets in their grant applications.

Selecting Disaster Mental Health Staff

Disaster mental health work is not for everyone. It is challenging and rewarding work which requires mental health professionals to be flexible and socially extroverted. Despite their altruism and sincere desire to help, *not all individuals are well-suited for disaster work*. Whether designating and training disaster staff prior to or during a disaster, the mental health manager should consider several selection issues.

Selection of professional or paraprofessional staff should consider the demographics of the disaster-affected population, including ethnicity and language; the personality characteristics and social skills of the staff member; the disaster phase; and the roles the worker may play in disaster response and recovery efforts. Workers who are selected for disaster response and recovery work should not be so severely impacted by the disaster that their responsibilities at home or their emotional reactions will interfere with participation in the program, or vice versa.

Population Demographics

Managers should choose staff who have special skills that match the needs of the population. For example, staff who have special expertise working with children and the local schools should be included. If there are many elderly persons in the community, the team should include persons skilled in working with older adults.

Ethnicity And Language

Survivors will react to and recover from disaster within the context of their ethnic background, cultural viewpoint, life experiences, and values. Those who have limited English-speaking skills may experience difficulty communicating needs and feelings except in their native language. All aspects of disaster operations must be sensitive to cultural issues, and services must be provided in ways that are culturally appropriate.

It is essential that mental health staff be both familiar and comfortable with the culture of the groups affected by the disaster. It is very desirable that they also be fluent in the languages of non-English speaking groups affected. Mental health staff should include individuals who are indigenous to specific cultural groups affected by the disaster. If such staff are not immediately available, mutual aid staff with the required ethnic backgrounds and language skills should be recruited from other community agencies or mental health jurisdictions for the immediate post-disaster phase. Indigenous personnel can be recruited and trained for the longer term recovery work at a later time.

Personality

The ability to remain focused and to respond appropriately are necessary qualities for individuals who participate directly in a disaster. Disaster mental health staff must be able to function well in confused, often chaotic environments. Workers must be able to "think on their feet", and have a common-sense, practical, flexible and often improvisational approach to problem-solving. They must be comfortable with changing situations. They must be able to function with role ambiguity, unclear lines of authority, and a minimum of structure. Many of the most successful disaster mental health workers perceive these factors as challenges rather than burdens. Initiative and stamina are required, as well as self-awareness and an ability to monitor and manage their own stress.

Workers need to be able to work cooperatively in a liaison capacity. They need to be aware of and comfortable with value systems and life experiences other than their own. An eagerness to reach out and explore the community to find people needing help, instead of a "wait and treat" attitude, is essential (Farberow and Frederick, 1978). Workers must enjoy people and not appear lacking in confidence. If the worker is shy or afraid, it will interfere with establishing a connection (DeWolfe, 1992). Staff must be comfortable initiating a conversation in any community setting. In addition, workers must be willing and able to "be with" survivors who may be suffering tragedy and enormous loss without being compelled to try to "fix" the situation.

Disaster Phases

In the immediate response phase of disaster, an "action orientation" is important. Workers who do well with the pace of crisis intervention do well in this phase. Personnel who have worked in emergency services in a local mental health center or a hospital emergency room are frequently well-suited to this phase of disaster work.

Some people cannot and do not function well when exposed to the sights and sounds of physical trauma. These staff should obviously not be asked to provide mental health services at the scene of injuries or in first aid stations, hospital emergency rooms, or morgues. This does not mean that they cannot be on the disaster response team. There are many other roles that they can play. Involved personnel should openly discuss such issues during initial formation of the team so that individuals best suited to these roles can be pre-designated.

Long-term mental health recovery programs, covering the period from about one month to one year post-disaster, are different in nature and pace from the immediate response phase. Mass care shelters and disaster application centers (DACs) are closed or closing. Locating disaster survivors is more difficult. Mental health workers need to be adept and creative with outreach in the community.

Results of outreach and education efforts are often difficult to measure. Survivors do not traditionally seek out mental health service. There are few "clients" to treat and count. Clinically oriented staff who are accustomed to an office-based practice often question their usefulness and effectiveness. "Action-oriented" staff who thrived in the immediate response phase may not enjoy or function well in the longer-term recovery phase where patience, perseverance, and an ability to function without seeing immediate results are assets.

Roles and Responsibilities of Mental Health Workers

Disaster mental health roles and responsibilities are diverse. Thoughtful matching of worker skills and personalities to the specific assignment can help ensure success of mental health efforts.

1. Outreach: Working in neighborhoods, mass care shelters, disaster application centers, or other community settings requires workers who are adept at such non-traditional mental health approaches as "aggressive hanging out" and "over a cup of coffee" assessments and interventions.

2. Public education: Public education efforts require staff who are interested and effective in public speaking and working with the media. Development of fliers and brochures requires good writing skills.

3. Community liaison: Establishing and maintaining liaison with community leaders requires someone who understands and is effective in dealing with organizational dynamics and the political process. Working successfully in the "grass roots" community requires someone who understands the local culture, social network, formal and informal leadership, and is effective in establishing relationships at the neighborhood level. Liaison activities might include everything from attending grange or church gatherings, participating in neighborhood meetings, or providing disaster mental health consultation to government officials.

4. Crisis counseling: For most disaster survivors, prolonged psychotherapy is not necessary or appropriate. Crisis intervention, brief treatment, support groups, and practical assistance are most effective. Mental health staff must have knowledge and skills in these modalities.

Disaster Mental Health Worker Qualifications

The disaster mental health team should be multi-disciplinary and multi-skilled. Staff should be experienced in triage, first aid, crisis intervention, and brief treatment. They should have knowledge of crisis, post-traumatic stress and grief reactions, and disaster psychology. Survivors are often reluctant to come to mental health centers for services. Therefore, staff must be able to provide their services in non-traditional, community-based settings. Prior disaster mental health training and experience are highly recommended. In situations of mutual aid where licensed professionals cross state lines to provide assistance in disaster, licensing in the impacted state may be waived under the Good Samaritan law. This issue should be investigated in instances of cross-state mutual aid.

Staff should be well-acquainted with the functions and dynamics of the community's human service organizations and agencies (Farberow and Frederick, 1978). They should have experience in consultation and community education. Excellent communication, problem-solving, conflict resolution, and group process skills are needed, in addition to an ability to establish rapport quickly with people from diverse backgrounds.

Managers should pay careful attention to the state's scope of practice laws for various mental health professional disciplines. Individuals providing formal assessment and counseling which fall into the definition of psychotherapy should be appropriately licensed and insured for professional liability.

Qualifications for Paraprofessionals

Paraprofessionals can be excellent choices for outreach and community workers. This is especially so if they are familiar with the community and trusted by its residents. They may already be employed by a mental health, social service, health, or other community-based agency, or they may be recruited from among community residents. Characteristics and qualifications should include the following (Collins and Pancoast, 1976; Farberow and Frederick, 1978; Tierney and Baisden, 1979):

1. Possess at least some high school education (to master information and concepts to be taught).

2. Are indigenous to the area, if possible.

3. Represent a cross section of the community/neighborhood members with regard to age, sex, ethnicity, occupation, length of residence in the community, etc.

4. Are motivated to help other people, like people, and have sensitivity and empathy for others.

5. Are functioning in a stable, mature, and logical manner.

6. Possess sufficient emotional and physical resources and receive sufficient personal rewards to be truly capable of helping.

7. Can work cooperatively with others.

8. Are able to work with people of other value systems without inflicting their own value system on others.

9. Are able to accept instructions and do not have ready-made, simplistic answers.

10. Have an optimistic, yet realistic, view of life, i.e., a "health engendering personality".

11. Have a high level of energy to remain active and resourceful in the face of stress.

12. Are committed to respecting the confidentiality of survivors and are not inclined to gossip.

13. Have special skills related to unique populations (e.g., children or older adults, particular ethnic groups) or useful to disaster recovery (e.g., understanding of insurance, building requirements).

14. Are able to set personal limits and not become too involved with survivor recovery (e.g., understand the difference between facilitating and empowering survivors as opposed to "taking over" for the survivor).

Why Training?

Mental health professionals often assume that their clinical training and experience are more than sufficient to enable them to respond adequately in disaster. Unfortunately, traditional mental health training does not address many issues found in disaster-affected populations (FEMA, 1988). While clinical expertise, especially in the field of crisis intervention, is valuable, it is not enough. Mental health personnel need to adopt new procedures and methods for delivering a highly specialized service in disaster. Training must be designed to prepare staff for the uniqueness of disaster mental health approaches.

Though disasters profoundly affect individuals, people rarely disintegrate or become incapable of coping with the situation. Nor does mental illness suddenly manifest in a full-blown florid state. Problems do appear. They vary in nature and intensity (Farberow, 1978). However, most of the problems and post-disaster symptomatology are *normal* reactions of *normal* people to *abnormal* events. Few require traditional psychotherapy. Very few people seek out mental health assistance following disaster, and mental health staff who simply open the doors of their clinics to clients or patients will have little to do.

As a result, outreach to the community is essential. Outreach is more than simply setting up decentralized clinical services in impacted areas, or sending out brochures advertising mental health services. Outreach also means mingling with survivors in shelters and DACs and meal sites and devastated neighborhoods. The key to effective outreach is the mental health worker's ability to establish rapport and to have therapeutic intervention with individuals in an informal, social context in which there is not a psychotherapeutic "contract".

In addition to the impact on individuals, disasters are political and bureaucratic events. They profoundly affect the community and its social systems. Everyday resources for basic human needs may be destroyed or damaged. Transportation and communication may be disrupted. In a large-scale disaster, specialized emergency response and recovery agencies move into action and exert a significant influence on the post-disaster environment. Resources, structures, and individuals change as specialized response groups finish their jobs and move on and as new, grassroots groups spring up. Mental health staff need to understand and be able to function effectively in a complex and fluid political and bureaucratic network.

Disaster mental health training will help staff to understand the impact of disaster on individuals and the community. It will provide information about the complex systems and resources in the post-disaster environment. It will also help staff to fine tune clinical skills that are relevant and useful in disaster. It will aid them in learning effective community-based approaches.

Through videotapes, role play, and other exercises, training allows staff to experience vicariously the emotional climate of disaster recovery work. Sometimes, staff may decide they are not well suited to this type of work. Usually, the experiential aspects of the training will provide workers with some measure of "emotional inoculation" that will help them to anticipate the emotional aspects of the work. Training must also provide staff with awareness of the personal impact of disaster work, and with strategies for stress management and self-care.

Before Training

It is essential for disaster mental health workers to begin to process their own emotions about the disaster before attempting to help survivors. While workers may talk about their own reactions during the training, *training is not designed to be a debriefing.* If workers come to the training with unmet needs related to their own feelings, the training will not be able to proceed effectively. A debriefing or other group format for discussion of workers' reactions to the disaster should be conducted for workers before training. A trained facilitator who has not been directly involved in service delivery, yet thoroughly understands the demands of disaster work, should provide the debriefing.

Debriefing and Other Approaches

The concept of debriefing has been popularized as a mental health intervention in the early phases of response to disaster. Raphael (2003) addresses several issues about psychological debriefing techniques and their place as mental health interventions in the immediate post-disaster or post-trauma phase. She clarifies the meaning of "debriefing" and reviews research that addresses the question of whether debriefing works. Special issues in early intervention and debriefing include such areas as physical needs; separation; loss of loved ones; dislocation, loss of home, and destruction of community; human malevolence; making meaning; personality and individual coping styles; timing; and culture. (2) concludes that any intervention must encompass principles such as psychological first aid, ensuring safety, security, survival, shelter, and other basics. Debriefing is not effective as a one-to-one early intervention, and group debriefing is mostly questions. For those at high risk following trauma and loss, specialized counseling may be beneficial.

Family health counseling, counseling in disasters, health interventions, transcultural/multicultural family counseling, and reimbursement with families of diverse cultures are all areas that have relevance for mental health professionals responding to disasters and similar crisis situations. The development of a therapeutic relationship with multicultural families, supervision and training for clinical practice with multicultural families, family assessment, legal and ethical issues, treatment plans for problem families and troubled families, and initiating family interventions are some approaches that can be implemented. It may also be relevant to explore the politics of gender in clinical practice, skills needed for transcultural/multicultural family counseling, the need for evidence-based treatments, issues related to reimbursement services, and family counseling in disasters such as the 9-11 crisis.

Emergency Management of Disasters

Figley, Giel & Borgo (1995) provide a concise summary of the key elements to consider when planning a course of action to implement within a disaster-stricken community. They categorize disasters according to two dimensions:

1) sudden vs long-term and

2) natural vs man-made.

These distinctions provide initial insights into the character of the disaster impact and the types of interventions that are likely to be helpful.

They emphasize that it is necessary to outline key types of information that need to be gathered.

Emergency management (EM), the decision making involved in directing the relief operation after a disaster or otherwise catastrophic accident is an issue of public and private concern because of the high stakes involved. Due to the nature of emergencies, and especially mass emergencies, EM teams are faced with decision making in stressful situations, information ambiguity and overload, and a significant level of uncertainty, whereby non-routine problem solving of a knowledge-based nature is required. An important characteristic of EM is that it is a team of teams; multiple teams that come from different organizations, with different organizational goals and different organizational cultures, that work together to minimize the negative effects of the emergency. As a consequence, EM requires good coordination and communication not just within, but also among the various teams involved. Coordination among teams should, therefore, be a key focus for training.

An application of program planning and evaluation was described within the larger domain of natural disaster planning and in relation to evacuation and relocation of residents of Montserrat, a British Dependent territory, to England (Kydd, 1999). It was anticipated that utilization of the program planning and evaluation process by an external consultant would involve clients and stakeholders in a series of sequential, interrelated activities, resulting in useful information for the eventual benefit of clearly defined groups of evacuees in relocation settings. Through this process, key clients and stakeholders were identified and involved, both in Montserrat and in England, subsequent to the eruption of the Soufriere Hills volcano, and the initiation of evacuation and relocation activities in that setting. Then, these individuals collaborated with the consultant in targeting evacuees, and in conducting an assessment of the psychological and psychosocial needs of this group, using multiple quantitative and qualitative methods, with resulting data analyzed and synthesized within the evacuation and relocation context according to program planning and evaluation protocols. This information was then used by clients and the consultant as the basis for the development and documentation of guidelines for evacuation and relocation for use by the British Government in further assisting the evacuees as well as for adaptation of the guidelines to other natural disaster planning situations. Data collected in response to a set of case study questions indicated that the program planning and evaluation process has potential to be a practical, useful, proper, and efficient means of contributing to sound natural disaster planning, within and across cultures.

DeVries (1995) reviewed the multiple, interacting processes that are relevant to individual and community stress in response to catastrophe. He outlines three stages of the community response to stress:

(1) inducing and legitimizing the communication of distress, and beginning to mobilize resources;

(2) facilitating resource mobilization, including cultural coping mechanisms; and

(3) maintaining support processes after the crisis has ended, including such resources as self-help healing strategies.

Culture plays a role in coping with stress in that:

(1) it organizes and provides meaning in stressful circumstances;

(2) maintains itself through rules, roles, and rituals; and,

(3) especially within traditional cultures, utilizes symbols to conceptualize the relationships between individuals, religious beliefs, body, and mind.

These illustrate the three processes of inducing, facilitating, and maintaining community-level support systems within traditional and developed cultures and the ritualization of social communication and coping responses.

Examples of Disaster–Related Emotional Problems

Frequently among responders, questions are raised about the types of emotional distress to be expected with disaster victims. There is also interest expressed about learning ways in which these problems can best be handled by responders in the field.

Responders should realize that they are not expected to become instant experts in the diagnosis and treatment of mental disorders. The responder's role is first to identify those in need of help and then to offer verbal support, information, and advice when requested. Sometimes physical assistance, such as moving a victim's belongings or helping to repair damage to homes and property, is most helpful in overcoming emotional distress.

Following are some case illustrations of the more typical types of disaster-related emotional distress along with a brief discussion of ways each situation might be handled.

Depression

A responder finds a middle-aged man pacing up and down in front of his flood-ravaged home. Some of the water-soaked furniture has been dragged out into the yard to let the sun dry it out. However, the man has apparently abandoned further attempts to salvage his furnishings and is now walking about aimlessly in what remains of the front yard, wringing his hands.

This illustration of depression differs somewhat from the usual picture of the individual suffering from apathy and withdrawal, with no interest in what is going on around him. The example demonstrates that depression is frequently masked by, or expressed in, agitated activity which is aimless or nonproductive. Unless the depression in this phase is recognized and helped, it may readily progress to more serious mental and physical problems.

Help for the depressed person in this instance might take the form of verbal help, such as reassurance, encouragement, giving information about where and how to get help, and offers of physical assistance in salvaging belongings, making sure he has had something to eat recently, and providing hot coffee or tea while conversing.

Grief

A man appears in a one-stop relief center in a small western city severely damaged by an earthquake. He asks for help in acquiring a set of mechanic's tools. He needs the tools because his set was lost with his house and all the rest of his possessions in the earthquake. While giving the required information to the disaster worker, he mentions in passing that his son was killed in the earthquake.

This man appears to be in complete control of his emotions. He seems to be going about the business of re-establishing his life in a well-organized fashion. However, such behavior would be considered healthy and desirable only after a suitable period of mourning or "working through" the grief reactions to the death of his son. In this instance, there had been no time for mourning. The father was busying himself with constructive tasks that actually served to screen the emotional pain in order to avoid dealing directly with his loss. One doesn't have to be a specialist in human behavior to anticipate that the father would probably at some point experience the flooding of emotions he was now damming up and that he would be overwhelmed by them.

What could be done in such a case? It would seem presumptuous and perhaps ill-advised to confront this man directly with his loss and to challenge his defense of suppressing his emotions under these circumstances. Perhaps a brief, gentle comment on his loss is all that can be done at this time. Such a comment might permit the beginning of the experience of grief. The bereaved father has thus felt the touch of gentle understanding and in a sense has received permission to deal directly with his loss. The responder would want to alert relatives or close friends to the probability that the father might need help in the future in dealing with his grief.

Depending on the situation, there are many approaches which might be appropriate for assisting those suffering grief. It often might be desirable to convey empathy through those close to the victim rather than directly. Again, depending on the circumstances, it might be more suitable to offer direct assistance in the form of making arrangements, notifying relatives, or dealing with insurance matters.

Anger

A rural valley with many small farms was devastated when a newly finished manmade dam gave way and flooded the area below it. Some citizens who had suffered losses in the flood were seen throwing rocks at trucks belonging to the construction company that had built the dam. Anger was also expressed by local relief workers whose efforts were hampered by bureaucratic red tape. Victims exhibited anger toward relief workers both for interfering with their lives and for not doing enough to help those in need.

Anger is one of the natural and expected reactions to adversity. The degree of anger felt and ways in which it is expressed are related to many things, some of which are external, as in the case of negligence which caused or contributed to the catastrophe; and some of which are a reflection of the individual's experience of helplessness and frustration in the disaster itself.

In dealing with anger in disaster victims, it is important for the responder to be aware of the value of "ventilation" as a means of reducing the excess emotion which interferes with constructive handling of the causes. That is, it is important that the angry victim be permitted to express his/her anger verbally. It is generally not desirable to take direct action while in the grips of such strong feelings. On the other hand, an understanding listener should not try to exhibit anxiety while listening to the angry outbursts and recitals and not try to "talk him out of" being angry, nor express disapproval or other guilt-inducing reactions. Many people find it uncomfortable and difficult to listen to angry reactions of others. If one is aware of its therapeutic value and is sufficiently motivated, however, this important service becomes easier with practice.

Guilt

A woman whose home miraculously escaped damage in the flood, while the home of a close friend and neighbor was completely destroyed, appears at the local health center with various physical symptoms such as stomach cramps, loss of appetite, and severe headaches. Medical examination provides no apparent basis for the complaints. It was concluded that the patient was experiencing a severe anxiety attack. Consultation with a mental health professional revealed that the woman was suffering an overwhelming sense of guilt because she was spared the tragic loss suffered by her friend. Counseling helped her to accept the unpredictable nature of the disaster which ruined one person and spared the next. The woman was able to overcome her guilt and to offer welcome assistance to her neighbor in coping with her losses.

Guilt is a frequent occurrence among survivors of a disaster. We all experience to some degree the uneasiness which accompanies sudden and unexplainable good fortune. Our own sense of worthiness is called into question. Why have we been spared misfortune when others have suffered? We are glad to have been so favored, of course, but at the same time feelings of guilt arise because secretly we are relieved that the losses occurred to someone else instead of us. The opportunity to talk about and confront directly these natural human reactions with someone who is understanding and shares the same weaknesses is of great value. The knowledge that such feelings occur with most people provides a sense of acceptance and belonging which permits one to go on and to do what can be done to help others who have been less fortunate.

Apathy

An elderly man owned and operated a small private fishing lake and boat rental concession at his home site. A flood destroyed his boats and equipment and completely filled the lake with mud. The old man, who lived alone, was discovered by neighbors several weeks later. He had taken to his bed, neglecting to eat or care for himself. At the time he was found, his weight and physical condition had deteriorated to the point where he was almost dead. At first he refused assistance. However, as a result of patient and persistent efforts by the neighbors, he was persuaded to allow himself to be taken to the hospital. Although he initially regained his health he did not survive long after being placed in a residence for the elderly.

In this case, the old man felt he could never regain what he had lost in the flood. There simply was not enough time or opportunity. He had little left to live for.

In disasters, apathy is frequently found in the elderly who have suffered significant losses of possessions, their homes, friends, and neighbors. There is a feeling, often all too real, that they will not again be able to recover or replace these losses. Assistance must take very concrete and immediate forms if it is to be of any value. Relatives or friends must be located if possible. Physical relocation should be as near as possible to what is familiar for the older person. Readjustment to new surroundings and strangers is often an overwhelming and sometimes impossible effort, as in the case illustrated above. As many people as possible should be involved, especially other elderly people who have gone through the same experience.

When apathy is encountered in the middle-aged person or in the adolescent, emphasis should be on immediate and active attempts to recover and replace the losses, to become involved in community rehabilitation, and to participate in social activities. The last mentioned is of particular importance for the adolescent.

Fears

An otherwise normal 6-year-old girl who has experienced an earthquake becomes terrified and cries when a heavy truck passes by the house, causing a slight vibration. A 4-year-old boy, who was suddenly evacuated just before the flood destroyed his home, develops the habit of sleeping with all his clothes on and his remaining belongings packed in a suitcase kept at the foot of his bed in the mobile home he and his family now occupy. A 7-year-old boy, who survived a flood caused by torrential rain, is found crying and crouched under a stairwell when a light rain starts to fall.

These persisting fears are often found among young children and sometimes among adolescents and adults following a disaster. They are referred to technically as "traumatic neuroses". With most otherwise healthy persons such persistent fears tend to subside as time passes. If they continue to appear some months after the disaster it is apparent that the intervention of a mental health specialist is needed. Much can be done, however, in the immediate post-disaster period to relieve these symptoms and prevent their continued self-reinforcement.

With children it is essential that the child be given additional warm affection and understanding when experiencing the recurrence. Above all, the child should not be scolded or punished for exhibiting these fears. Talking with the child in a gentle and reassuring manner is helpful. Permitting or encouraging the child to talk about what is frightening him is also important. For adolescents and adults who display recurrent fear symptoms, permitting the victim to relive the experience verbally, to become actively involved in recovery efforts, and to learn more about the causes and means of possible protection from future disasters are particularly useful.

The "Burn-out" Syndrome

Two police officers are on duty at a checkpoint for autos entering the disaster area. It is their job to permit entry only to those who have homes or businesses in the area or who are involved in relief activities. There is a constant stream of vehicles lined up in both directions. The officers must inspect identification and passes, answer questions about disaster recovery activities, reassure anxious homeowners, and placate angry citizens frustrated at the delay. The officers have had 12-hour duty days for the past week, with only brief periods of relief. Their faces show fatigue. Their efficiency is at a low ebb. One officer describes his concern about his family to a relief worker. Another officer is anxious about all the work that needs to be done at his house. His wife is upset at his absence during this critical period. He feels the accumulating frustrations and anger of the people he is trying to assist. His work requires him to ignore his personal priorities. There are not enough replacements to permit him to attend to his family responsibilities.

The man is exhibiting excessive fatigue, irritability, anxiety, impatience, and all symptoms of the beginning of the "burn-out" syndrome. Front-line responders typically overextend themselves in disasters. This most often occurs when there are not enough relief workers, and the ones available want to help as much as possible. Sometimes, however, even when replacements are available, responders refuse relief and push themselves beyond their effective limits. Such action might seem altruistic and commendable. In reality, the tired and inefficient relief worker can be more of a liability than an asset in rescue and recovery activities. The responders during and immediately following the disaster need all the strength and energy they can gather. They must have clear heads to make critical and sometimes life-saving decisions. They must be able to cope not only with the physical consequences of the disaster itself but with the fears, anger, and physical and emotional suffering of the victims.

It is essential, therefore, that the responder is not overtired or weak from lack of food or rest. Often the responder fails to recognize these signs in him/herself although they are obvious to others. Those responsible for supervision of front-line relief workers must do everything possible to forestall the occurrence of the "burn-out" syndrome.

Bizarre Behavior

A man whose entire herd of cattle was lost in a flood is apprehended while shooting his neighbor's surviving cattle. The man can offer no rational explanation for his behavior.

Sometimes the effects of the disaster can prove to be an overwhelming experience for victims. The excessive stress causes a breakdown of usually effective coping mechanisms. The individual exhibits irrational and bizarre behavior. He may temporarily "go crazy".

Contrary to popular misconception, this is an unusual rather than a usual occurrence during disasters. Most frequently, individuals who suffer emotional breakdowns are those who have had previous histories of breakdown and likely have had to be hospitalized for mental health treatment in the past. There are generally a few people in any community with histories of emotional breakdown. It is valuable for local mental health professionals to be aware of those who are more likely than most to suffer serious mental disturbance as a consequence of the disaster. Immediate assistance is required in the form of admittance to a hospital or emergency professional attention when the victim shows behavior which could be harmful to himself or others.

Suicide

A woman who lives alone is found dead of a self-inflicted gunshot wound following a flood which devastated the community where she lived.

As with mental breakdowns, suicide is not a common occurrence among disaster victims. The seriousness of this tragic aftermath is such that mental health and other relief workers need to be alert to those individuals who might be likely to react to excessive stress in this way. It has been found that those who do commit suicide usually have some previous history of attempts or communications to others about their intent to do away with themselves. Awareness of who in the community is susceptible to this sort of self-destruction is one of the vital roles the local mental health workers can play in alleviating the emotional suffering which accompanies all disasters.

Intervention Strategies

Basic Guidelines

People in crisis are extremely vulnerable. They are open to hurt as much as to help. The goal of crisis counseling should be to protect them from further harm, while providing them with immediate assistance in managing themselves and the situation. Crisis counselors provide brief, clear and gentle directions and support to distressed victims. As soon as possible, they help the victims take on responsibility for their own care. It is important to provide frequent reassurance and guidance when the situation is most threatening. The most important thing is to offer assistance to help the individual gain a sense of control of self and situation, and not to do everything for the victim.

Whenever possible, it is important to help the victim identify and focus on the problem, or the most important problem if there are several. This helps the individual gain a sense of perspective and to prioritize their recovery efforts. They need to be told what is happening and why to help reduce the sense of surprise or feeling that they are being lied to.

- Tears – Let the client know that it is normal, helpful and OK to cry.

- Touch – A gentle touch on the shoulder, hand, or a hug can be very supportive. It is generally a good idea to ask permission before touching.

- Talk – Encourage the individual to talk about the experience, not only with you, but with family and friends, or support groups. Talking helps one put the incident in perspective so they can put it behind them.

- Trust – You must build up a sense of trust between you and the individual. They need to know that what they share with you will be held confidential, and that you will be non-judgmental.

- Toil – Be willing to work with the client. Don't rush them. Give them the opportunity to work through their emotions and problems.

- Time – It takes time to sit with a client. Let them talk, and let them know that the recovery process does take time.

Fig. 7–1: The Six "Ts"

There are six "Ts" to providing support to those experiencing an emotional reaction to any crisis situation: Tears, Touch, Talk, Trust, Toil, and Time (Fig. 7-1).

Interventions

When working with the victims of a disaster, it is important that interventions focus on the resolution of the disaster-caused problems by adapting or reinforcing the victims' coping techniques to meet the need. Keep in mind that our goal is to decrease emotionality and increase functioning. Crisis Counselors can help victims stabilize emotionally by:

- Utilizing their available support structure (e.g. family, friends, etc.).

- Establishing a realistic perception of disaster recovery.

- Predicting future problems.

- Providing opportunities to vent their anger, fear, frustration, and grief.

- Reinforcing use of present coping strategies or developing new ones to prevent the recurrence of the same problems in the future.

Handouts on disaster related stress and self-help techniques help normalize the responses for disaster victims and should be made available.

When working with victims of a disaster, it is important that interventions must focus on resolution of the disaster-caused problems by adapting or reinforcing victims' coping techniques to meet the need. The goal is to decrease emotionality and increase functioning.

Psychological Implications for Disaster Workers

Factors Affecting Responders

Psychological effects are universally present to at least some degree in responders involved in disaster situations. Teams of responders on the spot of a disaster or following one have psychological reactions very similar to those of the victims. Their reactions vary with the magnitude of the event and the number of casualties. Consider, for example, the differences in effect between reactions of responders to a traffic accident vs an incident like the Oklahoma City bombing or Columbine High School.

There are a number of factors that affect the severity of responders' reactions to disasters and critical incidents.

- **The nature of the traumatic event:** What type of disaster or incident is it? Were there many deaths or injuries, gruesome sights or sounds?
- **Proximity of the responder to the event:** Did it happen in his/her own community? Was he/she also a victim, or had family or friends who are victims?
- **Nature of the responder's role:** Is he/she on the front lines or working behind the scenes? How much responsibility does the responder have, and how is he/she dealing with the responsibility?
- **Responder's prior experience** with crisis, critical incidents or disasters: Has he/she developed positive coping strategies due to prior experience, or is he/she still affected by past events?
- **Responder's current life situation:** Problems at home or with the job will be intensified by the stresses of disaster work or a critical incident.
- **Behavior of others at the incident**: This includes reactions of media as well as relationships with co-workers, supervisors, and clients.
- **Psychological preparedness for the incident:** How well was the responder prepared for the incident? Was he/she given enough information to be able to build protective barriers and effective coping strategies?

Fig. 7–2: Factors Affecting Severity of Responder Reactions

It is also important to consider that, in addition to their work with disaster victims, there are factors of occupational stress which include: the time factor, overload of responsibilities, physical demands, mental demands, emotional demands, the workplace, environmental factors, limited resources and the high level of expectations on the part of the public and the responders themselves. Generally, responders function well despite the responsibilities, dangers and stress factors which are inherent in their work. However, sometimes it happens that the intense stress of the event overcomes their previously used defenses.

Verbalization or debriefing sessions following a disaster, critical incident or tragedy are needed following an event to help responders deal with their personal reactions. These are used to help prevent development of delayed or lasting reactions. It is also important to recognize that some responders may listen and discuss more openly with peers than with mental health professionals. Individual crisis intervention, defusing, and debriefing are three of the elements of Critical Incident Stress Management (CISM).

The longer a worker is assigned to an acutely stressful situation, the more likely they are to develop some of the following problems.

Physical Signs Of Acute Stress	
• Exhaustion	• Tremors, rashes
• Loss of energy	• Headaches
• Gastrointestinal Distress	• Heart rate and blood pressure increases
• Hypochondria	• Chest pain
• Changes in appetite	• Psychological preparedness for the incident
• Sleep disturbances	

Emotional Signs
• Depression
• Irritability
• Anxiety
• Hyper-excitability
• Excessive rage reactions
• Isolation

Cognitive Signs
• Mental slowness or confusion
• Inability to make decisions
• Loss of ability to conceptualize thoughts or prioritize tasks
• Loss of objectivity in evaluating own functioning
• Decreased computational skills
• Decreased memory and attention span

Behavioral Signs
• Hyperactivity
• Excessive fatigue
• Inability to express self verbally or in writing

Fig. 7–3: Effects of Long Exposure to Stressors by Disaster Responders

Workers may experience post-traumatic stress syndrome days or weeks after the incident, or at the time of a similar incident.

Management Of Stress Responses
• Be aware of symptoms as they occur and take steps necessary to alleviate causative factors, or increase coping skills.
• Symptoms may appear early in disaster or later, possibly up to one year after incident.
• Seek out support from mental health responders for any reactions which last longer than six weeks, or interfere with your ability to function either on the job or at home.

There are many ways to deal with stress response syndrome, either during the disaster response or afterward. It is very important that responders and debriefers realize and communicate to the people they are working with that all of these signs and symptoms are normal reactions.

Remember, the majority of responders and victims will have only temporary problems associated with the stress they experience. They are normal people having normal reactions to an abnormal situation. These are understandable, warranted, and necessary feelings to recover. It is important to stress this to victims and responders who may otherwise see themselves as sick.

8	**Stress Management**	

Stress Responses

Everyone has experienced stress at one time or another. Pushing one-self for weeks to meet a deadline at work or school; going through a long divorce; caring for a sick relative or friend; over-exertion in too much physical training—these push the body too much and often result in getting sick.

Professionals in every field—executives, doctors, lawyers, people in positions where they must make frequent rapid decisions—learn how to take advantage of their stress response. They use it to bring their performance to a peak (consider athletes in competitive sports). However, these people also learn how to lower their stress response. This can be accomplished subconsciously or it can be trained. Anyone who has successfully learned how to juggle many tasks simultaneously has also learned to assess situations quickly, break them down into their most manageable parts, prioritizing components, and dealing with them in order of urgency. Examples include airplane pilots, stockbrokers, homemakers, secretaries, business executives, doctors in emergency rooms, etc. Whether learned by trial and error or through training, such a pattern of behavior minimizes stress responses, resulting in feeling more in control.

Stress can occur also over longer periods. There may be weeks, months or even years which are more turbulent than usual. This can be related to the stage of life or just with chance. For example, as the parent of an adolescent, you may experience difficulties letting go as your child grows. Your own aging parents may be ill at the same time. As a result, you find yourself constantly on call for unexpected responsibilities and difficult decisions. Another scenario related to phase of life might find you as the parent of a young child, your first, and simultaneously juggling a career with the attendant pressures to succeed. If, at such times, you experience another unexpected stress such as the loss of a loved one, you may not be able to cope.

If between stressful events your life settles down to a quiet baseline, your system will have a chance to recover and be ready for the next event. However, without a safety net, a chronic load of stress accumulates. This eventually takes a toll on your health because, unless the body has a chance to recuperate, the effects of stress accumulate and build up.

Inescapable exposure to many different stressors simultaneously (e.g. a move, caring for children and home, full-time work) over a period of time (usually months) can lead to a type of exhaustion known as burnout. Some professions tend to be more prone to burnout than others. These include teachers, emergency responders and others. They are faced with daily situations in their work lives that require important decisions and responses on their part. They often receive inadequate pay, inadequate assistance in their jobs, and too many patients, students or incidents on the job.

Stress can deplete the body's will to fight. Chronic illness is an example. Psychological stress is another. Additionally, strenuous, unaccustomed and prolonged physical stress (e.g. running to your max on a treadmill) lasting for days; or chronic physiological stresses (e.g. lack of sleep and food) all deplete the body's reserves. Initially, these chronic stresses keep the body's response switched on, working at its maximum as long as the stress remains. If these extremes persist, however, the response can fail, exhaustion is reached and burn-out results.

Chronic unrelenting stress can change the stress response itself. However, with sufficient rest, persons suffering from burnout can recover.

War is an experience in which all possible stresses combine in the extreme. They continue for prolonged periods and are unrelenting. These stressors include: physical stress; continuing strenuous exercise in harsh environments of extreme heat or cold; threat of unpredictable life-threatening attacks; lack of sleep (3 or 4 hours or less a night for days at a time); lack of food (one meal or less for days); and the psychological stress of life-depending need for peak performance. Many recover from these with minimal effect on their stress responses. However, some do not recover. They continue to suffer hormonal, physical and psychological effects long after peace has returned and they have gone home. Soldiers from all wars have experienced some form of this syndrome. It has been given different names at different times. In the Civil War it was called Da Costa's syndrome; in World War I, Shell Shock; in World War II, Battle Fatigue or "disordered action of the heart"; and Viet Nam and the Gulf War, Post-traumatic Stress Disorder (PTSD).

This syndrome does not just occur with soldiers. It is also seen in Holocaust survivors, those exposed to traumas resulting from bombs, fires, rape, natural and man-made disasters and other traumatic events, critical incidents, terrorist acts and losses. For every individual who is exposed to a traumatic event, there is a different interpretation of its stress-fulness.

There is another form of work stress—the demand for rapid-fire deci-sion making—involving frequent, short but high intensity bursts of stress. For example, consider a job in which you must be constantly vigilant. One second of inattention might result in the death of hundreds of people whose lives depend on your moment to moment judgments. Now, consider that you are working on this job at a small workstation surrounded by dozens of other co-workers, all trying to concentrate on their mission. All around you there is constant movement and distracting noise which you must ignore or lose your concentration. Your job requires lightning quick eye-hand coordination as well as an ability to react and give commands and directions in response to shifts in the tiny blips you see on the screen in front of you. Your job requires perfect performance for hours at a time—sometimes late into the night or in the early dawn. The job is that of an air traffic controller. It is a profession which places the worker un-der high stress and high pressure on a constant basis. Members of this profession are at risk for high blood pressure, stroke, heart disease, acci-dents and depression.

In 1983, air traffic controllers went on strike and thousands were laid off. A large percentage of controllers suddenly found themselves out of work. These were men in the prime of their lives, highly trained, heads of households, and skilled in a very specialized profession. They suddenly, and without warning, lost their jobs without any recourse or possibility of returning to their profession. As a result, many experienced clinical de-pressions during the first year following their lay-off. Others turned to drinking to mask their problems. Most found new and productive jobs and put the strike and depression behind them. Others did not.

Common stresses experienced by everyone can sometimes trigger emo-tional memories of stressful events, including all of the accompanying physiological responses. Prolonged stress (e.g. divorce, the end of a rela-tionship, a hostile workplace, death of a loved one) can trigger elements of PTSD.

Consider the following scenario. You awaken refreshed and happy. You relax over coffee and breakfast while reading the morning paper. As a bright sun lights up your kitchen, you feel happy and secure. You leave for work. Your workplace is a hostile environment. Day after day your boss disparages you inappropriately. Your job is in jeopardy because of downsizing. There is an inadequate infrastructure to support your pro-ductivity. Physical surroundings are noisy and cramped. You are not valued for your full worth. Your mood gradually deteriorates as you drive closer to your office. You become increasingly more tense the closer you get. You experience a rush of anxiety as you enter the parking lot. You feel mildly flushed and your heart rate increases. On top of all this, there are no parking spots because the company policy reserves spots only for those of higher rank. However, you park there anyway, knowing that when you return at the end of the day there will be a parking ticket on your windshield. As you leave your car and walk towards the office, you feel anxious, angry, demoralized and you dread the start of the work day.

Another example might be one in which you work on a job you love. You work in a clean, airy office with supportive co-workers and boss, enthusiastic management which values its workers. However, home life is falling apart. You are in the middle of a nasty divorce from a controlling spouse, someone who has emotionally or physically abused you during the marriage. For months, day after day, your soon-to-be ex-spouse's attorney who is known as a pit bull divorce attorney, a basher who takes pride in destroying lives rather than salvaging what may be left of the family's spirit, uses grinding tactics to wear you down. He uses repeated questions designed to trap you and to set you up against yourself. He waits a few days, then escalates the legal demands, threatening subpoena and depositions. His threats come in waves. As soon as you regain some balance, he hits you again. As a result, you feel like one of those inflatable, plastic punching toys that is slapped down the moment it pops up again. The threat this attorney is using to try to break your spirit is loss of custody of your children. As the target of these attacks, you might experience flushing, palpitations, an urgency to defecate every time the phone rings or when a letter is delivered to your door. You might have repeated nightmares about losing your children, searching for them and not finding them. You might wake up in a cold sweat and even continue to experience such physical symptoms and anxiety long after the divorce is over and a settlement reached.

These are some of the elements of PTSD which you might experience. The trigger for such symptoms doesn't have to be very complex, especially if the initial event was severe enough. A single visual element can sometimes expose a piece of memory which evokes a physiological response. Something as innocent as a lawn marker for a house address (e.g. a gray stone with the address painted on it) may, following the death of a loved one, remind one of a grave stone. For a few transient seconds it brings on a rush of hormones and despondent feelings experienced when the loved one died.

Situations do not have to entail the risk of life to be real and potent stressors. Conversely, an incident that involves risk of life may not necessarily be perceived by everyone as a major stress. Within hours of the Northridge, California earthquake immune and hormone responses were measured in people who had been at the earthquake epicenter. While some individuals seemed to respond with high stress and low immune responses, others did not.

Stress can cause sickness because hormones and nerve pathways which are activated by the stress change the way the immune system responds. It becomes less able to fight off invaders. Genetics and perceptions of the event also play important roles. Some people are high stress responders and others are low. We do have control over how we perceive events. We can learn how to tone down physiological responses to stress. By doing so, we can minimize the effects of stress on disease. Memories of what was or what should have been play an additional role along with learning.

In addition to the above stressful situations, there is another element that contributes to perceived stress. Interpersonal relationships in some cases contribute to job stress and in others may buffer us from it. These relationships can be the most powerful stressors most people encounter in their working lives.

Coping With Stress – Guidelines for Responders

One of the most important keys to managing stress in yourself is by first deciding if you want to be a "sprinter" where you work very hard for a short period of time and then burn out, or a "long distance runner". In order to be able to work effectively and stay healthy on disaster assignments, you must develop good stress management skills. Don't think, "I should manage my stress," and then ignore the signals as they appear. You must learn to take conscious steps to manage stress on the job in order to remain an effective member of the disaster response team.

How do you know when you or others are stressed? What suggestions do you have to help responders deal with stress? The following are some examples.

- Watch responders' functioning; the person watching can be the responder himself, a mental health professional, a peer working in a buddy system, or a supervisor.

- Breaks should be scheduled regularly when possible, or when function is impaired.

- Breaks should be taken away from the area so the responder is not reminded of the scene and is not interacting with the victims.

- Sleep breaks must be scheduled; otherwise they may not be taken.

- Responders should talk and share experiences with friends and colleagues as a way to let off steam. Included in this is "disaster humor".

- Recreational and leisure activities should be encouraged away from the disaster area to avoid constant reminders of the event.

Fig. 8-1: Suggestions to Help Responders Deal with Stress

Responders who are away from their home area or who will not be able to return home for an extended period of time, should be encouraged to bring personal items from home with them, and to call home often.

Interventions during a Disaster

Team Managers

The following are suggestions for team managers:

- During the Alarm Phase, provide responders with as much factual information as possible about what they will find at the scene. Provide this information via radio communications or in the form of a quick briefing as new personnel arrive at the scene. This forewarning can help personnel gear up emotionally for what they may find.

- Try to get information for responders about the location and well-being of their family members.

- Remember that early identification and intervention of stress reactions is the key in preventing responder burnout. Review lists of stress symptoms. Remember that multiple symptoms in each category indicate that responder effectiveness is diminishing.

- Use mental health assistance in field operations if plans have been made to do so. Mental health staff can observe responders' functioning, support responders, and give advice to command officers about responders' fatigue levels, stress, reactions, and need for breaks.

- Check in with responders by asking, "How are you doing?" Assess whether verbal response and responder's appearance and level of functioning jibe. For example, responders may say they are doing "fine", but may be exhibiting multiple stress symptoms.

- Try to rotate responders among low-stress assignments (such as staging areas), moderate-stress assignments, and high-stress tasks.

- Limit responders' time in high-stress assignments (such as triage or morgue) to an hour or so at a time, if at all possible. Provide breaks, rotation to less stressful assignments, and personal support.

- Ask responders to take breaks if effectiveness is diminishing. Order them to do so if necessary. Point out that the responder's ability to function is diminishing due to fatigue, and that you need him/her functioning at full potential to assist with the operation. Allow responder to return to the scene if he/she rests and functioning improves.

- On breaks, try to provide responders with the following:
  - Bathroom facilities
  - A place to sit or lie down away from the scene with quiet time alone
  - Food and beverages
  - Shelter from weather, dry clothes. Etc.
  - An opportunity to talk about their feelings—coworkers, chaplains, or mental health staff can assist

Workers

The following are suggestions for responders for management of stress during a disaster operation:

- Develop a "buddy" system with a co-worker. Agree to keep an eye on each other's functioning, fatigue level and stress symptoms. Tell the buddy how to know when you are getting stressed. For example: "If I start doing so-and-so, tell me to take a break." Make a pact with the buddy to take a break when he/she suggests it, if the situation and command officers allow.

- Encourage and support co-workers. Listen to each other's feelings. Don't take anger too personally. Hold criticism unless it's essential. Tell each other "You're doing great" and "good job". Give each other a touch or pat on the back. Bring each other a snack or something to drink.

- Try to get some activity and exercise.

- Try to eat frequently, in small quantities.

- Humor can break the tension and provide relief. Use it with care, however. People are highly susceptible in disaster situations. Victims or co-workers can take things personally and be hurt if they are the brunt of "disaster humor".

- Use positive "self-talk", such as "I'm doing fine" and "I'm using the skills I've been trained to use."

- Take deep breaths, hold them, then blow out forcefully.

- Take breaks if effectiveness is diminishing, or if asked to do so by commanding officer or supervisor.

- On long assignments away from home, remember the following:

  ➢ Try to make your living accommodations as personal, comfortable, and homey as possible. Unpack bags and pull out pictures of loved ones.

  ➢ Make new friends. Let off steam with co-workers.

  ➢ Get enough sleep.

  ➢ Enjoy some recreation away from the disaster scene.

  ➢ Remember things that were relaxing at home and try to do them now. Take a hot bath or shower, if possible. Read a good book. Go for a run. Listen to music.

  ➢ Stay in touch with people at home. Write or call often. Send pictures. Have family visit if at all possible and appropriate.

  ➢ Avoid excessive use of alcohol.

  ➢ Keep a journal. This will make a great story for grandchildren.

Interventions Following a Disaster

Team Leaders

The following are some things for team leaders to consider following a disaster:

- Arrange a debriefing for all responders involved in the disaster.

- Line personnel should have an opportunity to participate in a critique of the event. Often, a critique is limited to officers and supervisors. However, line staff participation can assure that responders are recognized for their contribution to the operation. Additionally, their viewpoints are valid and valuable input toward improving operations the next time around. DO NOT confuse debriefing with critique. These are separate functions and should not overlap.

- Formal recognition by the organization of a responder's participation in a disaster operation can mean a lot. A letter in the individual's personnel file, or a certificate of appreciation for contribution to an unusual and important job, lets the responder know that his/her participation meant something. Responders who remained at the office or station "minding the store" during the disaster should also receive recognition. Their contribution was also essential.

- Managers and supervisors should plan for the letdown their staff may experience. Discuss stress reactions in a staff meeting and emphasize that they do not imply weakness or incompetence. It is similar to being wounded in action.

- If responders' reactions are severe or last longer than 6 weeks, encourage them to use professional assistance. Again, this does not imply weakness. It simply means that the event was so traumatic that it has had a profound effect on the individual.

Survivors

Emergency and disaster responders are highly motivated and highly trained individuals. They perform strenuous, stressful, and often dangerous work. They seek to ease the suffering of victims. At the same time, they put themselves at high emotional risk for stress reactions that may be harmful to themselves, their work life, and their family life. It is important to remember and recognize the inherent strengths and qualities of the people who do this work. They embody the traits of the survivor personality. These traits include:

- A sense of commitment to and involvement in life; strong commitments; clear values; and things they believe in.

- Paradoxical traits of gentleness and strength, trust and caution, self-confidence and self-criticism, dependence and independence, toughness and sensitivity.

- A feeling of control over their circumstances, and the willingness to admit what can't be controlled.

- The ability to see change as a challenge, not just a threat; the commitment to meet challenges in a way that will make them stronger persons.

- Emergency and disaster responders are survivors. They can see both the positive and negative sides of any situation. They like to challenge themselves. They intend to survive, and to do so in good form.

Debriefings

A debriefing is an organized approach to the management of stress responses following a traumatic or critical incident. It is a specific, focused intervention to assist responders in dealing with the intense emotions that are common at such a time. It also assists responders by teaching them about normal stress responses, specific skills for coping with stress, and how to provide support for each other.

A debriefing involves a group meeting between the responders and trained facilitators. Group meetings are recommended, as they provide the added dimension of peer support.

A debriefing is not a critique. A critique is a meeting in which the incident is discussed, evaluated, and analyzed with regard to procedures, performance, and what could have been improved upon. A critique is a valid and important meeting. It can help responders to sort out facts, get questions answered, and plan for what to do in the future. A debriefing has a different focus: that of dealing with the emotional aspects of the experience.

It will not work to combine a critique and a debriefing in the same meeting. The goals and focus of the two meetings are entirely different. If an attempt is made to combine them, personnel may be much more comfortable analyzing logistics of the operation than dealing with the feelings involved, and the critique is all that occurs.

The basic ground rules for conducting a debriefing are outlined below.

Who Should Attend?

Everyone who participated in the incident should attend, unless the group is too big. In that case, it can be split into smaller groups. Multidisciplinary groups with police, firefighters, paramedics and EMTs, emergency room nurses, etc, are good. They bring together the whole team. Command officers and line staff should participate in the same debriefing. The media should be excluded if they wish only to observe. If they were part of the traumatic incident, they should participate in the debriefing as a participant and observe confidentiality like all other participants.

Mandatory vs Optional Debriefings

Opinions vary as to whether debriefings should be made mandatory. Many departments are moving in the direction of making debriefings routine and mandatory after any critical incident. This policy gives personnel the message that:

1) the organization is concerned for responders' well-being, and

2) the debriefing is a natural and routine procedure, with no stigma attached.

When debriefings are not mandatory, personnel who might benefit may not attend for fear of being labeled "weak".

Who Conducts the Debriefing?

The debriefing should be conducted by an experienced mental health facilitator and trained peer(s). A professional facilitator is recommended because the emotions expressed in a debriefing may overwhelm an untrained facilitator. The facilitators should be skilled in group dynamics and communications, use a crisis intervention approach, have a good knowledge of stress response syndromes and interventions, and be well-versed in operational procedures of emergency service organizations.

When a Debriefing Should Be Held

The best time to hold a debriefing is about 24 to 48 hours after the incident. Prior to that time, responders may still be emotionally "numb", either from the shock of the incident or because their feelings are still being suppressed. Responders are also in the process of intellectually restructuring the incident, often trying to figure out if they operated "by the books". At the 24-48 hour period, emotions are often surfacing in an intense form. This is a good time to deal with them. Effectiveness diminishes with the passage of time between the event and the debriefing. Every effort should be made to conduct the debriefing within 6 weeks of the event. However, successful debriefings have been conducted a year or more following a traumatic incident.

How Long Should a Debriefing Take?

Usually 2 to 4 hours should be allowed for a debriefing. In some situations, it may take longer. It is usually wise to block out a morning or afternoon to devote to the debriefing.

Incident Debriefing

The incident debriefing session is psycho-educational and takes different forms, depending on the age group involved.

It can be performed through activities including drawing, writing, or discussion. For example, it could be a puppet theater for very young children or an interactive story book for the 6-12 year olds. Adolescents could participate in a forum type meeting in which each person is given the opportunity to give their point of view. For adults, a regular debriefing session could be held; and, for the elderly, a round table type discussion. Even though the incident debriefing session may take different forms, the same rules should apply in order for the session to attain specific objectives.

The Goal of the Incident Debriefing Session

An incident debriefing session generally helps alleviate acute reactions to stress manifested during the incident or those which persist following it, thereby reducing or eliminating the delayed reactions to stress.

This intervention is a rational way of dealing with stress reactions.

Specific Objectives

The intervention model is based on three specific objectives:

1. to help the individuals express the feelings they experienced

2. to help them understand their emotional reactions and their behavior

3. to encourage the return to dynamic equilibrium

Debriefing Topics

These meetings are not sessions for discussing private grievances or offering a critical analysis of what happened. In general, they focus on what the people experienced and their subsequent reactions.

Confidentiality

These meetings are strictly confidential. A psychosocial practitioner who doesn't respect this rule will only undermine the quality of the intervention.

The Appropriate Time To Hold A Debriefing Session

Specialized literature suggests that this form of intervention has very good results if it is performed fairly rapidly after the disaster, critical incident or tragedy.

When should incident debriefing sessions be held?

The debriefing session can be held at any time. However, the lapse of time between the incident and the session can have a significant impact on the behavior of the individuals during the session. The impact of the session may also vary from one person to another.

Debriefing Guidelines

A. Never: within 24 hours of the incident

This period is required in order to allow the psychological defense mechanisms to subside. Only then can the individual come to terms with the psychological impacts underlying the traumatic incident. For the moment, all that can be done is to allow time for the emotions to "defuse".

B. Ideal: 24 to 72 hours after the traumatic incident

This period of time allows the individual to overcome the trauma and reflect on the incident, either at the conscious or unconscious level. If the person feels pain, this time is all the more necessary since it precedes the stage of suppression.

C. Good: within a few weeks of the traumatic incident

Suppression of the psychological effects caused by the traumatic incident is still minimal and the psycho-educational process is still effective.

D. Acceptable: within 12 weeks of the traumatic incident

Jeffrey Mitchell, the founder of formalized debriefings, states that a group debriefing within three months of the traumatic incident can work effectively. However, there is an increased chance of either suppression of symptoms or scapegoating through blaming. Most individuals, though, are able to access the psychological issues in a constructive and non-therapeutic manner.

E. Discouraged: 12 weeks or more after the traumatic incident

By this time, it is probable that a significant part of the psychological Impact of the traumatic incident has been suppressed to the subconscious. As a result individuals may react in a less than constructive fashion or require a more strategic debriefing performed on an individual basis. On the other hand, an educational session would be the intervention of choice. In this way, distressed individuals can still be advised of the signs and symptoms of critical incident stress and learn strategies for effective coping and stress management. This could also provide an opportunity to offer individual debriefing sessions.

13 Rules for an Incident Debriefing Session

1. **Confidentiality:** Confidentiality is essential.

2. **Freedom of speech:** Anyone is free to remain silent if that is his/her choice, but everyone is encouraged to participate.

3. **Speak about yourself:** Anyone who agrees to speak will speak only about him/herself. Hearsay is prohibited.

4. **Respect others:** Do not relate details which could embarrass other participants.

5. **Equality:** During the session, all participants are equal.

6. **Psycho-education rather than therapy:** The meeting is not a therapy session, but is designed to help the Participants return to their usual pace and recover their dynamic equilibrium as quickly as possible.

7. **Respect cultural aspects:** The cultural aspect of a group must be taken into consideration. Certain traditions, beliefs and customs can influence the expression of emotions.

8. **Expressing oneself during the session:** The practitioners are usually available after the session if necessary, but the participants are strongly encouraged to express themselves during the session.

9. **Direct relation with the incident:** Other than certain exceptions, only the people who had a direct relation with the incident are eligible.

10. **Pay attention to certain needs:** People who smoke can do so providing the other participants do not object.

11. **No interference:** "Pagers", including those belonging to the group leaders, must be turned off or placed on vibrate.

12. **Respect of the group's privacy:** Taking notes, or recording the session on tape, as well as the presence of media people are prohibited.

13. **Pay attention to the silent participants:** Attention must be paid to the people who do not speak but who seem to be disturbed. They can be approached privately later on, in the event that they are simply individuals who are reticent to express themselves in front of a group.

Organizational Aspects

The Optimal Intervention Should:
1. Be Held: as soon as possible following the appearance of symptoms (idea of "immediacy"); as close as possible to the site of the disaster or the place to which the disaster victims were evacuated (idea of "proximity").

2. Bring together: similar groups (idea of "community").

3. Create: a favorable climate which allows the message to be heard.

Whatever the people are experiencing is normal. They can recover from it and they will be able to return to their activities (idea of "expectancy").

It is also important to take into account the composition of the group. In order to encourage discussion, the composition of the group should be homogenous. The characteristics of the participants must be taken into account: primary clientele, secondary clientele and tertiary clientele and, if possible, age groups.

Who Should Be Grouped In An Incident Debriefing Session?

Anyone associated with a traumatic incident can participate in a debriefing session. The issue is: *who should be grouped with whom?*

A. Debrief those in the greatest need first.

Picture a target with concentric circles. The closer you are to the center, the more directly or more closely involved you were with the incident. Set your priorities so that those closest to the center get debriefed first. In this way, you ensure your energies go to those in greatest need. You have only so much energy and so many resources. Use them wisely.

B. Debrief homogenous groups

For debriefings to work, individuals need to feel safe. Debrief those who were present at an incident or those who witnessed one separately from those who did not. Those who were present at an incident often feel uncomfortable when people who were not directly involved in the incident participate. As well, details mentioned during a session could unnecessarily traumatize those who were not there. One way to ensure this is to debrief at a peer level. This means excluding one's superiors or subordinates. As well, when debriefing disaster service groups, it is important to ensure that they are professional equals. For example, professional firefighters, ambulance attendants and police officers can be debriefed in the same group. However, the session may not work if others not of similar professional status, such as volunteer workers or highways staff, were present. You must know your group and make your own decisions.

- **The Significant Person for the Group:** This person is recognized or identified as being helpful and significant for the group.

- **The Number Of Participants:** A group should be restricted to a maximum of twelve participants, or less if the emotional load is extremely heavy.

- **The Climate:** The meeting must take place in a favorable atmosphere of support and understanding. Each person's reactions are offered to the group and accepted.

- **A Basic Rule:** No one is allowed to criticize someone else.

Information Sessions

Information sessions (e.g., Crisis Management Briefings or CMB) presented jointly with the organizations involved are intended for the whole community. They consist of providing general information and dealing briefly with the current difficulties, the reactions that may be shown by the victims, services available, and the problems typically associated with returning to normal life. The activities suggested for information sessions are all optional. None are mandatory, neither for the disaster victims nor for the members of their families or witnesses of the event.

During these information sessions, the following messages are among those given with regard to physical and emotional reactions:

- The physical and emotional symptoms are part of a stress reaction and are considered normal;

- These symptoms occur in most people in a situation of stress, threat or loss. They are primitive reactions of the mind and body, and their purpose is to help the individual survive;

- Stress syndromes, although normal, can, however, present health risks if they persist, since they rob people of energy and make them vulnerable to illness. In some cases, they can even have repercussions on a person's whole life;

- There are many ways of dealing with stress reactions, such as surrounding oneself with people one feels good with and with whom it is easy to talk about what one is experiencing, doing vigorous physical exercise, or using relaxation techniques.

- The most effective way of relieving stress reaction syndrome is verbalization sessions on the event.

Verbalization Sessions

Verbalization sessions (e.g., CISD) on the event are a simple but effective method of assisting the population and responders to cope with and carry on with normal life. A verbalization session on the event usually permits the alleviation of acute stress reactions in order to reduce or prevent delayed stress reactions.

This method is a rational way of dealing with stress reactions. The intervention model focuses on three specific objectives:

- to help people express their feelings;

- to assist them in understanding their emotional reactions and their behavior;

- to promote a return to a state of equilibrium in each individual.

The specialized literature in this area suggests that this type of intervention gives very good results if it takes place quickly after the disaster or tragedy, that is between 24 and 72 hours following the event. At least 24 hours should be allowed to elapse before such a session, since the normal mechanisms of denial and avoidance are predominant immediately after the disaster, whereas after 24 hours, cognitive activity decreases to give way to feelings and emotions. Studies have shown the importance of holding these sessions promptly, because the longer one waits to carry out post-disaster intervention, the less effective is the intervention. Therefore it is important that it take place within 72 hours.

The optimal intervention should take place as soon as possible after the appearance of symptoms (the concept of immediacy) and as close as possible to the site of the disaster or the evacuation site of the disaster victims (the concept of proximity). It should bring together similar groups (the concept of community) and create a climate that carries a clear message: what they are experiencing is normal; it can be healed and they will be able to resume their activities (the concept of expectancy).

The make-up of the groups should be homogeneous and reflect the characteristics of the participants—men, women, the elderly, adolescents, responders, etc.—in order to facilitate discussion.

Groups should be restricted to a maximum of 12 participants, or fewer if there is too great an emotional charge. The atmosphere should be positive, supportive and understanding. The reactions of each participant are shared and accepted. The basic rule is that no one criticizes another person.

The verbalization sessions on the event should be led by competent mental health professionals and peers who are knowledgeable about this type of intervention and who have received the necessary training.

> It is important to demystify psychological help because it is too often confused with mental problems. It is essential that psychological help be offered and that it be offered at the time of the tragedy because people need to verbalize their emotions and be together to comfort each other.

Follow–up and Referral to Mental Health Resources

Each organization should have some means of monitoring individuals' recovery from traumatic events or incidents. This may take place as a routine follow-up meeting (group or individual) with the debriefing facilitators, a meeting between supervisor and employee, or a routine medical check with the employee health nurse or physician. The purpose of the follow-up is to allow the worker further opportunity to talk about feelings about the incident. It is also to assess with the individual whether the symptoms are diminishing. A good time to do a routine follow-up is about a month to 6 weeks following the event.

If workers are still having difficulties with stress symptoms at that time, a routine referral to a mental health counselor should be suggested. The organization should have a pre-established plan for referrals to counselors who are knowledgeable or specialize in working with emergency service personnel. Fee arrangements should be pre-established. The ideal arrangement is for mental health services to be available to emergency workers through their prepaid employee health plan or EAP. Many plans do not provide this coverage. Personnel are often angry if they find they must pay for counseling out of their own pocket when the trauma was a work-related event. This can produce a real barrier to personnel obtaining the services they need to remain functional and productive on the job.

Sometimes workers are unfamiliar with the process of counseling and what it entails and are therefore reluctant to seek help. They should know that most counselors prefer to work with emergency workers in a short-term, active approach. Counselors often use specific techniques which are aimed at symptom reduction. They usually do not use long-term, psychoanalytic approaches. Occasionally, depending on the nature of the problem, marital or family therapy may be suggested.

Post–Disaster Counseling for Individuals or Groups

Counseling should be offered to individuals who were unable to attend a verbalization session or debriefing. Counseling can also be offered to people who feel a need for individual help or for longer term help in a group.

This type of intervention usually consists of two or three meetings during which the counselor pursues the same objectives as during the verbalization session. In terms of the content, essentially the same techniques developed in the Mitchell Model seem to be effective. The major difference is that they are spread out over time rather than being concentrated in a single session.

Short Term Intervention

This type of intervention is based on the assumption that appropriate assistance provided at the appropriate time can, in the short term, bring an individual back to the level of his/her psychological and social functioning prior to the traumatic event.

Intervention in a crisis situation is designed to assist the disaster victim who is experiencing transitory difficulties associated with major psychological distress.

Once the crisis is confined, it lasts from four to six weeks. During this transition period there is both the danger of increased psychological vulnerability and the opportunity for personal growth. The outcome depends to a large degree on the ease of access to appropriate assistance and on the therapeutic climate. Such short term interventions are high intensity assistance generally consisting of two or three sessions a week. If the objectives are not met within four to six weeks the client should be considered for and offered medium or long term intervention.

Medium and Long Term Intervention

Resources providing the assistance required in medium and long term follow-up counseling should be provided as part of the services normally offered to victims and workers.

This follow-up is intended for disaster victims with severe difficulties associated with important psychological distress. It is also associated with a degree of impaired functioning such that it significantly interferes with their interpersonal relations and their basic social skills.

If the disequilibrium caused by the disaster has increased a pre-existing vulnerability in the individual, the intervention should aim not only to restore the previous level of functioning, but also to prevent and avoid the recurrence of psychological distress.

Collaboration between Emergency and Mental Health Services

A pre-disaster collaborative relationship can make training available for emergency workers in the mental health aspects of their work. This can help them to anticipate and effectively deal with their own mental health needs and those of victims. Such pre-disaster planning between mental health and emergency services also paves the way for effective collaboration during and after a disaster.

Psychological First Aid and Short Term Therapy

Most authorities agree that mass disasters leave in their wake a need for some form of acute mental health services. A review of current literature on crisis intervention and disaster mental health reveals differing points of view on the methods that should be employed (Raphael, 1986; NIMH, 2002). However, there has been a general endorsement of the value of psychological first aid (American Psychiatric Association, 1954; USDHHS, 2004; Raphael, 1986; NIMH, 2002; Institute of Medicine, 2003; WHO, 2003; DoD/VAPTSD, 2004; Ritchie, et al, 2004; Friedman, Hamblin, Foa, & Charney, 2004) as an acute mental health intervention. It seems uniquely applicable to public health settings, the workplace, the military, mass disasters, and even the demands of critical incidents (e.g., dealing with the psychological aftermath of accidents, robberies, homicide, or community violence). (Everly Jr. and Flynn, 2006)

Psychological First Aid

Psychological first aid is emerging as the crisis intervention of choice in the wake of critical incidents such as trauma and mass disaster. It is similar to the concept of physical first aid. Physical first aid is the preliminary physical care provided by members of the general population, not by medical professionals. In minor cases of physical injury, first aid can provide the care an individual needs for recovery. There may be no need for follow-up with a medical professional. In the same way, Psychological first aid is basic "grassroots" psychological support provided for family, friends, neighbors, and colleagues by members of the general population, not by mental health professionals. Just as physical first aid is used for injuries ranging from minor scratches to serious wounds, Psychological first aid is used to provide psychological support for experiences ranging from minor stressors in daily life to traumatic events. Physical first aid teaches participants how to know when an injury requires professional medical attention. Psychological first aid teaches providers when and how to make referrals for professional mental health care (Jacobs and Meyer 2006).

Nearly every survivor of mass violence, critical incidents or disasters experiences stress-related reactions in the immediate aftermath. Most recover. The emotional and psychological impact of disasters is not easily absorbed, and survivors may benefit from some immediate psychological support even under the best of conditions. However, it is no simple task to determine who should deliver what kind of support to whom and at what time. Disasters and wars are so dangerous and disruptive that it would be absurd to address people's psychological needs when their very lives are threatened. Moreover, even after the imminent threats have subsided, there continue to be imperative survival needs that must be given the utmost priority. Therefore, if immediate psychosocial support is to be supplied at all, it will most likely require an informal method of delivery that fits seamlessly with the provision of the most essential services (e.g., medical, nutritional, and sanitation) and must neither conflict with the priorities of the humanitarian operations nor the cultural values of the beneficiaries.

The role of mental health clinicians in the aftermath of disaster and terrorism is growing in importance. Assessment and treatment of acute responses to traumatic stress has received much attention since the World Trade Center incident on September 11, 2001. Those events underscore the value of having a trained and ready mental health workforce. Training in psychological first aid, crisis intervention, and early interventions may well become a part of graduate and postgraduate training in clinical programs in psychology, psychiatry, and social work. The scope and the depth of the psychological impact coming from these events warrants such an investment of time and resources. Coordinated efforts that cross geographic, political, and social lines would be welcome additions to societal efforts to understand the impact of mass violence and to provide the best possible interventions directed at recovery. It is clear that most survivors of traumatic events are resilient and do recover. However, a significant minority of survivors may endure prolonged periods of distress. It is for these people that interventions should be developed with the hope of minimizing the impact of trauma exposure, limiting disability and dysfunction, and maximizing optimal emotional recovery (Keane and Piwowarczyk, 2006).

Referral for Therapy

Much of today's psychological trauma can be identified as resulting from sudden and seemingly random events, and particularly from events that involve the loss of human life. Due to the often overwhelming and ongoing nature of disasters and the recovery efforts they necessitate, building competency in a variety of intervention techniques and prioritizing assessment and education is essential for effective response. Experts agree that most people will recover from the effects of a disaster with little or no formal psychological intervention (Norris, Friedman, Watson, Byrne, Diaz, et al., 2002). Providing well-planned and targeted psychological first aid may help many access coping skills and resources more quickly and may also allow disaster mental health providers to identify populations or individuals at greater risk for developing distressing psychosocial issues. In doing so, these individuals may be linked with the resources they need to ensure better outcomes. Different populations benefit from a variety of approaches applied at different stages of disaster response and recovery.

Traumatic Incident Reduction (TIR)

Traumatic Incident Reduction (TIR) is a brief, one-on-one, person-centered, simple and highly structured method designed to permanently eliminate the negative effects of past traumas. It involves repeated viewing of a traumatic memory under conditions designed to enhance safety and minimize distractions. Described as "person-centered", TIR provides the structure for the client to do all the work. The therapist or counselor offers no interpretations or negative or positive evaluations, but only gives appropriate instructions to the client to have him/her view a traumatic incident thoroughly from beginning to end. Hence, the term "viewer" is used to describe the client and "facilitator" to describe the person who is helping the client through the procedure by keeping the structure of the session intact and giving the viewer something definite to do at all times.

The facilitator confines her/himself to giving a series of set instructions to the viewer and offers no advice, interpretations, evaluations, or reassurances. TIR uses repetition to unsuppress the trauma being addressed to provide the viewer the opportunity to review and revise his/her perspective on it. TIR's uniqueness lies, in part, in the fact that a session continues until the viewer is completely relieved of whatever stress the target trauma originally provoked and any cognitive distortions (e.g., observations, decisions, conclusions) embedded within the incident have been restructured. (Gerbode, 1989).

A one-on-one guided imagery process, TIR is also useful in remediation of specific unwanted stress responses, such as panic attacks, that occur without significant provocation. "Thematic TIR" traces such conditioned responses back through the history of their occurrence in a client's life to the stressful incidents primarily responsible for their acquisition. The resolution of the primary incidents then reduces or eliminates the target stress response.

TIR is a systematic method of locating, reviewing and resolving traumatic events. Once a person has used TIR to fully and calmly view a painful memory or chain of related memories, life events no longer trigger it and cause distressing symptoms. TIR has been used in relieving a wide range of fears, limiting beliefs, suffering due to losses (including unresolved grief and mourning), depression, and PTSD symptoms. The TIR technique can be traced to roots in psychoanalytic theory and desensitization methods. However, it is carried out in a thoroughly person-centered, non-judgmental and respectful context.

Eye Movement Desensitization Reprocessing (EMDR)

EMDR is a psychotherapeutic approach developed by Francine Shapiro (Shapiro and Forrest, 2004) to resolve symptoms resulting from exposure to a traumatic or distressing event, such as rape. Although it is considered effective for civilian PTSD, no controlled evaluation of EMDR, or any other treatment for PTSD, has been conducted with adults in a natural disaster context.

EMDR integrates elements of many effective psychotherapies in structured protocols that are designed to maximize treatment effects. These include psychodynamic, cognitive behavioral, interpersonal, experiential, and body-centered therapies. EMDR is an information processing therapy and uses an eight phase approach.

During EMDR the client attends to past and present experiences in brief sequential doses while simultaneously focusing on an external stimulus. Then the client is instructed to let new material become the focus of the next set of dual attention. This sequence of dual attention and personal association is repeated many times in the session. Although eye movements are the most commonly used external stimulus, therapists often use auditory tones, tapping, or other types of tactile stimulation. The kind of dual attention and the length of each set is customized to the needs of the client. The client is instructed to just notice whatever happens. After this, the clinician instructs the client to let his/her mind go blank and to notice whatever thought, feeling, image, memory, or sensation comes to mind. Depending upon the client's report the clinician will facilitate the next focus of attention. In most cases a client-directed association process is encouraged.

After EMDR processing, clients generally report that the emotional distress related to the memory has been eliminated, or greatly decreased, and that they have gained important cognitive insights. Importantly, these emotional and cognitive changes usually result in spontaneous behavioral and personal change, which are further enhanced with standard EMDR procedures.

Clinical trials have demonstrated EMDR's efficacy in the treatment of post-traumatic stress disorder (PTSD). It has shown to be more effective than some alternative treatments and equivalent to cognitive behavioral and exposure therapies. Although some clinicians may use EMDR for various problems, its research support is primarily for disorders stemming from distressing life experiences.

The theoretical model underlying EMDR treatment hypothesizes that EMDR works by processing distressing memories. EMDR is based on a theoretical information processing model which posits that symptoms arise when events are inadequately processed, and can be eradicated when the memory is fully processed. It is an integrative therapy, synthesizing elements of many traditional psychological orientations, such as psychodynamic, cognitive behavioral, experiential, physiological, and interpersonal therapies. EMDR's most controversial aspect is an unusual component of dual attention stimulation, such as eye movements, bilateral sound, or bilateral tactile stimulation. Some individuals have criticized EMDR and consider the use of eye movements to be controversial.

Summary

Various other cognitive-behavioral approaches have varying degrees of reported success in alleviating post-traumatic stress. At present there does not seem to be any one technique that is effective in all situations. When making referrals following a mass disaster or critical incident, it is important to make sure that an adequate assessment be made by a mental health professional. It is also important to identify adequate and appropriate referral resources prior to an incident. An inappropriate referral has potential for doing more harm than good.

9 Coping and Resiliency

On September 11, 2001, tragedy struck New York, Washington, D.C. and Pennsylvania as well as the whole country. Immediate, short-term and long-range effects on victims, victims' families, responders and the general public can be expected to vary in intensity and emotional responses. How we face the tasks before us and how we respond—personally, as communities, as a nation, and world-wide—may very well determine the viability of the American vision and way of life for the remainder of the 21st century and beyond.

The United States is no stranger to adversity, tragedy, war and disaster. We have dealt with it before. Each generation has been tested and challenged—and each generation has risen to the occasion.

Our national unity was tested in a bloody Civil War that forever changed the future and the character of the country. In 1941 we were stunned by an attack by the Empire of Japan on our own soil. This led to our entrance into World War II. That event changed forever the world view of this country and our involvement in world affairs. We became a leader in the world with all of its attendant rewards and responsibilities.

In the 1950s, the long Cold War began with its threat of nuclear annihilation and resulting stresses and trauma in a society intent on survival, defense and the defeat of communism. The Korean War was fought to a stalemate not resolved to this day. Many grieved the losses of loved ones in uniform.

When John F. Kennedy became president in 1960, he represented a dramatic change in the leadership and direction of this country. He offered a vision and hope for a bright and prosperous future. He challenged us to move in new directions and provided impetus for the manned space program. The nation endured severe stress and real and perceived threat to our security and well-being during the Cuban Missile Crisis. Brinksmanship and a firm, strong resolve and message helped avert a possible direct threat to American cities.

On November 22, 1963 in Dallas, Texas, President John F. Kennedy was assassinated. This event shocked the nation and the world. In the days following this event the country felt vulnerable, grief-stricken and angry. Shaken to the core, we grieved for our loss and had our future changed forever. The leader who had challenged a generation to act had fallen. However, the ideals that he held out for the country have endured; the goals he set and the vision for the America he described have not been lost. The resolve of a generation was far stronger and had greater impact than the assassin's bullets. The inspiration of Kennedy's challenges to a generation has resulted in improved civil rights for all, many positive social changes, better opportunities for education for all citizens, more research and development in all the sciences and medicine, accomplishment of the goal of putting a man on the moon and returning him safely, and continuing positive international relations and development in other countries with assistance from numerous Peace Corps Volunteers.

During the 1960s the U.S. struggled with the issues surrounding the Viet Nam War and the ongoing mounting casualties. Civil Rights leader Martin Luther King was assassinated. Presidential candidate Robert F. Kennedy was assassinated. Riots in our cities tore at the very fabric and core of American values and life. Civil Rights and anti-Viet Nam War rallies and marches proliferated nationwide. Confusion, anger, grief, decreased morale, loss of a sense of direction, challenged traditional values, and cultural change all impacted a reeling society.

In the summer of 1966 in Austin, Texas, Charles Wittman went up into the Texas Tower on the campus of the University of Texas. He killed or wounded staff and tourists on his way to the top. Once there, with his arsenal of weapons and ammunition, he methodically began to pick off people on the campus and in town. He killed or wounded more that 40 people before being killed himself by 2 police officers and a civilian volunteer. This whole drama was viewed on live television throughout Texas and the country. It was the first time such an event had ever been seen live by so many people and was the worst "terrorist" event to occur in this country to that date. It shook the country and demonstrated the vulnerability of innocent people to such acts.

During the early 1970s, the country experienced the first significant fuel crisis. This awakened the country to the realities of oil sources and the control exerted by groups outside the U.S. such as OPEC. At Kent State University, the tragedy of students being shot by National Guardsmen shocked the nation. Photos and video of the events traumatized many vicariously, many of whom remain with residual problems to this day.

Also in the 1970s, our government system was challenged internally by the Watergate scandal and break-in. It resulted in the first resignation of a sitting president in the country's history. In 1979 the country endured the frustratingly long and drawn out daily drama of the Iranian Hostage Crisis. In many respects it paralyzed significant parts of the country. Its resolution partially depended on the election of a new president. While long, frustrating and drawn-out, the crisis resolved peacefully.

In the 1990s the country fought the Gulf War. In early 1993, New York reeled following a terrorist bombing of the World Trade Center. There were six casualties, repairs were made and New York recovered. A domestic terrorist, Timothy McVeigh, bombed the Murrah Federal Building in Oklahoma City in 1995. This was the worst act of terrorism in U.S. history to that date.

There have been other traumatic events that have shaken our consciousness in recent years. Columbine stands out, but there have been other violent events in our nation's schools in other parts of the country. Each of these events above resulted in direct and vicarious trauma in many individuals, communities and the nation. Each one has had significant long-range effects on the country. While each was followed by a period of grief and mourning and shock, each has also generated some positive and constructive changes. In all cases, the communities and the country as a whole have been very resilient and have recovered psychologically, emotionally and physically.

Resilience and Recovery

Resilience is the capacity of an individual, group, community, organization, or a nation to withstand loss or damage and to recover from the impact of an emergency, critical incident, or disaster. Vulnerability can be viewed as a measure of the susceptibility to suffer loss or damage. The higher the resilience, the less likely the damage will be and the faster and more effective will be the recovery. Conversely, the higher the vulnerability, the more exposed is the community, group, individual or nation to loss and damage.

Developing and using a resilience and vulnerability profile is an integral element in effectively planning the management of consequences to a community or country following an emergency, critical incident or disaster. Such a profile helps identify the strengths of particular areas, communities or groups in terms of resources, skills, networks and community agencies available. These strengths and local capabilities can be used and further developed to help minimize the negative consequences of an emergency, critical incident or disaster by supporting recovery activities.

When preparing to intervene, it is critical to assess which phase (heroic, honeymoon, disillusionment, recovery) the individual, community, or country is currently in. This will help in designing a general intervention.

The approach will be different for each phase. This is an example of community psychology at its best.

In the recent terrorist aftermath from the WTC in New York, the Pentagon and the plane crash in Pennsylvania, these phases will be increasingly difficult to characterize. At this point, observing from a distance, it appears that the heroic phase is concluding. With aid coming from around the country and the world, and measures (economic and legislative) being enacted by Congress, the affected areas appear to be entering a honeymoon phase. Plans for recovery and the future are being discussed. The country as a whole is making plans for a changed way of life.

While still uncertain about the future (immediate and long-term) the country is beginning to debate rational and effective responses and recovery efforts. These will require close scrutiny, observation, and continued re-evaluation.

What Can Mental Health Professionals Expect?

The responses of communities and individuals around the country will vary over the next 6 months to a year. Some will prove to be more resilient than others in recovering and getting on with life. Cultural differences and different economic levels will be variables that will affect recovery. Morale will be affected by both the real and perceived directions, actions, and goals voiced, outlined and acted upon by community and national leaders.

Individuals

Therapists can expect an increase in certain types of presenting problems. These will include, but not necessarily limited to: somatic complaints, depression, grief reactions, feelings of hopelessness and helplessness, generalized and specific anxiety, phobic reactions, trauma reactions, school phobias, fear of flying and travel, fear of elevators and other closed spaces, fear of strangers, increase in divorce rates, family problems, spousal and child abuse, intrusive thoughts and ruminations related to anxiety and fears, difficulties concentrating and making decisions, absenteeism, difficulties making plans, sleep problems, nightmares, disturbing dreams, difficulties relaxing, etc.

These and other related presenting problems can be expected to manifest in children as well as in adults. Some adults who have had direct relationships or exposure to the actual events may be at risk for feelings of survival guilt. Some veterans and others who have experienced post-traumatic stress from other previous events may re-experience symptoms.

Under most conditions with clients presenting, most developed therapeutic approaches will generally be sufficient with the caveat that this ongoing crisis will continue to generate certain feelings and responses. Individual adjustment and adaptation are a couple of the general goals in these cases. Another helpful approach is the use of support groups guided and/or facilitated by available mental health professionals. Ongoing discussions of feelings, current events and actions would be a useful approach. If symptoms persist and/or become more severe or present as severe, further and more intensive therapeutic approaches are indicated.

Communities

Contact on a regular ongoing basis with various community groups, formal and informal, by mental health professionals can help in the assessment of community morale, recovery and other responses as well as opportunities to promote morale, recovery, etc. by helping identify positive, constructive community actions and goals and suggesting other positive actions and activities. This is a time for mental health professionals to use their skills, knowledge and abilities to become active participants in their communities at many different levels other than the consulting room, workshops, and speeches.

While there are wide variations in the types of losses individuals, groups and communities may suffer, the following are the most common types of potential losses and damages:

- Safety: threats of death or injury.

- Home/Shelter: threats to safe, appropriate accommodation.

- Health/Well-Being: threats to short or long-term well-being in terms of physical health and psychological and emotional well-being.

- Food: threats to an adequate supply of food and to a supply that is uncontaminated.

- Contaminated Water: threats to an adequate supply of water and to a supply that is uncontaminated.

- Sewage/Waste Disposal: threats to a continued safe disposal of waste and an avoidance of environmental health risks.

- Social Links: threats to the networks and links which sustain daily community life, which provide a sense of order and meaning and which allow access to support and services.

- Information: threats to sources or outlets of information about existing or emergency management services.

- Access: threats to transport systems and utilities as well as to physical infrastructure such as roads and bridges.

- Income/Economic Opportunity: threats to the capacity to earn a livelihood through the loss of employment, loss of customers, or the loss of assets.

It is important to prioritize needs and the following is one possible way:

1. SUSTAINING LIFE: (including people on life support machines).: Essential medical facilities, medical equipment, "hospital in the home", medicines

2. SUSTAINING PHYSICAL WELL-BEING: Accommodation, food and water, clothing, etc.

3. SUSTAINING MENTAL WELL-BEING: Personal and psychological support and information.

4. REDUCING SOCIAL ISOLATION: Access to support networks as well as information and resources.

5. REDUCING PHYSICAL ISOLATION: Access to support networks as well as information and resources.

6. SUPPORTING EMERGENCY STAFF: Supporting staff whose job is to provide urgent, critical support to others.

7. SUPPORTING PEOPLE WHO HAVE FEW RESOURCES: Access to financial supplementation and resource supplementation.

8. ASSISTING PEOPLE WHO HAVE RESOURCES ADEQUATE TO MANAGE THEIR OWN RECOVERY: Access to assistance.

Some Issues

In terms of individual, group and community issues which support resilience and help to reduce vulnerability, there are some relevant broad principles to consider:

1. We are aware from the experience of many events that the affected community(s) will expect to contribute to their own recovery. If denied an opportunity, they may establish their own structures and processes to achieve that end. It is paramount, therefore, to support community involvement. Successful management of the consequences is not possible without community commitment and involvement.

2. It is useful to set out community issues in these terms because it places them in a management and operational framework. Issues of resilience, vulnerability and need are expressed in terms in which they can be operationalized and dealt with in a practical way.

3. These issues are a broad characterization of the types of assistance and support that individuals and groups may require after a significant emergency or disaster. They are a way of thinking about service provision in management and operational terms rather than simply in terms of the particular assistance measure.

Filling Needs:

The following are some of the major needs that should be addressed:

Information

- Information and advice about assistance measures and how to access them, including eligibility conditions and application procedures.
- The normal biopsychosocial reactions which can be expected and how they can deal and cope with these reactions in themselves, members of their family and their community.
- How to make sense of the event in terms of its cause and fitting it into their "view" of the world.

Resources

- Financial assistance where eligible to help restore losses. This may include, where appropriate, grants, loans, and insurance.
- Physical goods such as temporary accommodation, essential household items, temporary public transport, tools, etc.

Management Capacity

- Time and opportunity: to undertake recovery activities.
- Physical capacity: which may include the support of other people, machinery, or other support where there is a particular need.
- Access to services: through establishing support systems, locating service centers close to affected areas or access in terms of translator, interpreter, or other language and media services.
- Expertise: access to specialist services such as tradesmen, financial counselors, and other professional services.

Support

- Personal support: outreach services, personal advisors and counselors, specialist support services, advocates and gatekeepers.

- Community support: community development officers, etc.

Involvement

- Consultation in developing and implementing assistance and recovery programs.
- Encouragement in making a contribution to policy and program development.
- Engagement in monitoring and auditing the progress of recovery.

Recovery and Returning To Equilibrium

All survivors of disasters suffer loss. They suffer loss of safety and security, loss of property, loss of community. Loss of status, loss of beauty, loss of health, or loss of a loved one. Following a disaster, all individuals begin a natural and normal recovery process through mourning and grief.

Assessing Resilience

A number of factors support individuals, families and communities and help to minimize the consequences of disasters in terms of supporting sustaining recovery activities. Some of them are the reverse of vulnerability such as access and adequate resources. Identifying and assessing those positive factors possessed or shared by individuals, families, groups, communities and agencies which support resilience gives emergency planners and managers the opportunity to further develop resilience to increase the "disaster resistance" of the population. Some of the elements supporting resilience include:

1. **Shared community values**, aspirations and goals including a shared and positive sense of the future, a commitment to the community as a whole and agreement of community goals as well as a shared culture.

2. **Established social infrastructure** such as information channels, social networks and community organizations such as sporting and social clubs.

3. **Positive social and economic trends**, such as a stable or growing population, a healthy economic base.

4. **Sustainability of social and economic life** which embraces a capacity for the community to weather disruption.

5. **Partnerships** between agencies, between community groups and between commercial enterprises, or any combination of these may bring innovation, sharing of experience, knowledge, resources, and

common goals. This applies particularly where the partners play a dominant role in the social and economic life of the town such as towns dominated by a particular industry or economic activity.

6. **Communities of interest:** Where a group may exist over a wide area and be otherwise socially diverse but they share a common area of interest, skill or expertise. This includes communities bound together by faith and religious commitment as well as less formal groups such as business or commercial associations or sporting or recreational clubs.

7. **Established networks:** Clear, agreed and stable links between people and groups facilitate the exchange of information as well as the sharing of resources and the commitment of skills, time and effort to planning and preparedness.

8. **Resources and skills available locally** may be directly relevant to emergency management planning, preparedness and for community support when an emergency or disaster occurs. These can be identified by the type of resource or skill, its amount, the cost to use it, its availability, and by its location. Where useful resources or skills do not exist they may be developed or promoted as part of preparedness activities.

Where Do We Go From Here?

People in crisis are extremely vulnerable. They are open to hurt as much as to help. The goal of crisis counseling should be to protect them from further harm, while providing them with immediate assistance in managing themselves and the situation. Crisis counselors provide brief, clear, and gentle directions and support to distressed victims. As soon as possible, they help the victims take on responsibility for their own care. It is important to provide frequent reassurance and guidance when the situation is most threatening. The most important thing is to offer assistance to help the individual gain a sense of control of self and situation, and not to do everything for the victim.

Whenever possible, it is important to help the victim identify and focus on the problem, or the most important problem if there are several. This helps the individual gain a sense of perspective and to prioritize their recovery efforts. They need to be told what is happening and why to help reduce the sense of surprise or feeling that they are being lied to.

Provide Information Sessions

Information sessions presented jointly with the organizations involved are intended for the whole community. They consist of providing general information and dealing briefly with the current difficulties, the reactions that may be shown by the victims, services available, and the problems typically associated with returning to normal life. The activities suggested for information sessions are all optional. None are mandatory, neither for the disaster victims nor for the members of their families or witnesses of the event.

During these information sessions, the following messages are among those given with regard to physical and emotional reactions:

- The physical and emotional symptoms are part of a stress reaction and are considered normal;

- These symptoms occur in most people in a situation of stress, threat or loss. They are primitive reactions of the mind and body, and their purpose is to help the individual survive;

- Stress syndromes, although normal, can, however, present health risks if they persist, since they rob people of energy and make them vulnerable to illness. In some cases, they can even have repercussions on a person's whole life;

- There are many ways of dealing with stress reactions, such as surrounding oneself with people one feels good with and with whom it is easy to talk about what one is experiencing, doing vigorous physical exercise, or using relaxation techniques.

- The most effective way of relieving stress reaction syndrome is verbalization sessions on the event.

Provide Verbalization Sessions

Verbalization sessions on the event are a simple but effective method of assisting the population and responders to cope with and carry on with normal life. A verbalization session on the event usually permits the alleviation of acute stress reactions in order to reduce or prevent delayed stress reactions.

This method is a rational way of dealing with stress reactions. The intervention model focuses on 3 specific objectives:

- to help people express their feelings;

- to assist them in understanding their emotional reactions and their behavior;

- to promote a return to a state of equilibrium in each individual.

Specialized literature in this area suggests that this type of intervention gives very good results if it takes place quickly after the disaster or tragedy, that is, 24 to 72 hours following the event. The optimal intervention should take place as soon as possible after the appearance of symptoms (the concept of immediacy) and as close as possible to the site of the disaster or the evacuation site of the disaster victims (concept of proximity). It should bring together similar groups (concept of community) and create a climate that carries a clear message: what they are experiencing is normal; it can be healed and they will be able to resume their activities (concept of expectancy).

Groups should be homogenous and have a maximum of 12 participants. The atmosphere should be positive, supportive and understanding. The reactions of each participant are shared and accepted. The basic rule is that no one criticizes another person.

Verbalization sessions on the event should be led by competent mental health professionals who are knowledgeable about this type of intervention and who have received the necessary training.

Provide Follow–up and Referral to Mental Health Resources

Each organization should have some means of monitoring individuals' recovery from traumatic events or incidents. This may take place as a routine follow-up meeting (group or individual) with the debriefing facilitator. A meeting between supervisor and employee, or a routine medical check with the employee health nurse or physician. The purpose of the follow-up is to allow the worker further opportunity to talk about feelings about the incident. It is also to assess with the individual whether the symptoms are diminishing. A good time to do a routine follow-up is about a month to 6 weeks following the event.

If workers still have difficulties with stress symptoms at that time, a routine referral to a mental health counselor should be suggested. The organization should have a pre-established plan for referrals to counselors who are knowledgeable or specialize in working with emergency service personnel. Many EAP plans cover this.

Provide Post–disaster Counseling for Individuals or Groups

Counseling should be offered to individuals who were unable to attend a verbalization session or debriefing. Counseling can also be offered to people who feel a need for individual help or for longer term help in a group.

Finally, crisis presents an opportunity for change and re-evaluation. This can be a positive and constructive development.

A pre-disaster collaborative relationship can make training available for emergency workers in the mental health aspects of their work. This can help them to anticipate and effectively deal with their own mental health needs and those of victims. Such pre-disaster planning between mental health and emergency services also paves the way for effective collaboration during and after a disaster.

10	# War	

Fear and War

Over the past two decades, the world has witnessed an increasing number of disasters involving massive exposure of the population to radiation, chemical toxins, or other hazardous agents. Terrorist acts such as that on September 11, 2001 create apprehension about possible further attacks, perhaps with biological or chemical weapons. The term "ecological disaster" is used to indicate these incidents, which are often followed by widespread fear of future adverse health effects. Concerns or worries about health tend to facilitate the appearance of medically unexplained symptoms or syndromes. This mental health component has received relatively little attention in the disaster literature (Havenaar, Cwikel & Bromet, 2002).

Murphy, Wismar & Freeman (2003) examined stress reactions to the events of September 11, 2001 among African-American college students not directly exposed to the attacks. Within 3 days of September 11, 219 undergraduates (78.3% women; aged 18-32.9 yrs) completed self-report measures assessing stress symptoms and other reactions to the attacks. The results indicated that many students experienced a variety of stress symptoms and distressing thoughts and feelings in response to the events of September 11, including academic problems, concerns about family and friends in the military, and fear about war. Most students were highly distressed by specific attack-related news reports and images. Anger toward persons of Middle Eastern descent was not frequently reported. Later college year and having parents not currently together were predictors of overall stress symptom severity as assessed by the Posttraumatic Stress Disorder Checklist. Later college year also predicted academic problems after September 11.

Panic and fear appear to have different functions. Starcevic, Kolar, Latas, Bogojevic & Kelin (2002) assessed the impact of real danger on several aspects of panic disorder patients' psychopathology and level of disability. Their results suggest that there is no relationship between panic attacks and real danger and lend support to the notion that panic attacks and fear induced by real danger are different phenomena. Fear interrupts the continuum of memory. Examples of situation-specific amnesia, including severe depression, crimes of passion, disasters, war and child sexual abuse suggest that emotional memories may implicate amygdaloidal circuits. In extraordinary circumstances we may ask ourselves to recall far more detail than in normal circumstances (Kopelman, 2000).

Therapists have unique skills that are desperately needed in the prevention of and recovery from violence, war, and terror. They can heal, teach people how to hear and transform, and listen. Recent acts of terrorism and violence on U.S. soil have left citizens, politicians, and professionals asking similar questions. Why did this happen to us? What can we do to keep this from happening again? Witty (2002) provides one answer to those questions by calling for greater involvement of systemic therapists in violence prevention and intervention at home and abroad. Conflict resolution theory, steeped in realism, modernism, and a structural perspective of change, dominates conflict analysis abroad even though it has been largely ineffective. Structural changes in government do not address the fear, anger, and destruction of human relationships generated by war and terror. The transformation of the root causes of war, violence, and hatred lies in integrating the analytical and transformational perspectives of conflict resolution and systemic therapy, particularly the narrative deconstruction of hate, with existing structural problem-solving models.

Fear and Children

The potential for war is a pervasive threat to the security and family structure of children in military families and can result in anticipatory anxiety and other expressions of distress. For children living in war zones, they can express acute distress from various traumatic events through emotional problems that are not usually recognized. Thabet, Abed & Vostanis (2002) assessed the nature and severity of emotional problems Palestinian children (aged 9-18 yrs) exposed to home bombardment and demolition during the Al Aqsa Intifada and age-matched controls who had been exposed to other types of traumatic events related to political violence. They completed self-report measures of post-traumatic stress (PTS), anxiety, and fears. Significantly more children exposed to bombardment and home demolition reported symptoms of PTS and fear than controls. Exposure to bombardment was the strongest socioeconomic predictor of PTS reactions. In contrast, children exposed to other events, mainly through the media and adults, reported more anticipatory anxiety and cognitive expressions of distress than children who were directly exposed. Thabet et al (2002) suggest that health professionals and other agencies coming in contact with children who have been affected by war and political violence need to be trained in detection and treatment of emotional problems due to acute stress from traumatic events.

The use of children in combat situations is another source of fear, distress, and long-term trauma among those involved. Armed combat in childhood is a form of child abuse. de Silva, Hobbs & Hanks (2001) interviewed 19 former child soldiers (aged 16-24 yrs) using a standard questionnaire. Reasons cited for recruitment included: volunteered, hatred of enemy (revenge), virtue of being a freedom fighter (martyrdom), and as a means of supporting their family (economic). One child was abducted, 7 joined for fear of the 'enemy' abducting them, and in 5 a family member was killed by the 'enemy' or their own group. The children were involved in manual labor, guard duty, front-line fighting, bomb manufacture, setting sea/land mines and radio and communication. Fifteen were trained in firearms and fourteen in self-destruction. Twelve children attempted to or did run away and eleven refused to obey orders or argued. This led to various punishments, including kitchen duty, beatings, imprisonment, blackmail or death threats. A majority of the children felt sad and emotionally upset when they remembered their mother and family. de Silva, Hobbs & Hanks (2001) conclude that children's involvement in war, whatever the 'justifications' may be, should always be considered as forced, as they cannot truly comprehend their action in war. The responsibility must be taken by the adult caregivers. They suggest that firm international agreement on guidelines for the lower age limit of recruitment of children into armed forces should be required.

Fear and trauma among children can also occur as a result of vicarious exposure to traumatic events. Using telephone interviews with a random sample of 314 Dutch children between the ages of 7 and 12 years, Valkenburg, Cantor & Peeters (2000) investigated (a) the prevalence of TV-induced fright, (b) whether the fear-inducing capacity of different types of TV content (interpersonal violence, fantasy characters, war and suffering, and fires and accidents) is associated with the child's age and gender, and (c) how boys and girls in different age groups cope with their TV-induced fears. subjects were given open-ended questions about TV fright, the TV-induced fright scales, and questions dealing with the frequency with which they used various coping strategies to reduce fear from TV. Thirty-one percent of the children reported having been frightened by television during the preceding year. Both children's TV-induced fears and their coping strategies to reduce such fears varied by age and gender.

There are a number of suggested techniques for helping children who have been exposed to such severe traumatic events as war. Indirect methods, such as games or play seem to be more effective ways for children to communicate their feelings. For example, Herman (2000) examined the use of board games to teach effective ways of communicating, dealing with conflict and feelings of anger, and fear. Four games were designed as part of the curriculum for use with 112 fourth grade children at Vladimir Nazor School in Slavonski Brod, Croatia who were experiencing the trauma of war. They found that over repeated game playing, there was improvement in dealing with anger, conflict, and fears by the children who were using the games. Interviews supported the game as an effective way of teaching communication, and alternative ways of coping with anger, conflict, and fears.

Fear and Other Cultures

Fears can sometimes be transferred from older sources to newer or different ones once the original has been eliminated. Murray & Meyers (1999) used the collapse of the Soviet Union to test the hypothesis that some people are psychologically predisposed to "need enemies." The findings from the 1988-1992 Leadership Opinion Project (LOP) panel data show that those respondents who had been highly suspicious of Soviet motives before the end of the cold war are more likely to view other countries with suspicion and to perceive the international environment as dangerous after the Soviet collapse. There is no evidence that people have actually transferred old fears about the Soviet Union onto a replacement enemy. China is the country most frequently named as the US's main adversary following the cold war, making it the most likely object for the transference of hostility. However, even the most ardently anti-Soviet respondents do not exhibit greater fear or animosity toward China after they have lost their old enemy. However, it is possible that the need to have some sort of "enemy" has been transferred to Al Queda and Saddam Husein's Iraqi regime.

Culturally relevant approaches toward healing are important considerations when developing and implementing interventions within a culture not one's own. For example, among Somalis in Ethiopia, war-related distress is not interpreted in a medical framework aimed at healing. Rather, such violence is predominantly assimilated into the framework of Somali politics, in which individual injuries are considered injuries to a lineage or other defined group. The dominant emotion in this context is not sadness or fear, but anger, which has emotional, political and material importance in validating individuals as members of a group sharing mutual rights and obligations (Zarowsky, 2000). Before advocating trauma-based models of war-related distress, researchers and practitioners should consider whether a medical framework would do better at helping individuals and communities to deal with distress and re-construct meaningful lives and relationships in circumstances of long-standing collective violence. It is important to consider culturally relevant approaches before proceeding in any response.

In another example, Hinterhuber, Hartmann, Stern, Ross & Kemmler (2001) investigated attitudes toward warfare in the former Yugoslavia among refugees and emigrants. In 1995, 283 Serbs, Montenegrins, Croats, and Bosnians (mean ages 32.0-37.8 yrs) from the former Yugoslavia completed surveys concerning:

(1) feelings, values, political attitudes, and assessments of contemporary history;

(2) attitudes to the then ongoing war;

(3) prejudices; and

(4) perspectives for the future.

Results show that almost half of Croat subjects were happy when Yugoslavia started to disintegrate. The Serbs predominantly felt grief, followed by fear and uncertainty.

Dar, Kimhi, Stadler & Epstein (1999) studied the effects of military service during the Intifada on veterans from a kibbutz background. 184 Israeli Defense Forces veterans (133 males and 51 females) from a kibbutz background who had served in the occupied territories during the Intifada (1992-1998) were retrospectively asked in a semi-structured questionnaire how this service had affected them. The results showed some common themes:

1) service in the "territories" deepened Subjects' understanding of the Israeli-Palestinian conflict, but also increased their fear and hatred of Arabs;

2) most Subjects did not develop a new political position but were firmer in their original "leftist" position;

3) only a few Subjects based their position on support for the Palestinians' rights or suffering focusing mainly on a generally utilitarian consideration of the Israeli side's needs;

4) in order to cope with the conflict between their military duty and the internalized values of their kibbutz education, Subjects either sought shelter behind army orders or compartmentalized their humanistic values and military duty; and

5) Subjects regarded their military service during the Intifada as a most difficult experience but leaving only a situational, temporal psychological imprint.

Cultural values, exposure to traumatic events, civilian or military status, attitudes, history, prejudices, politics, education, and other variables all play a role in the experience of and effective responses to fears due to war situations.

Fear and Nuclear Threats

Not since 1945 has the world experienced nuclear warfare, although there has been the threat of nuclear terrorism and a large number of nuclear/radiological accidents. Most people fear a nuclear/radiological threat even more than a conventional explosion due to their inability to perceive the presence of radiation with the ordinary human senses and to concerns about perceived long-lasting radiation effects. Studies of radiological accidents have found that for every actually contaminated casualty, there may be as many as 500 people who are concerned, eager to be screened for contamination, sometimes panicked, and showing psychosomatic reactions mimicking actual radiation effects (Salter, 2001). Data from the Hiroshima and Nagasaki attacks revealed widespread acute reactions such as psychic numbing, severe anxiety, and disorganized behavior, and later there were chronic effects such as survivor guilt and psychosomatic reactions. Such responses would likely be common in any future nuclear/radiological accident, terrorist attack, or warfare.

Conclusions

The response to 'new security' risks requires significant changes in public behavior, and the legitimization of unpopular government policies. Public education is one means of achieving this. The need is reflected in initiatives such as environmental and development education, health promotion, and the public understanding of science. Current strategies are often based on commercial advertising, but mass communications theory does not directly encompass influencing perception, which is necessary to create awareness of the new 'invisible' risks. Recent evolutionary brain science is providing new insights into our species perception deficits, which can inform a more effective approach to public education. Williams (2002) places risk within the context of the post-Cold War 'global security' agenda. He proposes a theoretical framework—'brain lag'—to explain perceptual deficits. It draws on theories of information, adaptation and denial, and an understanding of the human senses including time-scale-latency. He proposes fundamental areas of evolutionary perception: fear and disgust, number perception, and cheating. This leads to a core concept for public education about new security risks, 'enhanced difference', and a set of hypotheses that can be applied to text or image.

Whatever approach, fear remains a potent motivator of behavior. It is one that is consistently utilized for control and is manipulated by others for maximum effects. Helping those traumatized by fears is a major task for psychologists and others attempting to help them readjust to the world and to achieve a level of equilibrium.

Children and War

With the recent advent of involvement of children in military conflicts such as in Africa (Mozambique), the Middle East (Palestine and Lebanon), and Southeast Asia (Cambodia), psychologists have taken a keen interest in examining the psychological effects such conflicts reap on children. Hence, a growing but modest body of literature has been amassed within the past 20 yrs on the subject.

Health professionals and other agencies coming in contact with children who have been affected by war and political violence need to be trained in detection and treatment of such presentations. Children living in war zones can express acute distress from various traumatic events through emotional problems that are not usually recognized. Vizek-Vidovic, Kuterovac-Jagodic & Arambasic, (2000) examined affective and behavioral symptomatology in children (aged 8-16 yrs) who were traumatized to different degrees during the war in Croatia. 1,034 children completed the Questionnaire on Children's Stressful and Traumatic War Experiences and other instruments. Their results show a cumulative effect of traumatic and stressful events, with higher levels of traumatic and stress reactions and less successful adaptation in subjects with more traumatic and stress experiences. Older females reported more posttraumatic stress reactions, psychosomatic reactions, and anxiety, but had higher scores on the measure of psychosocial adaptation than did males. Younger subjects reported more posttraumatic stress disorder symptoms than did older subjects.

As part of a UNICEF-sponsored Psychosocial Program in Bosnia, Smith, Perrin, Yule & Rabe-Hesketh (2001) collected data from a representative sample of 339 children aged 9-14 yrs, their mothers, and their teachers to investigate risk and moderating factors in children's psychological reactions to war. Self-report data from children revealed high levels of posttraumatic stress symptoms and grief reactions, but normal levels of depression and anxiety. Mothers' self-reports also indicated high levels of post-traumatic stress reactions, but normal levels of depression and anxiety. Child distress was related to both their level of exposure and to maternal reactions. Structural equation modeling was used to quantify the relationships between these risk factors and child distress, and to examine putative pathways to account for the association between child and maternal health. Children's adjustment was associated significantly with both exposure and maternal mental health. Modeling also revealed a significant distorting effect of mother's own mental health on behavioral ratings of her child. Results suggest that although evidence exists for an association between maternal mental health and mother rating errors, there is also a substantive association between maternal mental health and children's adjustment following war.

Smith, Perrin, Yule, Hacam & Stuvland (2002) collected data from a community sample of 2,976 children in Bosnia-Hercegovina aged between 9 and 14 years. Children completed standardized self-report measures of posttraumatic stress symptoms, depression, anxiety, and grief, as well as a report of the amount of their own exposure to war-related violence. Results showed that children reported high levels of posttraumatic stress symptoms and grief reactions. However, their self-reported levels of depression and anxiety were not raised. Levels of distress were related to children's amount and type of exposure. Girls reported more distress than boys, but there were few meaningful age effects within the age band studied. Results suggest methods for both service development for children in war and for more effective coping methods.

Thabet, Abed & Vostanis (2002) assessed the nature and severity of emotional problems in 91 Palestinian children (aged 9-18 yrs) exposed to home bombardment and demolition during Al Aqsa Intifada and 89 age-matched controls who had been exposed to other types of traumatic events related to political violence. The subjects completed self-report measures of post-traumatic stress (PTS), anxiety, and fears. Significantly more children exposed to bombardment and home demolition reported symptoms of PTS and fear than controls. 54 (59%) of 91 exposed children and 22 (25%) of 89 controls reported PTS reactions of clinical importance. Exposure to bombardment was the strongest socioeconomic predictor of PTS reactions. By contrast, children exposed to other events, mainly through the media and adults, reported more anticipatory anxiety and cognitive expressions of distress than children who were directly exposed.

MacMullin & Odeh (1999) used a 4-part method to identify and understand the things that worry children in the Gaza Strip. 194 Gazan children, aged 8-14 yrs, were asked to generate lists of the things about which they worried. These data were then used to construct a survey questionnaire which allowed a rank ordering of children's worries and the exploration of developmental and gender differences. The final part of the study employed focus groups in which the children elaborated on their worries, spoke about the strategies they use to manage these concerns, and proffered advice for younger children who might have to face similar concerns in the future. Issues about which the children worried ranged from politics, war and religion to personal friendships and exam anxiety.

In summary, these studies suggest that children's adjustment following a war is significantly associated with levels of exposure, maternal reactions, and maternal mental health. Children's age and sex appear to be significant variables in terms of stress levels experienced. Girls seem to become more distressed than do boys.

Gender, Age and Cultural Factors

Ronen & Rosenbaum (2003) assessed children's reactions to the stress induced by the 1991 Gulf War as a function of gender and age. They conducted their assessment during the third week of the 1991 Gulf War in Israel. The participants were 229 boys and 189 girls who attended the 2nd, 6th, and 10th grades (aged 8, 12, and 16 yrs, respectively). The children were asked to report behavior problems (for before and during the war), anxiety level (before and during the war), and war-related symptomatic behavior. The findings indicate that the war had an adverse effect on the well being of children, in particular girls. Girls in comparison to boys reported higher levels of anxiety and more behavior problems for the war period as well as more war related symptoms. Gender differences were mostly found for the data relating to the war period and not for the pre-war period. Age moderated the effect of gender on war related symptoms and on anxiety. Whereas among the younger children (2nd grade) no gender effects were found, among the older ones (6th and 10th grades) the gender effects were apparent. In summary the Gulf war had an adverse effect on the well being of children, in particular on the well being of girls and the gender effects appeared only among the older children.

Baker & Shalhoub-Kevorkian (1999) examined the universal and culture-specific correlates of political and military trauma. Specifically, they focused on the psychological symptoms children display following their exposure to such traumatic events. They suggest that special emphasis be placed on anxiety, phobic, psychosomatic, and depressive symptoms. Examination should be made to ascertain which factors (e.g. psychosocial, cultural, and political) serve to shield or predispose children to psychological dysfunction. Furthermore, the analyses should be gender specific. Attempts should be made to delineate a paradigm that explains the relationship between trauma, culture, and personality.

Al-Krenawi, Slonim-Nevo, Maymon, & Al-Krenawi (2001) investigated the well being of Arab adolescents who live under the threat of ongoing blood vengeance, and assessed the impact of socio-demographic characteristics, cultural context, and family functioning as mediating factors. Their sample consisted of 100 adolescents (aged 12-14 yrs) in grades 6-8. Self-reported standardized measures were used to assess the participants' level of self-esteem (Rosenberg's scale), mental health (the Brief Symptom Inventory BSI), and perceived family functioning (the McMaster Family Assessment Device FAD). The participants of this study demonstrated higher levels of distress and symptomatic behavior as compared to the Israeli norms. General Family Functioning emerged as the major predictor associated with mental health. Female participants reported a higher anxiety level than their male counterparts. Male participants, on the other hand, were more willing to continue the feud of blood vengeance. Their findings suggest that there are similarities among children and adolescents who live in war zones and those who live under a threatening blood vengeance. Family functioning appears as the major mediator of well being.

Papageorgiou, et al (2000) described the pattern of psychopathology in a sample of 95 children aged 8-13 yrs, who had experienced war in Bosnia. The children were assessed with a battery of standardized measures during a psychosocial support program in Northern Greece. They either came from refugee families or had suffered significant family loss (a parent had been killed in 28% and the father was injured or absent in 27% of cases). Children recalled a substantial number of war traumatic experiences. According to previously established cut-off scores on self-report measures, 45 children scored within the clinical range on the Depression Self-Rating Scale for Children, 28 on the Revised Children's Manifest Anxiety Scale, and 65 on the Impact of Event Scale (IES) measuring posttraumatic stress disorder (PTSD) reactions. There was a significant association between the number of war traumatic experiences and the intrusion and avoidance scores on the IES. Findings suggest setting up intervention programs for children who are victims of war and their families.

Stein, Comer, Gardner & Kelleher (1999) examined the psychological symptoms of Bosnian children exposed to war and trauma, and detected the changes in these symptoms over time. A total of 147 displaced children (5-12 yrs old) residing in refugee centers in Bosnia completed self-report assessments of anxiety, depressive, and posttraumatic stress disorder (PTSD) symptoms at two time points approximately eight months apart. Symptoms of PTSD, anxiety, and depression showed a greater decrease in boys relative to girls over time. Gender may be an important factor in the natural course of trauma-related symptoms among war traumatized children.

Oclander Goldie (1999) presents an interesting case study. She uses material from the treatment of a young child whose development became seriously arrested from the time of a traumatic experience during a war. This experience, combined with the impact of the birth of a younger sibling while he was still a baby himself, had catastrophic consequences. He could only communicate his feelings of terror and fear of dying through the use of projective identification. The persecutory anxiety of this child was such that for a while he could not tolerate hearing the interpretations, and was prone to violent outbursts. Oclander Goldie describes how she had to bear the projections and manage the physical attacks while trying to maintain the capacity to observe and think clearly. This setting produced an experience of containment that gradually allowed this child to accept and understand interpretations which diminished the power of feelings that had overwhelmed him in the past. Through introjections of the experience of being understood during his sessions, he began to develop the capacity to think about his feelings. This allowed him to gradually recover, develop, and make use of his intelligence and imagination, and the behavioral difficulties that brought him to treatment disappeared.

Military Families

The potential for war is a pervasive threat to the security and family structure of children in military families. Ryan-Wenger (2001) compared 91 children (8-11 yrs old) of active-duty, reserve, and civilian families with respect to their perceptions of war, origin of fears related to war, levels of manifest anxiety, coping strategies, and projection of emotional problems in human figure drawings. Her findings regarding the adaptation of children in military families suggest the need for further research from children's perspectives is important for understanding adaptations and responses of military children.

Children and Families

Van Ommeren, de Jong, Joop, Sharma, Komproe, Thapa & Cardena(2001) provide an overview of the effects of war on children during the 20th century in specific countries in Latin America, Asia, Africa, and the Middle East. They argue that wars have both direct and indirect effects on the population. Wars have changed from being conventional to being of low intensity. Under these latter circumstances civilians become targets, whereas in the past, the targets were usually only military ones. The effects of the strategy used in low intensity conflicts is the disruption of the medical, social, educational, and public services of a country and the terrorization of the population. Under these circumstances children suffer inordinately. Their homes are destroyed, their families disrupted, and their chances of becoming mature productive members of society are compromised.

Five years after the military operation "Anfal" in Iraqi Kurdistan, 45 families were randomly selected among the survivors in two displacement camps (Ahmad, Sofi, Sundelin-Wahlsten & von Knorring, 2000). The Post-traumatic Stress Symptoms for Children and the Harvard Trauma Questionnaire were administered to the oldest child and the caregiver in each family, respectively. Posttraumatic stress disorder (PTSD) was reported in 87% of children (aged 7-17 yrs) and 60% of their caregivers (aged 17-91 yrs). While childhood PTSD was only significantly predicted by child trauma score and the duration of captivity, it was neither predicted by maternal PTSD nor did it disappear after the reunion with the PTSD-free father (Ahmad et al. 2000). However, the small sample size makes the results hypotheses rather inconclusive.

Ford, Shaw, Sennhauser, Greaves et al. (1993) obtained interview and questionnaire data 2-6 mo after demobilization from Operation Desert Storm (ODS) from 26 veteran/veteran or veteran/civilian spouse couples who received conjoint time-limited therapy and 30 veterans from the same Reserve and National Guard units who received 1-to-1 time-limited therapy. 31 nontreatment-seeking control veterans and 7 nontreatment-seeking civilian spouses were also included in the sample. Further assessments were conducted 12-15 mo after demobilization from veterans deployed during ODS with the same military units. Their findings indicate that the trauma and strain of war-zone military service, family separation, and subsequent family and community readjustment take a toll on a significant minority of ODS veterans and their families. With timely psychosocial intervention, veterans and families in distress are able to substantially resolve symptoms of psychosocial malfunctioning.

Apellaniz (1999) studied the impact of war deployment & enforced separation during the Persian Gulf conflict on family & coping strategies, and wives of civilian soldiers from Puerto Rico. This study documents how spouses of Puerto Rican National Guard soldiers appraise the impact of war deployment and separation on their family lives. It examines the coping strategies they found most useful in adjusting to the demands of separation during 1989's Persian Gulf conflict. A combination of quantitative and qualitative methods was used. Emotional tension, concern about their husband's safety and having to assume new family roles and full care taking and household responsibilities without their husbands' support and for such a prolonged period of time were reported by wives as the most distressing aspects of separation. In contrast to women who reported having a satisfactory marital relationship, informants who described their marital relationship as poor evaluated the actual period of separation as less distressing than previous periods of military enforced separation. Overall, women in this study were resourceful and strongly committed to overcome the obstacles faced by their families during separation. Coping strategies aimed at maintaining families united were found to be extremely helpful in adapting to separation. Religious values, a positive outlook on life events, and support from family members also contributed to strengthen their capacity to endure separation. Cultural values and social expectations related to the role that traditionally Puerto Rican women play in the family served the respondents as instrumental guidelines for adapting to the demands and strains of prolonged separation. These findings have implications for planning intervention and support services for military families.

In summary, major factors affecting families with military members include war-zone military service, family separation, and readjustment back into the community by service members. Posttraumatic stress (including PTSD) and psychosocial malfunctioning are among problems encountered. Strengths that contribute to resiliency by all family members include religious values, a positive outlook on life events, family support and various forms of psycho-social interventions. Children living and surviving in war zones are affected adversely in a number of developmental ways and are at severely increased risk of becoming unproductive members of their society.

Resiliency Following War

The effects of war, torture, and disaster on the mental health problems of refugees, spouses, family members and military personnel are manifested in several ways, including adjustment problems, depression, anxiety disorders or posttraumatic stress disorder (PTSD). The stressful condition of a refugee could also worsen any underlying mental disorders such as psychotic illnesses. To address the mental health needs of the large number of refugees, specific management ability and approaches are required. Some basic tenets that should be followed are that interventions should be integrated with overall health care; they should be responsive to all severity and kinds of problems; they should be part of the redevelopment of mental health services; and they should be sustainable, culturally sensitive, evidence-based and cost effective. Saraceno, Saxena, Maulik, Sartorius, Gaebel, et al. (2002) describe some of the broad public health principles and strategies in mental health care in complex refugee emergencies, discuss the role of international agencies, and suggest areas for further research pertinent to the mental health of refugees. They address the mental health problems and care of asylum seekers, refugees, internally displaced and repatriated persons, and other non-displaced populations affected by war and organized violence.

Each refugee group experiences specific migration and resettlement experiences. For example, there are no epidemiological data on risk factors for psychiatric symptoms among adult Somalis in the UK. Bhui, Abdi, Abdi, Pereira, Dualeh, Robertson, Sathyamoorthy, & Ismail(Jan 2003) interviewed a community sample of 180 Somalis (aged 20-88 yrs). They assessed relationships between symptoms of psychosis (Brief Psychiatric Rating Schedule), anxiety and depression (Symptom and Complaints Checklist-90) and suicidal thinking (Beck Depression Inventory) and migration-related experiences such as traumatic events, immigration difficulties, employment and income. Anxiety and depression were incrementally more common with each pre-migration traumatic event. Shortages of food, being lost in a war situation, and being close to death and suffering serious injury were each related to specific psychiatric symptoms. Suicidal thinking was more common among Somalis who were unemployed before migration and those using Qat in the UK. War-related experiences, occupational status before migration and current Qat use are risk factors for psychiatric symptoms among Somali refugees.

Traumatic experiences associated with the war in Bosnia (1992-1995) impacted the lives of many Bosnian refugees and displaced people. Approximately 25% of Bosnians were forced to leave their homes and resettle in other areas of Bosnia or abroad. Plante, Simicic, Andersen, & Manuel (2002) describe war-related stress and the association of marital status, anxiety, depression and sensitivity levels. 82 displaced Bosnians living in the area of Tuzla, Bosnia, and 53 refugees living in the San Francisco Bay area completed the same questionnaire in the Bosnian language. Better self-reported health was related to being single, having lower anxiety ratings, finding and adapting to a new environment easily, and moving on with life. Findings also revealed that being divorced or separated, better self-reported health, and lower anxiety, depression, and sensitivity ratings were predictors of more effective coping.

Tang & Fox (2001) conducted a preliminary investigation into the experiences and mental health of Senegalese refugees. They noted that although research has established that refugees are more prone to psychiatric illnesses than the general population, little has been written about West African refugees. 80 adult refugees (18 yrs of age and older) from the Casamance region of Senegal were randomly selected from refugee camps in The Gambia. The Harvard Trauma Questionnaire and the Hopkins Symptom Checklist-25 were used to assess levels of traumatization and mental health status. Typical of refugees of war, participants reported suffering a large number of various traumas. High prevalence rates of anxiety, depression, and posttraumatic stress disorder were also found in this group. Tang & Fox conclude that a substantial mental health problem exists within the Senegalese refugee population that may signify a potential human crisis.

Van Ommeren, de Jong, Sharma, Komproe, Thapa & Cardena (2001) surveyed a population-based sample of 418 tortured and 392 non-tortured Bhutanese refugees living in camps in Nepal. Trained interviewers assessed International Classification of Diseases and Related Health Problems (ICD-10) disorders through structured diagnostic psychiatric interviews. Except for male sex, history of torture was not associated with demographics. Tortured refugees, compared with non-tortured refugees, were more likely to report 12-month ICD-10 posttraumatic stress disorder, persistent somatoform pain disorder, and dissociative (amnesia and conversion) disorders. In addition, tortured refugees were more likely to report lifetime posttraumatic stress disorder.

Bek, Buzov & Bilic (2001) evaluated differences in anxiety levels between groups of refugees and non-refugees in Croatia. subjects were 90 subjects (similar in age, gender, and education, and each with a history of missing family members) divided into 3 groups (30 subjects each). Group 1 included subjects who lost close family members, Group 2 included non-refugees subjects, and Group 3 comprised of subjects whose immediate family members were reported as "missing." subjects were assessed using the Hamilton Anxiety Scale (M. Hamilton, 1986). The results revealed the most significant differences in anxiety levels in Groups 2 and 3. subjects grief over "missing" family members manifested itself as psychosomatic illness, somatic depression, and anxiety.

Deane, MacDonald, Chamberlain, Long & Davin(1998) reviewed research concerned with the association between combat-related posttraumatic stress disorder (PTSD) and interpersonal functioning, before describing the development of a pilot program established to provide mental health services for Vietnam veteran family members. The results of a brief program evaluation were also presented. 60 clients (aged 11-77 yrs) provided post treatment and 6-mo follow-up data on a variety of outcome measures which were compared with independent ratings returned by 33 therapists. On average, clients reported that counseling had been beneficial and indicated satisfaction with services received. However, at posttest, therapists indicated that approximately 50% of clients were in need of continued treatment. There was a decrease in satisfaction with services over the posttest follow-up period, but no change on most measures of psychotherapy outcome.

In summary, across various cultures and populations affected by war situations, major mental health related problems include: depression, anxiety, posttraumatic stress (including PTSD), various somatic complaints (including psychosomatic illness and persistent somatoform pain disorders), and dissociative disorders.

Conclusion

Cultural differences, age, sex, family structure, maternal mental health, anxiety and depression levels are among the variables that need to be addressed when assessing and treating children following war-related trauma. The role of the father was not adequately addressed in these studies in terms of effects on children's post-war adjustment. Further research is needed to better understand the psychological effects of war trauma on children, and the natural course of posttraumatic symptoms, so as to improve interventions targeted to this vulnerable population.

11	Terrorism and Terrorists	

Early Background

Following their defeat in 1918, Germany underwent a psychological change. As a result, they regressed to the militarism of Prussia and the power politics of Frederick the Great and Bismarck. Nationalism was deliberately fostered. It was intensified in reaction to Communism and alleged international Jewry (Brown, 1944). On the crest of this primitive reaction, Adolf Hitler rose to power. He was helped by both industrialists and the military. The mass mind of the nation accepted this. There was a mutual interaction between the leader and the led. This brought about a unification of the nation at a primitive level resulting in liberation and encouragement of a sadistic aggressiveness which horrified the civilized world. This appears to be somewhat supported by Colombio and Moccio (1961). It was their contention that, when group anxiety rises in circumstances of economic disruption, terrorism, etc, members of the group apply a learned mechanism and resolve the anxiety by transferring their unconscious aggressiveness to a paranoid projection.

What was important here was the psychology of the group mind, what Alfred Rosenberg (1982) called the community consciousness and what Hitler (1925) called the folk community. Hitler's *Mein Kampf* and Rosenberg's *Myth of the Twentieth Century* epitomized the psychology and philosophy of the Nazi movement.

Brown (1944) suggested that the hysterical and paranoid tendencies that were so manifest in Hitler had their counterpart in the reactions of the entire nation. He suggested that the post-war treatment of Germany should be adjusted to these psychopathological facts. He believed that the deliberate cruelty of the police and the terrorism of the spy system called for condign punishment. He suggested that the later stages of the war would bring stern re-education to the mass of the German nation regardless of whatever post-war measures might also be applied.

The public consciousness that the world is under threat of becoming involved in a terrible and devastating war has been manifested over the years in gigantic demonstrations, peace marches, and public petitions. In every part of the world, economists, philosophers, sociologists, and psychologists have noted increased anxiety and stress levels (Schiopu, 1983).

This growing panic has been aggravated by economic depression, the growing rate of unemployment, and monetary conflicts. This latent and diffuse panic has, over the years, increased the rate of accidents, suicides, terrorism, and delinquency, as well as the use of alcohol, drugs, and psychotropic medications.

What Is Terrorism And Who Are The Terrorists?

Whereas atomic weapons threaten death through an impersonal mechanism, in death dealt by terrorism, the action provides the terrorist the feeling of self-determination and individualism. The effect of *both* of these institutions on human feelings of insecurity and the obvious need to recognize the reality of these threats are critical to helping understand the terrorist and his/her motivations (Slochower, 1982).

The increasing attention being given to study of the political, social, and psychological antecedents of terrorism was presented at the International Scientific Conference on Terrorism in December 1978 (Holden, 1979). Although there was general agreement as to the nonexistence of a "terrorist personality," the need for further study of the dynamics of terrorist groups was noted. The 1981 conference dealt with international terrorism and discussed participation in terrorist groups in relation to the attraction to violent behavior and destructiveness; feelings of justification; the backgrounds of members; and feelings of hopeless, inner-directed anger that are related to the insecurity of the sociocultural climate. The involvement of both psychopathic and relatively "normal" individuals in terrorism was noted, and the formation of a specific type of subculture was considered. A panel discussion on the psychology of the leaders of terrorist groups was presented. Areas considered included the backgrounds of actual leaders in such organizations, the importance of charisma in the leadership of terrorist groups, pathways leading to the involvement in a deviant culture, and the roles of feelings of power and hostility in involvement in terrorist activities (International Scientific Conference on Terror & Terrorism: International Terrorism, 1982).

Gorney (1981) has suggested that psychosocial identity and self-esteem have grown out of conditions of competition and low social synergy, leading to the conflict and terrorism that now jeopardizes the human race. He maintains that humankind faces extinction within a shift toward greater cooperation and high social synergy, because humans cannot become conscious of and implement what they have learned about the route of survival. He examines elements of this thesis, such as scarcity and cooperation vs competition, and presents clinical examples as illustrative material.

The psychological roots of modern terrorism have been traced to the youth movements and countercultures of the late 1960s; the erosion of traditional moral and religious values; and young people's need for new ideologies to replace old, moribund ones (Bartalotta, 1981). The typical terrorist is characterized as someone who is young, well-educated, and of middle-socio-economic status, and who is skillfully manipulated by ruthless and power-crazed international leaders. Bartalotta (1981) hypothesized that terrorism operates in the realm of Jung's archetypal and personal "shadow." Recalling Jung's plea for understanding and acceptance of the shadow, he argues that Jungian psychotherapists should be able to confront the evil of terrorism through the recognition that it is one of the aspects of the evil embodied by the shadow in all persons.

Von Raffay (1980) discusses hope as the source of terrorism. Whereas progressive hope tries to bring about better conditions than those presently existing, regressive hope derives from the mother complex and from its inner inactivity, waiting eternally for a tomorrow that never comes. Hope is an archetype and as such belongs to the realm of fantasy, while the terrorists are determined to force it into the concreteness of reality. The terrorists fight for a new human, the Anthropos, thus rationalizing the violence and unjust means they are using in this fight. The terrorists' mentality is related to the old fascist one, and the myths of Pandora and Prometheus illustrate the archetypal background of these problems. It is concluded that the myth of Sisyphus, as interpreted by A. Camus (1991) might indicate a solution of how to overcome regressive hope.

Wright & Wright (1982) reviewed relevant empirical studies and theoretical formulations to gain insight into violence- prone groups that have come to public attention over the years (e.g., the Weather Underground, the Black Liberation Army, and the Charles Manson group). Research findings show group members tend to score high on variables like "anger at family members" and "overcontrolled hostility," and are often in developmental transition at the time they join the groups, and gain relief from significant emotional distress through group membership. They describe leader characteristics, group norm-forming, and group control processes particular to these kinds of groups.

Terror and terrorism are extraordinarily difficult concepts to handle in normative terms (Cooper, 1976). Terror is certainly an element in the commission of many easily identifiable crimes of universal recognition and condemnation. Terrorism, however, is an entity quite distinct in character and purpose from the criminality which is its vehicle. It thrives on the postulate that there are more horrible human fates than death. Cooper (1976) offers an analysis of the various types of terrorism, their modus operandi, and their victims, and makes speculations on the use of terrorism in the future. Political terrorism is distinguished from state, criminal, and psychopathic terrorism and from that of urban guerillas. Its main aim is psychological: to spread fear and undermine morale for political blackmail. It can be argued that the free world must combine against terrorist attacks on innocent civilians, taking of hostages, hijacking of aircraft, and involvement of 3rd-party countries (Comay, 1976).

Hutchinson (1972) presents a definition and explanation of the concept of revolutionary terrorism, considered a part of insurgent strategy in internal war. She argues that such terrorism is a rational method of action, which employs acts of extraordinary violence against selected physical victims, deliberately creates a psychological effect, and thereby influences political behavior and attitudes. This definition is tested against the activity of the National Liberation Front during the Algerian War and used as a basis to explain the theoretical and empirical significance of terrorism. She compares the relative costs and benefits of a terrorist strategy from the revolutionary point of view. Hutchinson concluded that the attractiveness of terrorism derives from the combination of economy and facility of means with high psychological and political effectiveness. The risks of the strategy are controllable, and the results are predictable. Revolutionary terrorism combines low cost with potentially high yield.

Kent & Nicholls (1977) propose a dynamic and social explanation for the "malignant aggression" of the terrorist. No specific terrorist character is to be looked for. Rather, terrorism can occur whenever political conditions provide social legitimacy for acting out deeply repressed hatred. The origins of this hatred lie in parental abuse, leading to murderous rage in the child, which must be deflected onto safer targets than the terrifying parent (e.g., the parent's enemies, or the authorities of one's country). Kent & Nicholls argue that political terrorism involves the exploitation of mental illness, connived at in turn by the international public through the media. However, Giegerich (1979) maintains that terrorism cannot be adequately explained by the individual terrorist's life history. He argues that the open brutality exhibited by terrorists mirrors a subtle and covert brutality in public life. The anarchist misunderstands the idea of anarchy as a political idea and does not see its actual psychological meaning.

Fields (1979) proposes that persons exposed to terrorism in childhood often develop into adult terrorists. To explain why this does not occur in every country or period, she argues that when institutions and legal codes are an outgrowth of the indigenous culture, they provide support for the population in times of stress. When the legal system and institutions are imposed on the population by an alien group, they tend to actively alienate the young, as has happened in Northern Ireland. Based on experience administering standardized tests to hundreds of children in Northern Ireland since 1971, Fields believes that children exposed to terrorism have suffered a severe disruption in the development of moral judgment. She discusses the developmental process of changing from a victim to a terrorist within this context.

In another attempt to explain and understand terrorism, Wilkinson (1977) addressed three sets of problems:

   a) The relation of terrorism to the basic values and processes of liberal democracies.

   b) The underlying and precipitating causes of terrorist action and the internal and external defenses open to liberal governments against terrorism.

   c) The growth and implications of international terrorism.

Topics that may be of interest to psychologists include

   a) modes of conflict, opposition, and protest;

   b) a typology of political violence;

   c) causes of political violence in liberal states;

   d) the relation between terrorism and criminality;

   e) a typology of terror and terrorism;

   f) targets, technology, and tolerance of terrorism; and

   g) barricade and hostage situations.

How much existing psychological theories can explain and control the behavior of terrorists was explored by Hilke & Kaiser (1979). Classical aggression theories and traditional individual psychology have had little success. Better answers may be provided by a social theory of action in which acts of violence are interpreted as rational in the sense of being a means to an end. Important progress in the analysis of terrorism, its causes and background, is expected from interdisciplinary research (Hilke & Kaiser, 1979).

Female Terrorists

In an article about women as terrorists, Galvin (1983) contended that there is no archetypal female terrorist. She described women terrorists as being varied from their physique to their role within the organization to their physiological make-up. She suggests that women become involved in terrorism either by their own initiative or through a secondary other and are most often introduced into it by a male. Although women terrorists have the equality to fight or die by the side of their male counterparts, their position frequently is less than that of the male. The female's sexuality plays an important role in the group dynamics and alters the nature of terrorism itself. Galvin suggests that many terrorist women are "counter-phobic" and, in their manufactured role as terrorists, are attempting to ward off inner and often unconscious feelings of dependency and vulner-ability.

Counteracting Terrorism

Two conflicting views of terrorist motivation are discussed by Corrado (1981): One holds that terrorists are driven by mental disorders (MDs), while the other argues that they are driven by political idealism. Psychiatric concepts and propositions (e.g., sociopathy, narcissism, the death-wish) used by MD theorists are presented, and their data are assessed. Clinical observations supporting the rational-idealist (RI) perspective are discussed to distinguish social deviance from MDs. Corrado concludes that the MD perspective appears important in understanding certain ex-pressions of terrorist-like behavior and describes a minority of political terrorists. Political terrorism generally requires an environment of either long-standing historical problems or the potentially radicalizing experi-ence of the university. Frustrated idealism probably motivates individuals into a variety of acts, including terrorism. The validity of both the MD and the RI perspectives remains tentative given the inadequate data available for their assessment. Newcomer & Adkins (1980) suggest prevention and counteraction techniques against terrorist activities and analyze short profiles of 3 types of terrorists; the political, the criminal, and the men-tally deranged. They note that the 3rd type is likely to be especially erratic, but with proper negotiating techniques, the deranged terrorist of-ten suddenly surrenders, or in some cases commits suicide.

One form of related suicide that has been studied is self-incineration. Crosby, Rhee & Holland (1977) explored the history of self-incineration by examining all cases of suicide by fire reported in the London Times and New York Times between 1970 and 1972. 71% occurred during 1963-1972, with all cases of political self-incineration also occurring during this time. The sociocultural context in which this form of protest may occur and psychological factors in individuals who choose this method of sui-cide are discussed. It is suggested that the occurrence of self- incineration as a means of political protest may be yielding to more aggressive acts of terrorism as popular methods of forcing political change.

Shelby, Hoyle & Whitacre (1981) develop a speculative framework as to how learning under the computerized instructional system ILIA (M. Shelly et al, 1981) might take place. The framework assumes a network of associations that preserves its own "logic," particularly when the network is complex. Learning occurs through the changes that are required to preserve this logic when the material being taught is introduced through the ILIA system. It is also suggested that the ILIA system could be used by an agent in search of a particular terrorist.

Corsi (1981) presents a typology of terrorist events and characteristics. He examines the negotiations involved in hostage situations with emphasis on government/terrorist response options and event outcomes. Assumptions of the theoretical model are tested utilizing the ITERATE data set, which covers 539 events of international terrorism occurring between January 1970 and July 1974.

Media and Terrorism

Mosse(1977) discusses research on the mass media which indicated that TV mainly provides audiovisual conditioning to violence. Natural and spontaneous actions of children have been moved toward cynicism, callousness, and indifference. TV has the potential for aiding viewers to participate in the cultural and intellectual life of mankind. However, the magnetic pull of violence has led to increased terrorism in the schools, to race hatred, and to a blunted sense of the horror of violence. Fourteen suicides that were publicized in the newspaper triggered additional, imitative suicides (Mazur, 1982; Phillips, 1974). To further investigate the effect of the mass media on human behavior, Mazur (1982) examined data on the incidence of bomb threats against nuclear energy facilities over 11 yrs. Results confirm previous findings, in that threat incidence closely followed fluctuations in mass media coverage of nuclear power issues.

Francis (1983) presented information about the treatment of stories in the media about terrorism, bomb alerts, accidents, and other catastrophes as well as requests for the suppression of specific information. Aner (1983) discussed the results of research on the effects of violence in the media and the means of establishing a European strategy to reduce the portrayal of violence in the media. His recommendations addressed such areas as terrorism, the role of the media, violence in sports, and the role of education in promoting socially constructive behavior.

Weimann (1983) examined the effects of media exposure on changes in images of terrorists. He compared the evaluative attitudes of 80 Jewish undergraduates before and after they read press clippings describing two separate terrorist incidents. Findings suggested that exposure to press coverage of terrorist events tended to slightly enhance evaluations of the terrorists. Subjects with moderate objections to terrorism tended to change their evaluations after being exposed to the press clippings. Those with extreme objections tended to hold to the image that they had before reading them. Results confirmed the existence of a "status conferral" effect. Weimann concluded that press attention appeared to be sufficient to enhance the status of the people, problem, or cause behind a terrorist event.

Role of Psychology in Coping with Terrorism

Current terrorist operations pose a greater potential threat to liberal democracies than their historical forebears did. Many of the reasons for terrorist potential are grounded in physical technological innovation and its consequences. Long-term or crisis-oriented solutions are rooted in behavioral considerations. Current anti-terrorist measures tend to rely on physical technological solutions and are unable to provide useful answers to questions surrounding terrorism. It is vital to assess the contribution that can be made by psychology to the resolution of the problems posed by terrorism. Wardlaw (1983) outlined areas in which psychology has, or could have, a significant role in the investigation and control of terrorist activities. He discusses psychologists as hostage negotiators as well as other terrorism-related roles. He concludes that there should be more appreciation by law enforcement and security experts of the potential contributions of psychology. By the same token, he also suggests that there should be more appreciation by psychologists of the practical problems of security personnel.

Behavioral scientists work with law enforcement personnel on the problem of terrorism in 3 general contexts: clinical help for victims, training and consultation for hostage negotiation, and profiling and institutional consultation. In a study of 115 senior police officers working in the area of terrorism, subjects valued psychological counseling for crime victims within a broad framework of financial and criminal justice services (Eichelman & Hartwig, 1983; Lebowitz, 1983). When describing a past personal victim experience, they valued direct physical action in their own coping, but expressions of sympathy and reassurance when provided by others. Problems encountered by behavioral scientists working in this area have usually involved difficulties in maintaining an effective consultant role, over-identification with the law enforcement identity, or inappropriate media statements.

In reference to coping with terrorism, Schiopu (1983) discussed the effects on general mental health of the political and global tensions that threaten to lead to war. She suggested that during the early 1980s psychological studies had slowly shifted from themes specific to peacetime (e.g. aptitude, learning processes, motivation) to human personality themes involving psychopathology, psychodiagnosis, and psychotherapies. She contends that this shift was due to mutations in the life space and personality structure of contemporary humans. She comments that during this period the need for disarmament and the reduction of global tensions was emphasized so that nations could concentrate on problems associated with the technical and information revolutions that meant unemployment for thousands of workers as well as a shift in the educational needs of future workers.

Kats (1982) compared a 1975 survey of human concerns (779 subjects; 18 yrs old and older) with a 1962 survey (531 subjects; 20 yrs old and older). subjects also completed the Self-Anchoring Striving Scale. It was hypothesized that in the interval between surveys, concerns and their salience would have changed in response to major social changes that occurred during this period. Basic concerns were expected to remain stable. Shifts in concerns were found, both on the personal and the national level. There was a drop in the general mood. Issues directly concerning war and its consequences were mentioned more frequently in the later survey; and new, related issues became relevant (fear of terrorism, prolonged army reserve service, fear of destruction of the State). Economic issues, formerly concerned with productivity, now centered on inflation and standard of living. Basic concerns with health, children, and the family remained, overarched by the wish for peace and fear of war, the most important concerns of the 1970s.

Lahad and Abraham (1983) tested the effectiveness of a program of intervention which was aimed at preparing teachers and students to cope with ongoing acute stress caused by war and terrorist activity. Their results suggested that intervention led to a decrease in situational anxiety in experimental classes and an increase in the control classes. They found that, in the experimental classes, changes occurred in the internal organization of the "self" towards greater openness and readiness to admit anxiety and to cope with it in sublimated, resourceful ways.

Rofe & Lewin (1982) studied terrorist effects on Israeli high school students. In 1976, 486 high school students (14-17 year-olds) completed questionnaires on
(a) dreams and sleep disturbances,
(b) content of their dreams,
(c) waking and sleeping times, and
(d) a revised version of Byrne's Repression-Sensitization scale.

216 subjects lived in an Israeli border town with a history of terrorist activity and 270 lived in a town in central Israel that had never experienced terrorist activity. Factor analyses of responses to the 20 items on the dream-and-sleep-disturbance questionnaire during periods of calm yielded 4 main factors—Horror Dreams, Sexual Dreams, Positive Attitude toward Dreams, and Aggressive Dreams—accounting for 24.7, 9.8, 7.9, and 6% of the variance, respectively. A second factor analysis, conducted on responses during a period of war, showed 3 factors identical to the first, second, and fourth ones in the first analysis. Multiple regression ANOVAs indicate that continuous living in a war environment since early childhood may induce

a) development of a repressive personality type, which makes life more tolerable;

b) a reduction in horror, sexual, aggressive, and unpleasant dreams (as well as daydreams);

c) a reduction in the number of dreams; and

d) the adoption of repressive and denial mechanisms among all inhabitants, repressors and sensitizers alike.

In addition, findings suggest that border-town subjects, as well as repressors, were more adjusted individuals than the non-border-town subjects and sensitizers, respectively.

In another study on the effects of terrorism on Israeli communities, Zuckerman-Bareli (1982) studied the effect of bombing and terrorist attacks on the way of life in 6 settlements—3 kibbutzim (communal settlements) and 3 moshavim of olim (noncommunal settlements founded by non-Western immigrants after 1949 and based on cooperative supply and marketing)—near the Lebanese border. Cultural, social, and personal factors that affect resistance to stress and the ability to carry on with the regular way of life were assessed among 100 residents of each type of settlement. Path analyses show that 4 variables directly affected emotional disturbance (in descending order of importance): anxiousness, sex, country of origin, and economic satisfaction. When combined, these variables predicted 38% of the variance in emotional and social disturbances. A Western, compared with an Eastern, background directly raised the level of education, satisfaction, and identification with community and lowered anxiousness; a similar pattern was found for the kibbutz compared to the moshav residence. A path model of the exogenous factors of kibbutz vs moshav, country of origin, and intensity of border incidents is presented.

Zafrir (1982) describes the psychological consequences of a 1978 terrorist attack on 2 public buses and private cars traveling on the main highway to Tel Aviv. He outlines psychological characteristics of this extremely stressful situation: lack of warning, the surprise factor, ambiguity, absence of leadership, confrontation with insoluble dilemmas, and shattered hopes of rescue. The range of reactions of the people involved are described, and the measures taken by the cooperative that operated the buses to support the victims of the attack are discussed as well as the various roles of the psychologist in the support system.

Ben-Eli & Sela (1980) engaged 60 children in therapy who, as a result of the 1979 terrorist attack on Nahariya, Israel, evidenced the following symptoms: fear of noise, the dark, and the seashore; lack of concentration; and difficulty sleeping. subjects were divided into small groups (6-8 members) that met close to the time of original crisis. Strong emphasis was placed on catharsis and cognitive reconstruction of the traumatic events. Feelings of anger, terror, and blame were allowed to be vented freely. Results of this active coping with the stress situation and application of relaxation and desensitization techniques indicate that most subjects' school and home functioning improved.

Children's Responses to Terrorism

Introduction

School shootings. Devastating earthquakes. Severe floods. Deadly motor vehicle crashes. Terrorist attacks. Many communities and individuals endure these and other extraordinary experiences so horrifying in their effects that we call them disasters. Over the past two decades, the world has witnessed an increasing number of disasters involving massive exposure of the population to radiation, chemical toxins, or other hazardous agents. Terrorist acts such as that on September 11, 2001 create apprehension about possible further attacks, perhaps with biological or chemical weapons. The term "ecological disaster" is used to indicate these incidents, which are often followed by widespread fear of future adverse health effects (Havenaar et al, 2002). Concerns or worries about health tend to facilitate the appearance of medically unexplained symptoms or syndromes. This mental health component has received relatively little attention in the disaster literature. The events of September 11, 2001 highlighted the realities of terrorism for most Americans and underscored the importance of understanding how children and adolescents react to disasters and terrorism.

The tragedies of September 2001 and subsequent events are still too recent to have yielded an empirical perspective on their impact on children, adolescents, and families. LaGreca et al (2002) reviewed the current state of knowledge regarding children's reactions to disaster and terrorism, and provide the background and conceptualization needed for framing mental health interventions and future research efforts. They provide a systematic review of children's and adolescents' reactions to specific disasters and the factors that contribute to those reactions. They also reviewed the current state of interventions that have been developed to address children's and adolescents' mental health needs following disasters.

Background

The recent wave of terrorism affecting the United States and other countries raises concerns about the welfare of children and adolescents. Prior studies suggest that level of exposure, evidence of psychopathology before trauma exposure, and disruption in social support networks consistently emerge as strong predictors of psychopathology following trauma exposure (Pine and Cohen, 2002). Clinicians may wish to monitor children exposed to trauma most closely when they present with these risk factors. When combined with other data from open studies and controlled trials in non-traumatized children, studies suggest that Cognitive Behavioral Therapy (CBT) is an option for children developing anxiety symptoms following terrorism events (Pine and Cohen, 2002).

There are a number of relevant studies with children following recent terrorist events both within and outside the United States. Nineteen infants and children were killed in the 1995 terrorist bombing in Oklahoma City, and many were injured. More than 200 children lost one or both parents. These casualties focused attention on children in the disaster response efforts. Pfefferbaum, Call and Sconzo(1999) describe the development and implementation of a school-based mental health program that provided accessible services to children affected by the bombing, with an emphasis on normalization. A clinical needs assessment of all children in the Oklahoma City public school system was carried out, and clinicians provided emergency and crisis services, counseling, and support groups.

Several thousand children were suddenly bereaved by the terrorist attacks on the United States on September 11, 2001. The New York Times estimated that possibly 15,000 children lost a father or a mother who, in many cases, was a single parent. The exact number of missing and dead changed daily after the disaster, as body parts were retrieved in the rubble and identified through DNA testing. This was a very slow process, however, and three months following September 11 there were still 3,045 persons reported dead or missing at the New York World Trade Center and 495 death certificates issued by the medical examiner's office. An additional 1,976 death certificates were issued at the request of families. At the Pentagon, 189 were dead or missing three months after September 11. In addition there were 246 passengers and crew who perished on the four hijacked planes and 19 hijackers. Several hundred police, firefighters, and other rescue personnel were also among the victims (Webb, 2002).

Brown (2002) discusses mental health trauma responses to the events of September 11th. He maintains that like most trauma responses, reactions to the events of September 11th occurred in three phases: crisis intervention, short-term reactions, and long-term planning. He reflects on observations as a New York City (NYC) mental health professional, Director of Trauma Services and Program Evaluation for the New York University Child Study Center's Child and Family Recovery Program, and as an NYC resident. He concludes that mental health professionals have not yet begun to understand the mental health impact of September 11th on children in NYC and around the country. He suggests that as needs are identified, strategies for service delivery must continue to change.

Studies of health care use after the September 11 terrorist attacks complement prior research on the subject. Hoge, Pavlin and Milliken (2002) used the Electronic Surveillance System for the Early Notification of Community-based Epidemics (ESSENCE) database to conduct behavioral health surveillance among military health system beneficiaries in the Washington, D.C., area following the September 11 attack on the Pentagon. Diagnostic groups for depression, anxiety, acute and posttraumatic stress disorders, substance-use disorders, and other behavioral health problems were defined according to the ICD-9. Although there was no significant increase in the total number of visits to behavioral health clinics, there were significant increases in the number of visits for anxiety disorder and acute stress reactions in children and for adjustment reactions in adults.

The goals of short-term intervention in the setting of a crisis event are to help children understand and accept the events that have occurred; to identify, express, and comprehend their emotions; to begin to regain a sense of control and mastery over their life; and to resume developmentally appropriate activities. Schonfeld (2002) discusses what the developmental-behavioral pediatrics field has learned since September 11, 2001 about the management of posttraumatic symptoms and reactions of children in the setting of terrorism. He notes that parents and other adults who support children, such as teachers, often underestimate the extent of children's' reactions to a crisis situation, especially those related to internalizing symptoms.

Research

Child-focused disaster research is a relatively new area of study. It has grown substantially in recent years and will continue to develop in the aftermath of the September 11th terrorist attacks. The first generation of studies has focused predominantly on documenting children's and adolescents' reactions to disasters and identifying factors that correlate with or predict severe disaster reactions. Studies have begun to examine interventions for children following disasters. However, this line of research is still in a preliminary stage (LaGreca et al, 2002). The field has yet to develop empirically supported interventions for children and youth following disasters. A broadened research agenda is needed to advance our understanding of how children are affected by disasters, which youth are most at risk, and when and how to intervene. Key issues include the need for researchers and clinicians in the child mental health field to help advance knowledge of the effects of disasters on children and youth and the need to develop and evaluate empirically based treatments for child disaster victims. Researchers and clinicians need to become advocates for children's needs following disasters and to become attentive to public policy.

Fields (1979) proposed that persons exposed to terrorism in childhood often develop into adult terrorists. To explain why this does not occur in every country or period, it is argued that when institutions and legal codes are an outgrowth of the indigenous culture, they provide support for the population in times of stress. When the legal system and institutions are imposed on the population by an alien group, they tend to actively alienate the young, as has happened in Northern Ireland. Based on experience administering standardized tests to hundreds of children in Northern Ireland since 1971, Fields believes that children exposed to terrorism have suffered a severe disruption in the development of moral judgment. The developmental process of changing from a victim to a terrorist is discussed in this context.

Ben-Eli and Sela (1980) engaged 60 children in therapy who, as a result of the 1979 terrorist attack on Nahariya, Israel, evidenced the following symptoms: fear of noise, the dark, and the seashore; lack of concentration; and difficulty sleeping. subjects were divided into small groups (6-8 members) that met close to the time of original crisis. Strong emphasis was placed on catharsis and cognitive reconstruction of the traumatic events. Feelings of anger, terror, and blame were allowed to be vented freely. Results of this active coping with the stress situation and application of relaxation and desensitization techniques indicate that most subjects' school and home functioning improved.

Dreman and Cohen (1982) suggest that much of the trauma precipitated by terrorist activities is a result of their suddenness, their salience in the public consciousness, and the consequent stigma they produce toward survivors and/or relatives of victims. A number of specific issues were common in the 2 case studies presented and in other families affected by terrorism. These included dealing with the need to be a "superparent" and correcting unrealistic expectations; teaching effective limit setting, including giving permission to be a parent and an adult; and dealing with guilt and phobic reactions, and family and network reorganization. Therapy concentrated on promoting family strengths and coping, and it deemphasized individual pathology. Common to most families treated was the strong desire of the victim's children to be treated as normal and not as psychological casualties. Family therapy proved to be an ideal treatment modality for dealing with the tragic loss. By focusing on the problems of day-to-day living, the mourning work evolved naturally in the course of therapy. Specific therapy modalities, such as co-therapy and network intervention, facilitated family adjustment.

Lahad and Abraham (1983) tested the effectiveness of a program of intervention aimed at preparing teachers and pupils to cope with the continual acute stress caused by war and terrorist activity. 86 experimental and 82 control 3rd, 5th, 6th, and 7th graders in parallel classes; 8 teachers; and 3 school staff members were studied. Experimental subjects completed a situation anxiety scale, a variation of the Q-Sorts method, guided observations, and a personal questionnaire. Teachers completed a personal questionnaire, and observation data were also obtained on them. Before and after the program there was a simulated alarm, after which the children stayed in the shelter for two hours. In the shelter, the children's behavior was observed. After leaving the shelter, the various questionnaires were administered. Observations were also made of the same children under an authentic alarm situation. The teachers' preparatory program spanned 2 trimesters of the school year. The classroom interventions were conducted by the teacher and program leader in 9 weekly two-hour meetings. Results indicate that the intervention program led to a decrease in situational anxiety in the experimental classes, whereas in the control classes the situational anxiety increased. In the experimental classes, changes occurred in the internal organization of the "self" toward greater openness and readiness to admit anxiety and to cope with it in sublimated, resourceful ways.

Rigamer (1986) described a 6-month intervention program conducted for teachers, parents, and 122 children (kindergarten-12th grade) in an American diplomatic community following the assassination of the American ambassador in Kabul. Adults' initial response to the effect of the trauma on the children was denial, a dynamic that had to be addressed before suggestions could be utilized. Most of the children mastered the psychological effects of the trauma through repetitive narrations, drawings, and play, activities that seemed necessary to restore emotional equilibrium. A small number of children appeared to adapt by shutting out all stimuli emanating from the event.

Kollwitz et al (2002) evaluated children's symptoms three and nine months after the 1993 bombing of the World Trade Center, and the relationship between parent and child reactions when only the children had been in the building. Nine children who had been trapped in an elevator, 13 who had been on the observation deck, and 27 controls completed the Posttraumatic Stress Reaction Index and a Fear Inventory. Parents completed these measures about the children and comparable measures about themselves. Exposed children reported posttraumatic stress disorder (PTSD) symptoms and disaster- related fears; their parents reported experiencing PTSD symptoms. Only parents rated children's symptoms as decreasing significantly over time. Association between child symptoms and parent symptoms increased over time. Children's initial distress predicted parents' distress nine months post-disaster.

Gurwitch et al (2002) describe how the bombing of the Murrah Building in Oklahoma City led to some of the first investigations of the effects of terrorism on U.S. children. They examined the prevalence of posttraumatic stress disorder (PTSD) symptoms among children and adolescents following the bombing and point out how subsequent events related to the bombing (namely, the constant media attention to the bombing and the later criminal proceedings) took their toll on the victims and families who lost loved ones. Their findings highlight that the crisis- intervention model of handling disasters is insufficient. They call for ongoing involvement by mental health professionals who have expertise in working with traumatized individuals and communities. Given that most children received no systematic help from a mental health professional to deal with their reactions soon after the bombing, it is reasonable to assume that most children also received little or no attention to deal with the events that occurred subsequent to the bombing (e.g., the trial and the execution). Gurwitch et al (2002) suggest that the crisis-intervention model is too narrow and too brief, and it fails to recognize the various psychological experiences that victims likely go through as different phases of the event unfold.

In a previous study, Pfefferbaum et al (2000) describe Posttraumatic Stress Disorder (PTSD) symptomatology in 69 sixth-grade youths who resided within 100 miles of Oklahoma City at the time of the 1995 bombing of the Alfred P. Murrah Federal Building. These youths neither had any direct physical exposure nor personally knew anyone killed or injured in the explosion. A survey conducted 2 yrs after the bombing assessed exposure, PTSD symptoms, and functioning. PTSD symptom frequency was measured with the Impact of Event Scale-Revised. Criteria for defining PTSD case was modeled after Mental Disorders-IV (DSM-IV) B, C, and D (BCD) criteria requiring 1 re-experiencing, 3 avoidance/numbing, and 2 arousal symptoms for diagnosis. Those who met BCD criteria had significantly higher PTSD symptom scores than those who did not. Both increased mean PTSD symptom score and meeting the authors' case definition were associated with increased functioning difficulties. Media exposure and indirect interpersonal exposure (having a friend who knew someone killed or injured) were significant predictors of symptomatology. Findings suggest that children geographically distant from disaster who have not directly experienced an interpersonal loss report PTSD symptoms and functional impairment associated with increased media exposure and indirect loss.

Schlenger et al (2002) assessed psychological symptom levels in the United States following the events of September 11 and examined the association between post-attack symptoms and indices of exposure to the events. One and two months after the attacks, 2,273 adults, including over samples of the New York, NY, and Washington, DC, metropolitan areas, responded to a Web-based survey that included the Posttraumatic Stress Disorder (PTSD) Checklist and the Brief Symptom Inventory. Outcome measures included self-reports of the symptoms of PTSD and of nonspecific psychological distress, as well as adult reports of symptoms of distress among children living in their households. The prevalence of probable PTSD was significantly higher in the New York City area than in Washington, DC and the rest of the country. Overall distress levels across the country, however, were within expected ranges. Sex, age, direct exposure to the attacks, and the amount of time spent viewing TV coverage of the attacks on September 11 and the few days afterward were associated with PTSD symptom levels. Sex, the number of hours of TV coverage viewed, and the content of that coverage were associated with the broader distress measure. Over 60% of adults in New York City households with children reported that one or more children were upset by the attacks.

Stuber et al (2002) assessed the prevalence and correlates of counseling received by 4-17 yr olds living in Manhattan for experiences related to the September 11, 2001 terrorist attacks. 112 parents or primary caretakers were interviewed about their child's level of exposure to the disaster, the extent of loss, receipt of counseling services, and behavioral reaction. Results show that 22% of the children had received some form of counseling related to their experiences after the disaster. 58% of the counseling received was delivered in schools. Predictors of counseling in a multivariate model were male sex, having a parent with current post-traumatic stress disorder (PTSD) related to the attacks, and having at least one sibling living in the household. Stuber et al concluded that parents' own level of posttraumatic stress was associated with whether their children received counseling related to the attacks.

Dreman and Cohen (1990) reported a 10-yr follow-up of early intervention with four children exposed at ages 6-11 yrs to the killing of one or both of their parents by terrorists. subjects were aged 20-22 yrs at follow-up, permitting examination of the effects of trauma and early intervention on long- term adjustment. Interviews suggested that psychic remnants of trauma may negatively affect adjustment throughout children's lives. Long term adjustment of three of the subjects had the following characteristics: fear of loss of control, pessimism, re-enactment behavior, situational triggered anxiety, stigma, shame, guilt, denial, impulse control problems, antisocial behavior, and interpersonal relationship problems.

In a previous study, Dreman (1989) conducted a 10-yr follow-up of Israeli children whose parents were killed in terrorist activities to determine posttraumatic adjustment. Therapy at the time of the trauma concentrated on promoting family strengths and coping. subjects, however, demonstrated considerable psychopathology. Two cases presented, together with previous findings, suggest that early abreactive intrapsychic intervention may help prevent long-term pathology, but interpersonal intervention may also be necessary to prevent manipulative antisocial behavior. In the Israeli context, adjustment is likely to be strongly influenced by recurring events such as military reserve duty, war, or terrorist activities that re-trigger or exacerbate existing posttraumatic symptomatology.

Vicarious Stress

Mosse (1977) discusses F. Wertham's work on the mass media, which indicated that TV mainly provides audiovisual conditioning to violence.

Natural and spontaneous actions of children have been moved toward cynicism, callousness, and indifference. TV has the potential for aiding viewers to participate in the cultural and intellectual life of mankind. However, the magnetic pull of violence has led to increased terrorism in the schools, to race hatred, and to a blunted sense of the horror of violence.

Pfefferbaum et al (2001) examined the influence of bomb-related television viewing in the context of physical and emotional exposure on posttraumatic stress symptoms—intrusion, avoidance, and arousal—in middle school students following the 1995 Oklahoma City bombing. Over 2,000 middle school students in Oklahoma City were surveyed seven weeks after the incident. The primary outcome measures were the total posttraumatic stress symptom score and symptom cluster scores at the time of assessment. Bomb- related television viewing in the aftermath of the disaster was extensive. Both emotional and television exposure were associated with posttraumatic stress at seven weeks. Among children with no physical or emotional exposure, the degree of television exposure was directly related to posttraumatic stress symptomatology.

In a related study, Pfefferbaum (2001) examined the influence of exposure on posttraumatic stress disorder (PTSD) symptomatology in children following the 1995 Oklahoma City bombing. Over 2,000 middle school students were surveyed seven weeks after the bombing. Initial reaction and emotional exposure were important predictors of PTSD symptomatology in the full sample. Children/adolescents who reported no physical or emotional exposure had significantly lower scores than exposed children on television viewing, initial reaction, and PTSD symptomatology. Within the unexposed group, those with high television exposure had significantly more PTSD symptoms.

Both studies suggest that children and adolescents with strong initial reactions should be followed over time, and disaster-related television viewing should be carefully monitored. The findings also suggest that television viewing in the aftermath of a disaster may make a small contribution to subsequent posttraumatic stress symptomatology in children or that increased television viewing may be a sign of current distress and that it should be monitored. Future research should examine further whether early symptoms predict increased television viewing and/or whether television viewing predicts subsequent symptoms.

Schuster et al (2001) assessed the immediate mental health effects of the terrorist attacks on September 11, 2001. Using random-digit dialing 3-5 days after September 11, they interviewed a nationally representative sample of 560 US adults about their reactions to the terrorist attacks and their perceptions of the reactions of their children (aged 5-18 yrs). Forty-four percent of the adults reported one or more substantial symptoms of stress. Ninety percent had one or more symptoms to at least some degree. Respondents throughout the country reported stress symptoms. They coped by talking with others (98%), turning to religion (90%), participating in group activities (60%), and making donations (36%). Eighty-four percent of parents reported that they or other adults in the household had talked to their children about the attacks for an hour or more. Thirty-four percent restricted their children's TV viewing. Thirty-five percent of children had one or more stress symptoms. Forty-seven percent were worried about their own safety or the safety of loved ones. They concluded that after the September 11 terrorist attacks, Americans across the country, including children, had substantial symptoms of stress. They suggest that even clinicians who practice in regions that are far from the recent attacks should be prepared to assist people with trauma-related symptoms of stress.

The events of September 11, 2001 have affected us in different ways. PTSD symptoms have been reported in children who have watched TV coverage related to Halloween, war, industrial disaster, and terrorist bombing. Duggal, Berezkin and John (2002) report the case of an 11-yr-old boy who developed posttraumatic stress disorder (PTSD) along with major depression after watching the terrorist attacks on the World Trade Center on TV. The patient was in the 7th grade in a boarding school. Overwhelmed by the events, he impulsively decided to commit suicide, but was prevented from doing so. This case demonstrates that a child who is exposed to traumatic events on TV can develop PTSD symptoms and has implications for media personnel, teachers, parents, and clinicians.

Previously, Vila et al (2000) presented a clinical case of posttraumatic stress disorder (PTSD) by indirect exposure to the trauma and data from follow-up in a department of child psychiatry of 10 of 29 children who were taken hostage and their parents. These children (directly exposed to the aggression) and their parents (indirectly exposed since they were not taken hostage but had a great empathy) were examined to assess mental disorders using Mental Disorders-IV (DSM-IV) diagnostic criteria. Children were assessed also with self-administered questionnaires for anxiety and traumatic stress. Nine pupils presented a PTSD, incomplete or full syndrome. In five families (50%), the parents had post-traumatic disorders: seven fathers or mothers. One mother had an acute stress disorder. Another had an adaptation disorder with anti-depressive symptoms and symptoms of PTSD. In conclusion, their results demonstrate the reality of PTSD by indirect exposure. From a nosological viewpoint, they raise the question of the limits of the concept of traumatic stress. From a practical point of view, when a child has been directly victim of an aggression, it seems important to also examine his parents and siblings, who are indirectly exposed and may induce or maintain post-traumatic disorders of the child, particularly when other risk factors are present.

Pfefferbaum et al (2000) examined effects of traumatic loss on children who reported a friend or acquaintance killed in the 1995 Oklahoma City bombing of a federal office building. Twenty-seven 3rd-5th grade children who lost a friend or acquaintance and 27 demographically matched controls were assessed 8-10 months after the bombing. All but three of the children continued to experience posttraumatic stress symptoms. Those who lost a friend watched significantly more bombing-related television coverage than those without losses. Those who lost a friend had significantly more posttraumatic stress symptoms at the time of the assessment than those who lost an acquaintance. She concluded that parents and those working with children should be alert to the impact of loss even when it involves non-relatives.

Following the terrorist bombing in Oklahoma City in 1995, a bombing exposure screening questionnaire was developed for children and adolescents who lived in Oklahoma City at that time (Peak, 2000). It was administered throughout the school system and was completed by approximately 3,000 students in grades six through twelve. The purpose of this study was to determine the severity of PTSD symptoms reported by children and adolescents at seven weeks after the bombing. Relationships between gender, severity of vicarious exposure, and PTSD severity were also examined. This study controlled for effects of direct personal exposure by including only those participants who did not hear or feel the blast (N = 817). Results showed that females reported significantly higher posttraumatic stress severity scores than males. Additionally, those children and adolescents who knew someone who was injured or killed by the blast (vicarious exposure) reported higher posttraumatic stress severity than those who did not. However, no significant interaction of gender by vicarious exposure for PTSD severity was found. The results of this study suggest that further research is needed to define how best to assist children and adolescents in processing their reactions following a traumatic event of this extent.

Cultural Factors

Violence stemming from ethnic and political tensions is a problem of increasing proportions throughout the world, and many indicators show that large numbers of children are directly or indirectly exposed to war, political repression, torture, and terrorism. There is growing evidence to suggest that children are at risk under these conditions, and that the consequences of growing up amid danger, chaos, and deprivation can be severe (Ladd, 1996).

Since the establishment of the State of Israel in 1948, the civilian population has endured many terrorist attacks. This reality, together with an expanded network of mental and social services, has led to the development of extensive interventions directed toward helping those people who experienced these terrorist attacks. Over a period of many years, Shalif and Leibler (2002) have worked extensively with children and adults in Jewish communities in Judea and Samaria who have been subjected to terrorist attacks. They describe how narrative therapy ideas and practices aid their work. They also present a deconstructive analysis of existing discourses on trauma and crisis, demonstrating the use of narrative ideas and practices, and present a number of vignettes of people dealing with the hardships related to ongoing peril and terror.

Melville and Lykes (1992) describe the emotional, social, and cultural effects of government-sponsored terrorism on 32 Mayan children in Guatemala and 36 Guatemalan children who were exiled in Mexico (aged 8-16 yrs). The two groups were compared with respect to the negative effects of civil war and the adaptive capabilities of children who had experienced the trauma of loss of immediate family members, the witnessing of violent crimes, and displacement from their homes. Open-ended interviews, observations, taped personal stories, and traditional psychological instruments were used to examine the subjects' well-being. subjects experiencing the most fear were in Guatemalan villages. subjects in Mexican refugee camps were less fearful.

Miller (1996) Examined the mental health and psychosocial development of 58 Guatemalan Mayan Indian children (aged 7-16 yrs) living in two refugee camps in Chiapas, Mexico. Assessment instruments and semi-structured interviews were utilized to gather phenomenological data from subjects regarding developmental, sociocultural, and political topics. Results show minimal evidence of psychological trauma in this sample. Various factors are suggested to account for this finding. A positive relationship between subjects' mental health and the physical and mental health status of their mothers was found. A strong association between depressive symptomatology in girls and poor health status in their mothers was also found. Qualitative data from the interviews are presented, focusing on subjects' understanding of why their families fled Guatemala, the nature and causes of the violence, and their thoughts and feelings regarding the prospect of returning to Guatemala in the future.

Sack et al (1986) studied 40 Cambodian students (average age 17 yrs) who survived four yrs under the Pol Pot regime and six age-matched controls who escaped prior to Pol Pot, using home interviews and school teacher ratings. In their findings, subjects reported more distress with school grades, peers, and themselves than was observed by their caretakers. Many family members exhibited similar posttraumatic stress and depressive symptoms. In school, subjects receiving a psychiatric diagnosis were more likely to be rated by their teachers as withdrawn than as disruptive. A case vignette of a 16-yr-old girl is presented. Results emphasize the crucial role of the school and responsibilities and opportunities for ESL teachers in helping refugee students to make a major and difficult transition.

Kinzie et al (1986) described the psychiatric effects on 40 Cambodian students (average age 17 yrs) in the US who suffered massive trauma from 1975 to 1979 compared with 6 age-matched refugees who escaped the Pol Pot regime. subjects endured separation from family, forced labor, and starvation, and witnessed many deaths. After 2 yrs of living in refugee camps, they immigrated at about age 14 yrs. Four years after leaving Cambodia, 20 subjects developed posttraumatic stress disorder; mild, but prolonged depressive symptoms were common. Psychiatric effects were more common and more severe when subjects did not reside with a family member.

Militant Islam and Terrorism

Western foreign policy makers have not fared well with Islamic fundamentalist groups. Why? Kreidie (2001) argues that Islamic fundamentalists pose such difficulties for Western governments not because the Islamic fundamentalists are terrorists prone to violence, for they are not simply that, but rather because the Islamic world view represents a different cognitive worldview, or 'Weltenschang'. This worldview differs in critical ways from the post-Enlightenment rationalist worldview prevalent in Western democracies. Kreidie attempts to explain the Islamic worldview through a narrative analysis of in-depth interviews with Islamic Fundamentalists conducted between July 1995 and August 1999. Kreidie's central argument is that Islamic fundamentalists differ from other social and political groups prevalent in the Middle East and Asia in their cognitive world views and their resultant attitudes toward the political process. Kreidie suggests treating Islamic fundamentalism as a form of ethical-political behavior that can best be explained through a social psychological approach. In a previous study, Monroe and Kreidie (1997) provided an empirical analysis of how fundamentalists see the world. They illustrated the importance of cognitive differences in worldviews held by fundamentalists. They used a narrative and survey interview technique to contrast the worldviews of 9 fundamentalists (aged 19-50 yrs) in the US or Lebanon with those of 5 comparable Muslims who were not fundamentalists. Their data suggest that Islamic fundamentalism attracts because it provides a basic identity, an identity which in turn provides the foundation for daily living. They suggest that the fundamentalist perspective itself is best understood through reference to a worldview which makes no distinction between public and private, in which truth is revealed by revelation, and reason is subservient to religious doctrine. Religious dictates dominate on all basic issues, and only within the confines of the fundamentalist identity are choices decided by a cost/benefit calculus (Kreidie, 2001).

Some Cultural Sketches

As elsewhere in the Middle East, the Yemeni family is described as patrilineal, virilocal, and extended. This generalization is often inaccurate, but in the central highlands of the (former) Yemen Arab Republic, this family type represents both the cultural ideal and the social norm. Drawing on data from 10 rural communities, Stevenson (1997) examined the convergence of family form and household composition. Recognizing that internal dynamics are probably central to household unity or division, he discusses five activities, including, co-residence, production, transmission of property, reproduction, and distribution of resources. The extended family household as the cultural ideal and the decline in migration of the Yemen family are also discussed. Stevenson suggested that the confluence of cultural values, Islamic fundamentalism, and economic factors account for the high prevalence of extended or multiple family households.

Harik (1996) tested whether a hypothesis explaining popular support for Middle Eastern fundamentalist movements adequately describes the grassroots appeal of Hezbollah, Lebanon's radical Shiite organization. 1993 survey data from 405 respondents showed that Hezbollah adherents were less likely than expected to be deeply religious, to have a low SES, and to have a strong political alienation. She suggests that constraints imposed on Islamic goals by Lebanon's pluralist society and its powerful neighbor Syria have influenced the moderate trend of Hezbollah. Harik concludes that Islamist success in carving a niche in a community still seeking self-identity and adequate national representation means that Islamists are unlikely to lose external backers' support should Middle East peace negotiations reduce Hezbollah's resistance role.

Psychology of World Views

Bohleber (2002) examined the convictions and motives acted upon by the perpetrators of the September 11 attacks. He identified the ideological/religious factor as a crucial component because it appears to be the operative force behind the combination of narcissistic ideal condition and terrorist mass murder. He made general observations on the connection between religion, purity, and violence and enlarged upon the religious world view and mentality of Islamic fundamentalism (T. Reik, 1924; Grunberger, 1988). Bohleber found surprising similarities with ethnocentric German nationalism and radical nationalism after WWI. Some common traits include the same ubiquitous unconscious fantasies, such as care fantasies and sibling rivalry, purity and the idea of the other, visions of unity and fantasies of fusion. He offers some psychoanalytical thoughts on biographical material pertaining to two members of the circle close to the Al Qaeda terrorists.

Euben (1995) argues that the rational actor theory (RAT) and Islamic fundamentalism hold competing, inimical assumptions about human behavior. She contends that such differences suggest that the RAT reaches its limits when applied to fundamentalism and that such limitations must be seen as an expression of a deeper clash of worldviews—a clash between a world defined by divine sovereignty, and a world defined by human knowledge and power. The RAT cannot but misinterpret Islamic fundamentalism because RAT assumptions and the rationalist worldview of which they are an expression exclude fundamentalists' own conceptions of human nature and action. Euben suggests that the failure by American policy-makers to understand such essential differences accounts for misguided American policies in the Middle East.

The attainment of global shared values and norms is difficult because peoples of the world still embrace ideas of separateness reinforced by their normative systems. Michael and Anderson (1989) discuss six competing world views in the postmodern world they suggest are inadequate as normative frameworks for a global society. These are Western-style progress, Christian and Islamic fundamentalism, Marxist ideology, Green politics (identified with environmental values), and the new paradigm of superprogress. They note that conflict and stress will accompany the emergence of a global information system and that humanistic psychology may contribute to the understanding of this historical moment and the human need to find and create social meaning.

Growing Fundamentalism

One-fifth of the world's population currently follows the teachings of Islam. The believers are not just within the Middle East. China has three times as many Muslims as Saudi Arabia. Altogether, thirty-two countries have Muslim majorities of 85 percent or higher. Of the total Muslim population, about 10 percent is Shia, which have constituted the most deadly religious terrorist groups in the past (Wright, 1986). The Shia represent about 95 percent of Iran's population, 60 percent of Iraq's population, and a large share in Lebanon, Bahrain, and Qatar (Musacchio and Rozen, 1988). Additionally, near the border of Paraguay, Brazil, and Argentina there is a community of about 100,000 Shiites that has already been infiltrated by terrorists (Weiner, 1995). It has been speculated that the bombers of the Jewish Center in Rio de Janeiro came from this region of South America. Of Shiite religious leaders in recent history, Iran's Ayatollah Khomeini made some of the most provocative statements, encouraging militancy among his followers. In 1979 he declared,

> "Islam is the religion of militant individuals who are committed to truth and justice. It is the religion of those who desire freedom and independence. It is the school of those who struggle against imperialism.... Weapons in our hands are used to realize divine and Islamic aspirations." (Wright, 1986; Tehran Radio, 1989).

Islam is the fastest growing religion in the United States today. Additionally, most major Middle East terrorist organizations have a presence in the United States. Three of the more active and well-known groups are Abu Nidal, Hezbollah, and Hamas. Hezbollah, primarily a Shiite group, is considered by Washington to be today's most aggressive and lethal terrorist organization. The Federal Bureau of Investigation (FBI) has also intensified investigations of pro-Hamas organizations in the United States in recent years. Hamas, as a leading opponent of the Middle East peace talks, has been very active with terrorist strikes in the Israeli occupied territories. One Palestinian arrested by Israeli security forces claimed that he received bomb training during a pro-Hamas conference in Kansas City (Chesnoff, 1993; Jenkins, 1993). On 26 October 1995 Fathi Shiqaqi, leader of the militant Islamic Jihad movement, was traveling on a Libyan passport under the alias of Ibrahim Ali Shawash, a businessman, when he was shot in broad daylight in Malta by two men riding a motorcycle. He was shot five times in the head with a silenced gun. The assailants later abandoned their vehicle, which had false license plates. In another case, Yahya Ayyash, a Hamas member said by Israel to be the brains behind a wave of suicide bomb attacks against Israel, and also known as the "Engineer," was killed on 5 January 1996, apparently by a booby-trapped cellular telephone in PLO-ruled Gaza (Reuters News Media, 6 January 1996, Gaza)(LaGuardia and Gozani, 1995).

The defeat of Iraq in Desert Storm seems to have contributed to a regional ideological shift toward pan-Islamic fundamentalism. After the demise of Saddam Hussein's secular pan-Arab ideology, Islamic fundamentalism has filled the void and offered a theological explanation for Iraq's defeat. The conflict also called into question Iraq's methods of warfare against the high-technology weapons of the West (Anderson, 1992).

Martyrdom has been and will continue to be one of the signatures of the Islamic terrorists. According to David Rapoport,

> "A martyr has six privileges with God: he is forgiven his sins, he is shown a place in paradise, he is redeemed from the torments of the grave, he is made secure from the fear of hell, and a crown of glory is placed on his head of which one ruby is worth more than the world and all that is in it, he will marry 72 of the huris with black eyes, and his intercession will be accepted for 70 of his kinsmen." (Rapoport, 1990).

Hamza akl Hamieh, one of the most fearless fighters for Islam and a military commander for Amal, made the following statement shortly after the bombing of the U.S. Marine barracks in Beirut in 1983:

> "None of us are afraid. God is with us and gives us strength. We are making a race like horses to see who goes to God first. I want to die before my friends. They want to die before me. We want to see our God. We welcome the bombs of Reagan." (Wright, 1986).

The probability is good that the intensity of the religious terrorism threat will increase as the disparity grows between the wealthy secular nations and the destitute Islamic nations (Finnegan and Holzer, 1996; Hedges, 1995).

Summary and Conclusions

Much of the trauma precipitated by terrorist activities is a result of their suddenness, their salience in the public consciousness, and the consequent stigma they produce toward survivors and/or relatives of victims. A number of specific issues were common in two case studies presented by Dreman & Cohen (1982) and in other families affected by terrorism. These included dealing with the need to be a "superparent" and correcting unrealistic expectations; teaching effective limit setting, including giving permission to be a parent and an adult; and dealing with guilt and phobic reactions, and family and network reorganization. Therapy concentrated on promoting family strengths and coping, and it deemphasized individual pathology. Common to most families treated was the strong desire of the victim's children to be treated as normal and not as psychological casualties. Family therapy proved to be an ideal treatment modality for dealing with the tragic loss. By focusing on the problems of day-to-day living, the mourning work evolved naturally in the course of therapy. Specific therapy modalities, such as co-therapy and network intervention, facilitated family adjustment.

Because of present threatening political and economic developments both around the world and within individual nations and communities (e.g., inflation, unemployment, oil shortage, threat of biological warfare, bombings, aggression, nuclear energy, terrorism, and environmental problems), most knowledgeable individuals experience insecurity and anxiety, standing on one side or another of these issues, or wavering uncertainly in the middle. Indeed, the person without some anxiety these days may not be normal. Existential anxiety is thus commonplace, and the problem arises of distinguishing among reasonable concern, existential anxiety, and neurotic anxiety. Lindner (1982) uses an analysis of concepts from both philosophy and psychology to make such distinctions. Reorganization of the symbols used by human beings may result in a reduction in the degree of subjectivity in such problems, and the psychotherapist may thus assist the client in striving for increased self-determination in his/her own existence.

Finally, Clark (1980) defines empathy as the unique capacity of the human being to feel the experiences, needs, aspirations, frustrations, sorrows, joys, anxieties, hurt, or hunger of others as if they were his/her own. It is speculated that individuals vary in the degree of cortical development necessary to sustain functional empathy. It is also suggested that most individuals can be trained to that level of empathy necessary to counterbalance the more primitive animalistic determinants of behavior. Clark concludes that the blockage of functional empathy by power drives forms the basis of interpersonal and social tensions, conflicts, violence, terrorism, and war. Control of these destructive forces will require development of techniques to increase functional empathy among human beings.

Coping, Resiliency, and Recovery

On September 11, 2001, tragedy struck New York, Washington, D.C. and Pennsylvania as well as the whole country. Immediate, short-term and long-range effects on victims, victims' families, responders and the general public can be expected to vary in intensity and emotional responses. How we face the tasks before us and how we respond—personally, as communities, as a nation, and world-wide—may very well determine the viability of the American vision and way of life for the remainder of the 21st century and beyond.

The United States is no stranger to adversity, tragedy, war and disaster. We have dealt with it before. Each generation has been tested and challenged—and each generation has risen to the occasion.

Our national unity was tested in a bloody Civil War that forever changed the future and the character of the country. In 1941 we were stunned by an attack by the Empire of Japan on our own soil. This led to our entrance into World War II. That event changed forever the world view of this country and our involvement in world affairs. We became a leader in the world with all of its attendant rewards and responsibilities.

In the 1950s, the long Cold War began with its threat of nuclear annihilation and resulting stresses and trauma in a society intent on survival, defense and the defeat of communism. The Korean War was fought to a stalemate not resolved to this day. Many grieved the losses of loved ones in uniform.

When John F. Kennedy became president in 1960, he represented a dramatic change in the leadership and direction of this country. He offered a vision and hope for a bright and prosperous future. He challenged us to move in new directions and provided impetus for the manned space program. The nation endured severe stress and real and perceived threat to our security and well-being during the Cuban Missile Crisis. Brinksmanship and a firm, strong resolve and message helped avert a possible direct threat to American cities.

On November 22, 1963 in Dallas, Texas, President John F. Kennedy was assassinated. This event shocked the nation and the world. In the days following this event the country felt vulnerable, grief-stricken and angry. Shaken to the core, we grieved for our loss and had our future changed forever. The leader who had challenged a generation to act had fallen. However, the ideals that he held out for the country have endured; the goals he set and the vision for the America he described have not been lost. The resolve of a generation was far stronger and had greater impact than the assassin's bullets. The inspiration of Kennedy's challenges to a generation has resulted in improved civil rights for all, many positive social changes, better opportunities for education for all citizens, more research and development in all the sciences and medicine, accomplishment of the goal of putting a man on the moon and returning him safely, and continuing positive international relations and development in other countries with assistance from numerous Peace Corps Volunteers.

During the 1960s the U.S. struggled with the issues surrounding the Viet Nam War and the ongoing mounting casualties. Civil Rights leader Martin Luther King was assassinated. Presidential candidate Robert F. Kennedy was assassinated. Riots in our cities tore at the very fabric and core of American values and life. Civil Rights and anti-Viet Nam War rallies and marches proliferated nationwide. Confusion, anger, grief, decreased morale, loss of a sense of direction, challenged traditional values, and cultural change all impacted a reeling society.

In the summer of 1966 in Austin, Texas, Charles Wittman went up into the Texas Tower on the campus of the University of Texas. He killed or wounded staff and tourists on his way to the top. Once there, with his arsenal of weapons and ammunition, he methodically began to pick off people on the campus and in town. He killed or wounded more that 40 people before being killed himself by 2 police officers and a civilian volunteer. This whole drama was viewed on live television throughout Texas and the country. It was the first time such an event had ever been seen live by so many people and was the worst "terrorist" event to occur in this country to that date. It shook the country and demonstrated the vulnerability of innocent people to such acts.

During the early 1970s the country experienced the first significant fuel crisis. This awakened the country to the realities of oil sources and the control exerted by groups outside the U.S. such as OPEC. At Kent State University, the tragedy of students being shot by National Guardsmen shocked the nation. Photos and video of the events traumatized many vicariously, many of whom remain with residual problems to this day.

Also in the 1970s our government system was challenged internally by the Watergate scandal and break-in. It resulted in the first resignation of a sitting president in the country's history. In 1979 the country endured the frustratingly long and drawn out daily drama of the Iranian Hostage Crisis. In many respects it paralyzed significant parts of the country. Its resolution partially depended on the election of a new president. While long, frustrating and drawn-out, the crisis resolved peacefully.

In the 1990s the country fought the Gulf War. In early 1993, New York reeled following a terrorist bombing of the World Trade Center. There were six casualties, repairs were made and New York recovered. A domestic terrorist, Timothy McVeigh, bombed the Murrah Federal Building in Oklahoma City in 1995. This was the worst act of terrorism in U.S. history to that date.

There have been other traumatic events that have shaken our consciousness in recent years. Columbine stands out, but there have been other violent events in our nation's schools in other parts of the country. Each of these events above resulted in direct and vicarious trauma in many individuals, communities and the nation. Each one has had significant long-range effects on the country. While each was followed by a period of grief and mourning and shock, each has also generated some positive and constructive changes. In all cases, the communities and the country as a whole have been very resilient and have recovered psychologically, emotionally and physically.

Selected References

The following are some selected further readings available in the field of Disaster Mental Health. You might also wish to search for books in the field by going to:

http://www.angelfire.com/biz/odochartaigh/searchbooks.html

Place descriptors in the search box. You can also order the books online at this site via Amazon.com.

Other search resources include The Cochrane Library, PsychInfo and ERIC.

Ahmad, A., Sofi, M. A., Sundelin-Wahlsten, V. & von Knorring, A. -L. (2000). Post-traumatic stress disorder in children after the military operation 'Anfal' in Iraqi Kurdistan. *European Child & Adolescent Psychiatry*, Vol 9(4), pp. 235-243. Journal URL: http://link.springer.de/link/service/journals/00787/index.htm

Al-Krenawi, Alean, Slonim-Nevo, Vered, Maymon, Yaniv & Al-Krenawi, Salem (Apr 2001). Psychological responses to blood vengeance among Arab adolescents. *Child Abuse & Neglect*, Vol 25(4), pp. 457-472. Journal URL: http://www.elsevier.com/inca/publications/store/5/8/6/

American Psychiatric Association. (1954). *Psychological first aid in community disasters*. Washington, D.C.,

Anderson, Sean K. (1992). Iran: Terrorism and Islamic Fundamentalism. In *Low-Intensity Conflict: Old Threats in a New World*, ed. Edwin G. Corr and Stephen Sloan, Boulder, CO: Westview Press,), pp. 176-177.

Aner, Kerstin (Oct-Dec 1983). Violence and the media/La violence et les medias. *Revue Internationale de Criminologie et de Police Technique*. Vol 36(4), pp. 72-83.

Apellaniz, Ilia Maria (April 1999). Coping with war enforced separation: A pilot study on the account of wives of Puerto Rican civilian soldiers. *Dissertation Abstracts International: Section B: The Sciences & Engineering*, Vol 59(10-B),pp. 5567.

Apfelbaum, Erika (2000). The impact of culture in the face of genocide: Struggling between a silenced home culture and a foreign host culture. In: Squire, Corinne (Ed). *Culture in psychology*. New York, NY, US: Routledge. pp. 163-174.

Aptekar, L. & Boore, J.A. (1990). The emotional effects of disaster on children: A review of the literature. *International Journal of Mental Health*, 19: 77-90.

Aptekar, Lewis & Stoecklin, Daniel (1997). Children in particularly difficult circumstances. In: Berry, John W. (Ed); Dasen, Pierre R. (Ed). *Handbook of cross-cultural psychology, Vol. 2: Basic processes and human development* (2nd ed.). pp. 377-412.

Asai, A. & Barnlund, D. C. (1998). Boundaries of the unconscious private, and public self in Japanese and Americans: A cross-cultural comparison. *International Journal of Intercultural Relations*, 22: 431-452.

Asker, James R. (5 February 1996). What's Iran Up To? *Aviation Week & Space Technology*, p. 25.

Author (5 June 1989). Part I of Will and Testament. *Tehran Radio, Foreign Broadcast Information Service*, pp. 41-47.

Author (No authorship indicated) (1981). Psychology of leaders of terrorist groups. *International Scientific Conference on Terror and Terrorism: International Terrorism.* New York, NY.

Author (No authorship indicated) (1981). Psychology of the followers. *International Scientific Conference on Terror and Terrorism: International Terrorism.* New York, NY.

Baker, Ahmad & Shalhoub-Kevorkian, Nadera (Dec 1999). Effects of political and military traumas on children: The Palestinian case. *Clinical Psychology Review*, Vol 19(8), Special Issue: Mental health issues in middle east societies. pp. 935-950. Journal URL: http://www.elsevier.com/inca/publications/store/6/5/2/

Barbopoulos, Anastasia & Clark, James M. (Nov 2003). Practising Psychology in Rural Settings: Issues and Guidelines. *Canadian Psychology*, Vol 44(4), pp. 410-424.

Bartalotta, Giuseppe (Oct 1981). Analytical psychology and political terrorism/Psicologia analitica e terrorismo politico. *Rivista di Psicologia Analitica.* Vol 12(24), pp. 21-30.

Bek, Renata, Buzov, Ivan & Bilic, Vedran (Mar 2001). Anksiozne reakcije u ratu. Translated Title: Anxiety reactions in war. *Socijalna Psihijatrija*, Vol 29(1). pp. 3-8.

Belter, R.W., Foster, K.Y., Imm, P.S. et al. (1991). Parent vs child reports of PTSD symptoms related to a catastrophic natural disaster. In Children's responses to Natural Disasters: The aftermath of Hurricane Hugo and the 1989 Bay Area Earthquake. Presented at the Society for Research in Child Development, Seattle, April, 1991.

Ben-Eli, Tzion, Sela, Miriam (Sep 1980). Terrorists in Nahariya: Description of coping under stress. *Israeli Journal of Psychology & Counseling in Education*, No 13, pp. 94-101.

Benjamin, Jessica (2002). Terror and guilt: Beyond them and us. *Psychoanalytic Dialogues*, Vol 12(3). pp. 473-484. Journal URL: http://www.analyticpress.com/psychoanalytic_dialogues.html

Benswanger, Ellen G.; Baider, Lea; Cornely, Paul J. (Spr 1980). Infant death in rural community: Implications for research and intervention. *Journal of Rural Community Psychology*, Vol 1(1), pp. 25-46.

Bertolote, Jose M. & Fleischmann, Alexandra (Jun 2002). "Suicide rates in China, 1995-99": Comment. *Lancet*, Vol 359(9325), pp. 2274.

Bhui, Kamaldeep, Abdi, Abdisalama, Abdi, Mahad, Pereira, Stephen, Dualeh, Mohammed, Robertson, David, Sathyamoorthy, Ganesh, Ismail, Hellena (Jan 2003). Traumatic events, migration characteristics and psychiatric symptoms among Somali refugees: Preliminary communication. *Social Psychiatry & Psychiatric Epidemiology*, Vol 38(1). pp. 35-43. Journal URL: http://link.springer.de/link/service/journals/00127/index.htm

Bisson, J., Jenkins, P. Alexander, J. & Bannister, C. (1997). A randomised controlled trial of psychological debriefing for victims of acute burn trauma. British Journal of Psychiatry 171, 78-81.

Bohleber, Werner (2002). Kollektive Phantasmen, Destruktivitaet und Terrorismus. (Collective phantasms, destructivism, terrorism). *Psyche: Zeitschrift fuer Psychoanalyse und ihre Anwendungen*, Vol 56(8). pp. 699-720.

Brady, Kristine Lynn & Caraway, S. Jean (Nov 2002). Home away from home: Factors associated with current functioning in children living in a residential treatment setting. *Child Abuse & Neglect*, Vol 26(11), pp. 1149-1163.

Brown, Elissa J. (Sum 2002). Mental health trauma response to the events of September 11th: Challenges and lessons learned. *Journal of Child & Adolescent Psychopharmacology*, Vol 12(2), pp. 77-82. Journal URL: http://www.liebertpub.com/CAP/default1.asp

Brown, W (1944). The psychology of modern Germany. *British Journal of Psychology.* 34, pp. 43-59.

Bruner, Jerome S. (Nov-Dec 1990). Culture and human development: A new look. *Human Development*, Vol 33(6). *Special Topic: Jerome Bruner: Construction of a scientist.* pp. 344-355.

Butcher, J.N. (1980). The role of crisis intervention in an airport disaster plan. Aviation, Space, and Environmental Medicine, 51, 1260-1262.

Butler, Robert N. (1963). Psychiatric evaluation of the aged. *Geriatrics*, 18(3), pp. 220-232.

Campbell, Lisa Cecilia (Oct 2002). Life stories altered: The effect of clinical depression on reminiscence functions in rural older adults. *Dissertation Abstracts International: Section B: The Sciences & Engineering*, Vol 63(4-B), pp. 2050.

Camus, A. (1991). The Myth of Sisyphus and Other Essays. Vintage Books.

Canino, G.J.; Bravo, M.; Rubio-Stipec, M,; & Woodbury, M. (1990). The impact of disaster on mental health: Prospective and retrospective analyses. *International Journal of Mental Health*, 19: 51-69.

Caplan, G. (1964). Principles of preventive psychiatry. New York. Basic Books, Inc.

Carson, David K.; Araquistain, Mary & Ide, Betty (Jun 1994). Stress, strain, and hardiness as predictors of adaptation in farm and ranch families. *Journal of Child & Family Studies*, Vol 3(2), pp. 157-174.

Cecil, Harry F. (Win 1988). Stress: Country Style: Illinois response to farm stress. *Journal of Rural Community Psychology*, Vol 9(2), *Special Issue: Mental health and the crisis of rural America.* pp. 51-60.

Center for Disease Control and Prevention. (2004). MMWR. Mental health status of World Trade Center rescue and recovery workers and volunteers - New York City, July 2002-August 2004. September 10, 2004, 53 (35), 812-815.

Chemtob, Claude M. (1996). Posttraumatic stress disorder, trauma, and culture. In: Mak, Felice Lieh (Ed); Nadelson, Carol C. (Ed. *International review of psychiatry, Vol. 2.* Washington, DC, US: American Psychiatric Association. pp. 257-292.

Chesnoff, Richard Z. (20 September 1993). Between Bombers and Believers. *U.S. News & World Report*, vol. 115, p. 35. This story was also reported in the 19 April 1993 issue of *Security Intelligence Report*, p. 3, in which it added that the conference also included training in Israeli intelligence methods.

Chrzanowski, G. (1977). The occurrence of emergencies and crisis in psychoanalytic therapy. *Contemporary Psychoanalysis*, 13, 85-93.

Clark, Kenneth B (Feb 1980). Empathy: A neglected topic in psychological research. American Psychologist. Vol 35(2), pp. 187-190. von Raffay, Anita (1980). Hope, a principle of terrorism. Analytische Psychologie. Vol 11(1), pp. 38-52.

Cohler, Bertram J. (1993). Aging, morale, and meaning: The nexus of narrative. In: Cole, Thomas R. (Ed); Achenbaum, W. Andrew (Ed). *Voices and visions of aging: Toward a critical gerontology.* New York, NY, US: Springer Publishing Co. pp. 107-133.

Collomb, H.(1973). L'avenir de la psychiatrie en Afrique. Psychopathologie Africaine, 9, 343-370.

Colombo, Eduardo R; Moccio, Fidel (1961). The vampire: Study of a rumor/El vampiro: Estudio de un rumor. *Acta Neuropsiquiatrica Argentina.* 7, pp. 12-19.

Comay, Michael (1976). Political terrorism. Mental Health & Society. Vol 3(5-sup-6), pp. 249-261.

Comfort, L.K. (1989). The San Salvador earthquake. In Rosenthal, U. (Ed.); Charles, M.T. (Ed.); wt al. Coping with crises: The management of disasters, riots and terrorism (pp.323-339). Springfield, IL, USA: Charles C. Thomas, Publisher.

Conger, Katherine Jewsbury; Rueter, Martha A. & Conger, Rand D. (2000). The role of economic pressure in the lives of parents and their adolescents: The Family Stress Model. In: Crockett, Lisa J. (Ed); Silbereisen, Rainer K. (Ed); *Negotiating adolescence in times of social change.* New York, NY, US: Cambridge University Press. pp. 201-223.

Conger, Rand D.; Elder, Glen H. Jr. & Lorenz, Frederick O. (1994). *Families in troubled times: Adapting to change in rural America.* Hawthorne, NY, US: Aldine de Gruyter. xi, 303 pp.

Connery, Hilary Smith (Jan-Feb 2003). Acute symptoms and functional impairment related to September 11 terrorist attacks among rural community outpatients with severe mental illness. *Harvard Review of Psychiatry*, Vol 11(1), pp. 37-42.

Cook, John R. & Tyler, John D. (Sum 1989). Help-seeking attitudes of North Dakota farm couples. *Journal of Rural Community Psychology*, Vol 10(1), pp. 17-28.

Cook, Stephen W. & Heppner, P. Paul (Jan 1997). Coping, control. problem-solving appraisal, and depressive symptoms during a farm crisis. *Journal of Mental Health Counseling*, Vol 19(1), pp. 64-77.

Corsi, Jerome R (Mar 1981). Terrorism as a desperate game: Fear, bargaining, and communication in the terrorist event. Journal of Conflict Resolution. Vol 25(1), pp. 47-85.

Cox, Ruth P.; Farr, Ken; Parrish, Eddie (2003). Family health counseling, counseling in disasters, health interventions, and reimbursement with families of diverse cultures. ; In:

Cox, Ruth P. (Ed). *Health related counseling with families of diverse cultures: Family, health, and cultural competencies.* Westport, CT, US: Greenwood Press/Greenwood Publishing Group, Inc. pp. 169-191.

Crosby, Kevin; Rhee, Joong-oh; Holland, Jimmie (Spr 1977). Suicide by fire: A contemporary method of political protest. International Journal of Social Psychiatry. Vol 23(1), pp. 60-69. Cooper, H Anthony (Sum 1976). The terrorist and the victim. Victimology. Vol 1(2), pp. 229-239.

Dar, Yechezkel, Kimhi, Shaul, Stadler, Nurit & Epstein, Alek (May 1999). Imprint of the Intifada: Response of kibbutz born veterans to military service in the West Bank and Gaza. *Megamot*, Vol 39(4), pp. 420-444. URL: http://www.szold.org.il

David, K.H. (1976). The use of social learning theory in preventing intercultural adjustment problems. In Pedersen, P., Lonner, W.J. & Draguns, J.G. (Eds.), Counseling across cultures. Honolulu: University of Hawaii Press.

Davis, Helen Miller (Jan 2002). Play and culture: Peer social organizations in three Costa Rican preschools. *Dissertation Abstracts International: Section B: The Sciences & Engineering*, Vol 63(6-B), pp. 3040.

Davis, J. A. and Stewart, L. M. (Apr 1999). The PSA 182 airflight disaster twenty years later: What have we learned about disaster response and recovery? *Human Performance in Extreme Environments*, Vol 4(1), pp. 30-34.

Davis-Brown, Karen & Salamon, Sonya (Oct 1987). Farm families in crisis: An application of stress theory to farm family research. *Family Relations: Journal of Applied Family & Child Studies*, Vol 36(4), *Special Issue: Rural families: Stability and Change.* pp. 368-373.

De Girolamo, G. (1993). International perspectives on the treatment and prevention pf posttraumatic stress disorder. In J.P. Wilson, and B. Raphael, (Eds.). *International handbook of traumatic stress syndromes.* The Plenum series on stress and coping. (pp. 935-946). New York: Plenum Press.

De la Fuente, R. (1990). The mental health consequences of the 1985 earthquake in Mexico. International Journal of Mental Health, 19, 21-29.

de Silva, Harendra, Hobbs, Chris & Hanks, Helga (Mar-Apr 2001). Conscription of children in armed conflict—a form of child abuse. A study of 19 former child soldiers. *Child Abuse Review*, Vol 10(2), pp. 125-134. Journal URL: http://www.interscience.wiley.com/jpages/0952-9136/

de Silva, Padmal (1993). Post-traumatic stress disorder: Cross-cultural aspects. *International Review of Psychiatry*, Vol 5(2-3), pp. 217-229.

de Silva, Padmal (1999). Cultural aspects of post-traumatic stress disorder. In: Yule, William (Ed). *Post-traumatic stress disorders: Concepts and therapy.* New York, NY, US: John Wiley & Sons Ltd. pp. 116-138.

Deane, Frank P., MacDonald, Carol, Chamberlain, Kerry, Long, Nigel & Davin, Lorna (Mar 1998). New Zealand Vietnam veteran's family programme, nga whanau a tu (families of war): Development and outcome. *Australian & New Zealand Journal of Family Therapy,* Vol 19(1), pp. 1-10. Journal URL: http://www.blackwellpublishers.co.uk/asp/journal.asp?ref=0814-723X

DeFrain, John & Schroff, Jan A. (1991). Environment and fatherhood: Rural and urban influences. In: Bozett, Frederick W. (Ed); Hanson, Shirley M. H. (Ed); *Fatherhood and families in cultural context.* New York, NY, US: Springer Publishing Co. pp. 162-186.

Delamater, A. & Applegate, E.B. (1999). Child development and Post-traumatic Stress Disorder after hurricane exposure. TRAUMATOLOGYe. http://www.fsu.edu/trauma/a3v5i3.html Vol. 5, Issue 3, Art. 3, Retrieved May 1999.

deMause, Lloyd (Spr 2002). The childhood origins of terrorism. *Journal of Psychohistory*, Vol 29(4), pp. 340-348.

Department of Veterans' Affairs, Department of Defense. (2004). *VA/DoD guideline for the management of post-traumatic stress.* Washington, D.C.

Derosa, Ruth Reed (Dec 1995). Post-traumatic stress disorder and the subjective experience of disaster: The Hamlet fire. *Dissertation Abstracts International: Section B: The Sciences & Engineering*, Vol 56(6-B), pp. 3441.

Derr, Victoria (Mar-Jun 2002). Children's sense of place in northern New Mexico. Journal of Environmental Psychology, Vol 22(1-2), Special Issue: Children and the environment. pp. 125-137.

Derr, Victoria Leigh (May 2002). Voices from the mountains: Children's sense of place in three communities of northern New Mexico. *Dissertation Abstracts International Section A: Humanities & Social Sciences*, Vol 62(10-A), pp. 3454.

Deveraux, G. (1969). Reality and the dream: Psychotherapy of a Plains Indian. Garden City, NY: Doubleday.

deVries, Marten W. (1995). Culture, community and catastrophe: Issues in understanding communities under difficult conditions. In: Hobfoll, Stevan E. (Ed); deVries, Marten W. (Ed). *Extreme stress and communities: Impact and intervention.* New York, NY, US: Kluwer Academic/Plenum Publishers. pp. 375-393.

deVries, Marten W. (1996). Trauma in cultural perspective. In: van der Kolk, Bessel A. (Ed); McFarlane, Alexander C. (Ed). *Traumatic stress: The effects of overwhelming experience on mind, body, and society.* New York, NY, US: Guilford Press. pp. 398-413.

Diop, B., Collignon, R. & Gueye, E. (1976). Presentation de l'etude concertee de l'O.M.S. sur les strategies pour l'extension pes soins de sante mentale. Psychopathologie Africaine, 12, 173-188.

Doherty, G.W. (1987). *Extended Families.* http://www.angelfire.com/biz/odochartaigh/xfam.html

Doherty, G.W. (1999). Cross-cultural counseling in disaster settings. *Australasian Journal of Disaster and Trauma Studies, Volume 1999-2.* http://www.massey.ac.nz/~trauma/issues/1999-2/doherty.htm Retrieved 9/9/99.

Doherty, G.W. (1999*). From the field: A sample of disaster mental health*

Doherty, G.W. (1999). Towards the next millennium: Disaster mental health - Learning

Draguns, J.G. (1975). Resocialization into culture: The complexities of taking a worldwide view of psychotherapy. In Brislin, R.W., Bochner, S. & Lonner, W.J. (Eds.), Cross-cultural perspectives on learning. New York: Sage Publications.

Draguns, J.G. (1981). Cross-cultural counseling and psychotherapy: History, issues, current status. In Marsella, A.J. & Pedersen, P.B. (Eds.), Cross-cultural counseling and psychotherapy. New York: Pergamon Press.

Dreman, Solly (1989). Children of victims of terrorism in Israel: Coping and adjustment in the face of trauma. *Israel Journal of Psychiatry & Related Sciences*, Vol 26(4), pp. 212-222.

Dreman, Solly B., Cohen, Esther C. (Sum 1982). Children of victims of terrorist activities: A family approach to dealing with tragedy. *American Journal of Family Therapy*, Vol 10(2), pp. 39-47. Journal URL: http://www.tandf.co.uk/journals/pp/01926187.html

Dreman, Solly, Cohen, Esther (Apr 1990). Children of victims of terrorism revisited: Integrating individual and family treatment approaches. *American Journal of Orthopsychiatry*, Vol 60(2), pp. 204-209.

Dudley-Grant, G. Rita; Mendez, Gloria I. & Zinn, Juliana (Aug 2000). Strategies for anticipating and preventing psychological trauma of hurricanes through community education. *Professional Psychology: Research & Practice*, Vol 31(4), pp. 387-392.

Duggal, Harpreet S., Berezkin, Gennady, John, Vineeth (May 2002). PTSD and TV viewing of World Trade Center. *Journal of the American Academy of Child & Adolescent Psychiatry*, Vol 41(5), pp. 494-495. Journal URL: http://www.jaacap.com/

Dyregrov, A. (1989). Caring for helpers in disaster situations: Psychological debriefing. Disaster Management 2, 25-30.

Ecevit, Mehmet & Kasapoglu, Aytuel (2002). Demographic and psychosocial features and their effects on the survivors of the 1999 earthquake in Turkey. *Social Behavior & Personality*, Vol 30(2), pp. 195-202.

Eichelman, Burr; Hartwig, Anne C (1983). Ethical and consultation issues in the behavioral sciences and terrorism. *Behavioral Sciences & the Law*. Vol 1(2), pp. 9-18.

Elder, Glen H. Jr. & Russell, Stephen T. (2000). Surmounting life's disadvantage. In: Crockett, Lisa J. (Ed); Silbereisen, Rainer K. (Ed); *Negotiating adolescence in times of social change*. New York, NY, US: Cambridge University Press. pp. 17-35.

Elder, Glen H. Jr.; King, Valarie & Conger, Rand D. (1996). Attachment to place and migration prospects: A developmental perspective. *Journal of Research on Adolescence*, Vol 6(4), pp. 397-425.

Elder, Glen H. Jr.; Robertson, Elizabeth B. & Ardelt, Monika (1994). In: Conger, Rand D.; Elder, Glen H. Jr.; *Families under economic pressure. Families in troubled times: Adapting to change in rural America*. Hawthorne, NY, US: Aldine de Gruyter. pp. 79-103.

Elhai, J.D., Jacobs, G.A., Kashdan T.B., DeJong G.L., Meyer, L. , Frueh, B. (2006 Jun). Mental health service use among American Red Cross disaster workers responding to the September 11, 2001 U.S. terrorist attacks. *Psychiatry Research*. Vol 143(1) 29-34

Erikson, E. (1959). Identity and the life cycle. *Psychol Issues Monographs 1*.

Escobar, J.I.; Canino, G.; Rubio-Stipec, M.; & Bravo, M. (1992). Somatic symptoms after a natural disaster: A prospective study. *American Journal of Psychiatry*, 149: 965-967.

Euben, Roxanne (1995). When worldviews collide: Conflicting assumptions about human behavior held by rational actor theory and Islamic fundamentalism. *Political Psychology*, Vol 16(1). Special Issue: Political economy and political psychology. pp. 157-178. Journal URL: http://www.blackwellpublishers.co.uk/asp/journal.asp?ref=0162-895X Blackwell Publishers.

Everly, Jr., G.S. & Mitchell, J.T. (1999). Critical Incident Stress Management (CISM):A new era and standard of care in crisis intervention (2nd Ed.). Ellicott City, MD: Chevron Publishing.

Everly Jr., G. S.; Flynn, B. W. (2006 Spr). Principles and Practical Procedures for Acute Psychological First Aid Training for Personnel Without Mental Health Experience. *International Journal of Emergency Mental Health*. Vol 8(2) 93-100.

Fabrega, Horacio & Nutini, Hugo (Dec 1994). Tlaxcalan constructions of acute grief. *Culture, Medicine & Psychiatry*, Vol 18(4), pp. 405-431.

Falicki, Zdzislaw; Borowski, Tadeusz; Kalinowski, Antoni (1972). The opinions of rural population on psychic diseases. *Polish Medical Journal*, Vol. 11(1), pp. 213-219.

Farmer, Val (Apr 1986). Broken heartland. *Psychology Today*, Vol 20(4), pp. 54-57, 60-62.

Ferguson, Stanley B. & Engels, Dennis W. (Mar 1989). American farmers: Workers in transition. *Career Development Quarterly*, Vol 37(3), pp. 240-248.

Fiasche, Angel (1967). Investigation of a chain of suicides in a rural community. *Psychotherapy & Psychosomatics*, 15(1), pp. 20.

Fields, Rona M (Sum 1979). Child terror victims and adult terrorists. Journal of Psychohistory. Vol 7(1), pp. 71-75.

Fields, Rona M. (Sum 1979). Child terror victims and adult terrorists. *Journal of Psychohistory*, Vol 7(1), pp. 71-75.

Figley, Charles R.; Giel, Robert & Borgo, Stefania (1995). Prevention and treatment of community stress: How to be a mental health expert at the time of disaster. In: Hobfoll,

Finnegan, Philip and Holzer, Robert (6-12 February 1995). Iran Arms Cache on Disputed Islands Vexes U.S. *Defense News*, p. 1.

Flannery, Jr., R.B. & Everly, Jr., G.S. (2000). Crisis intervention: A review. International Journal of Emergency Mental Health, 2 (2), 119-125.

Flannery, Jr., R.B. (1998). The Assaulted Staff Action Program: Coping with the psychological aftermath of violence. Ellicott City, MD: Chevron Publishing.

Ford, Julian D., Shaw, David, Sennhauser, Shirley, Greaves, David et al. (Win 1993). Psychosocial debriefing after Operation Desert Storm: Marital and family assessment and intervention. *Journal of Social Issues*, Vol 49(4), pp. 73-102. Journal URL: http://www.blackwellpublishers.co.uk/asp/journal.asp?ref=0022-4537

Forducey, Pamela G.; Ruwe, William D.; Dawson, Stephen J. (2003). Using telerehabilitation to promote TBI recovery and transfer of knowledge. *NeuroRehabilitation*, Vol 18(2), pp. 103-111.

Form, William H.; Loomis, Charles P.; Clifford, Roy A. (1956). The persistence and emergence of social and cultural systems in disasters. *American Sociological Review*, 21, pp. 180-185.

Francis, Richard (Oct-Dec 1983). BBC policy regarding the presentation of television violence/La politique de la BBC en matiere de presentation de la violence. *Revue Internationale de Criminologie et de Police Technique*. Vol 36(4), pp. 91-99.

Friedman, M. J., Hamblen, J., Foa, E., & Charney, D. (2004). Fighting the war on terrorism. *Psychiatry*, 67, 105-117.

from the past and planning for the future. Traumatology-e, Volume 5, No. 2,

Galvin, Deborah M. (1983). The female terrorist: A socio-psychological perspective. *Behavioral Sciences & the Law*. Vol 1(2), pp. 19-32.

Gavin, Bea (May 2003). Open space. Some thoughts on moving west. *Psychodynamic Practice: Individuals, groups & organisations*, Vol 9(2), pp. 195-199 .

Gerbode, F. A. (1989). *Beyond psychology: An introduction to metapsychology*. Ann Arbor, MI: IRM Press.

Gergen, Kenneth J. (1996). Beyond life narratives in the therapeutic encounter. In: Birren, James E. (Ed); Kenyon, Gary M. (Ed). *Aging and biography: Explorations in adult development*. New York, NY, US: Springer Publishing Co. pp. 205-223.

Giegerich, Wolfgang (1979). Terrorism as task and responsibility: Reflections of a depth-psychologist. Analytische Psychologie. Vol 10(3), pp. 190-215.

Giordano, J. & Giordano, G.P. (1976). Ethnicity and community mental health. Community Mental Health Review, 3, 4-14, 15.

Goldson, Edward (Sep 1996). The effect of war on children. *Child Abuse & Neglect*, Vol 20(9), pp. 809-819. Journal URL: http://www.elsevier.com/inca/publications/store/5/8/6/

Gorgievski-Duijvesteijn, Marjan J. (Apr 1999). Job-involvement and stress in farm-couples; *Gedrag & Gezondheid: Tijdschrift voor Psychologie & Gezondheid*, Vol 27(1-2), pp. 109-117.

Gorney, Roderic (Apr 1981). The human agenda: Peril and survival. *Journal of the American Academy of Psychoanalysis*. Vol 9(2), pp. 185-209.

Goss, R. E. & Klass, D. (1997). Tibetan Buddhism and the resolution of grief: The Bardo-thodo for the dying and the grieving. Death Studies, 21: 377-395.

Grunberger, Bela (1988). "The Oedipal conflicts of the analyst" In: Pollock, George H. (Ed); Ross, John Munder (Ed) . The Oedipus papers. pp. 261-282.

Guarnaccia, P.J. (1993). Ataques de nervios in Puerto Rico: Culture-bound syndrome or popular illness? *Medical Anthropology*, Apr, 15: 157-170.

Guarnaccia, Peter J.; Canino, Glorisa & Rubio-Stipec, Maritza (Mar 1993). The prevalence of ataques de nervios in the Puerto Rico Disaster Study: The role of culture in psychiatric epidemiology. *Journal of Nervous & Mental Disease*, Vol 181(3), pp. 157-165.

Gurwitch, Robin H., Sitterle, Karen A., Young, Bruce H., Pfefferbaum (2002). The aftermath of terrorism. In La Greca, Annette M. (Ed); Silverman, Wendy K. (Ed); et al. *Helping children cope with disasters and terrorism*. Washington, DC, US: American Psychological Association. pp. 327-357.

Hagman, G. (1995). Mourning: A review and reconsideration. International Journal of Psycho Analysis, 76: 909-925.

Hall, Alan (May 1998). Sustainable agriculture and conservation tillage: Managing the contradictions. *Canadian Review of Sociology & Anthropology*, Vol 35(2), pp. 221-251.

Hargrove, David S. (Win 1986). Rural community psychology and the farm foreclosure crisis. *Journal of Rural Community Psychology*, Vol 7(2), *Special Issue: Prevention and promotion.* pp. 16-26.

Harik, Judith Palmer (1996). Between Islam and the system: Sources and implications of popular support for Lebanon's Hizballah. *Journal of Conflict Resolution*, Vol 40(1). pp. 41-67. Sage Publications. http://www.sagepub.com

Havenaar, Johan M., (Ed), Cwikel, Julie G., (Ed), Bromet, Evelyn J., (Ed)(2002). *Toxic turmoil: Psychological and societal consequences of ecological disasters*. Series Title: *Plenum series on stress and coping*. New York, NY, US: Kluwer Academic/Plenum Publishers. xiii, 279 pp.

Health Canada's Emergency Services Division's Disaster Mental Health Manual

Hedges, Chris (5 January 1995). Iran May Be Able to Build an Atomic Bomb in 5 Years, U.S. and Israeli Officials Fear. *New York Times*, p. 10.

Herman, Patricia (Sep 2000). Children and the trauma of war: Exploring the use of games in transforming attitudes and behaviors. *Dissertation Abstracts International: Section B: The Sciences & Engineering*, Vol 61(3-B), pp. 1637.

Higginbotham, H.N. (1976). A conceptual model for the delivery of psychological services in non-western settings. Topics in Culture Learning, 4, 44-52.

Higginbotham, H.N. (1979a). Culture and the delivery of psychological services in developing nations. Transcultural Psychiatric Research Review, 16, 7-27.

Higginbotham, H.N. (1979b). Culture and mental health services in developing countries. In A.J. Marsella, Ciborowski, T. & Tharp, R. (Eds.), Perspectives in cross-cultural psychology. New York: Academic Press.

Hilke, Reinhard; Kaiser, Heinz J (Apr 1979). Terrorism: Can psychology offer a solution to this problem? Psychologische Rundschau. Vol 30(2), pp. 88-98.

Hill, Michele B. (2000). Building sustainable reconciliation in South African communities experiencing witch burnings. *Dissertation Abstracts International: Section B: The Sciences & Engineering*, Vol 60(12-B), pp. 6018.

Hinterhuber, Hartmann, Stern, Milan, Ross, Thomas & Kemmler, Georg (Oct 2001). The tragedy of wars in former Yugoslavia seen through the eyes of refugees and emigrants. *Psychiatria Danubina*, Vol 13(1-4), pp. 3-14.

Hitler, A. (1925/1998). *Mein Kampf*. Houghton Mifflin Co.

Hoffman, Bruce (March 1990). Recent Trends and Future Prospects of Iranian Sponsored International Terrorism. Santa Monica: RAND, Report R-3783-USDP.

Hoge, Charles W., Pavlin, Julie A., Milliken, Charles S. (Aug 2002). Psychological sequelae of September 11. *New England Journal of Medicine*, Vol 347(6), pp. 443-444.

Holden, Constance (Jan 1979). Study of terrorism emerging as an international endeavor. Science. Vol 203(4375), pp. 33-35.
http://www.blackwellpublishers.co.uk/asp/journal.asp?ref=0036-5564

Minister of National Health and Welfare.. Personal Services: Psychosocial Planning for Disasters. Retrieved May 20, 1999.
http://www.phac-aspc.gc.ca/emergency-urgence/pdf/pers_e.pdf

Hutchinson, Martha C (Sep 1972). The concept of revolutionary terrorism. Journal of Conflict Resolution. Vol. 16(3), pp. 383-396.

Institute of Medicine. (2003). *Preparing for the Psychological Consequences of Terrorism.* Washington, D.C.: National Academies Press.

International Symposium on Technology and Terrorism in Palm Springs, CA, 23-24 February 1994.

Jacobs, G.A.; Meyer, .D.L. (2006. Psychological First Aid: Clarifying the Concept. In Barbanel, L.. (Ed); Sternberg, R. J. (Ed). *Psychological interventions in times of crisis.* (pp. 57-71). New York, NY, US: Springer Publishing Co xxix, 289 pp.

Jacobs, J. L. (1992). Relgious ritual and mental health. In Schumaker, John F. (Ed); et al. Religion and mental health. (pp. 291-299). New York, NY, USA: Oxford University Press. viii, 320 pp.

Jenkins, Robert M. (July 1993). The Islamic Connection. *Security Management*, vol. 37, p. 28.

Jensen, Gail M. & Royeen, Charlotte B. (May 2002). Improved rural access to care: Dimensions of best practice. *Journal of Interprofessional Care*, Vol 16(2) pp. 117-128.

Jilek-Aal, W. (1978). Native renaissance: The survival and revival of indigenous therapeutic ceremonials among North American Indians. Transcultural Psychiatric Research Review, 15, 117-148.

Joh, H. (1997). Disaster stress of the 1995 Kobe earthquake. Japan Psychologia: An International Journal of Psychology in the Orient. 40: 192-200.

Jurich, Anthony P. & Russell, Candyce S. (Oct 1987). Family therapy with rural families in a time of farm crisis. *Family Relations: Journal of Applied Family & Child Studies*, Vol 36(4), *Special Issue: Rural families: Stability and Change.* pp. 364-367.

Kardiner, A. & Spiegel, H. (1947). War, stress, and neurotic illness. New York:Hoeber.

Kats, Rachel (Feb 1982). Concerns of the Israeli: Change and stability from 1962 to 1975. *Human Relations.* Vol 35(2), pp. 83-100.

Keane, T. M.; Piwowarczyk, L. A. (2006). Trauma, Terror, and Fear: Mental Health Professionals Respond to the Impact of 9/11—An Overview. In Schein, L. A. (Ed); Spitz, H. I. (Ed); Burlingame, G. M. (Ed); Muskin, P. R. (Ed); Vargo, S. (Col). *Psychological effects of catastrophic disasters: Group approaches to treatment.* (pp. 3-16). New York, NY, US: Haworth Press xxiv, 940 pp.

Keating, Norah C. & Munro, Brenda (Apr 1989). Transferring the family farm: Process and implications. *Family Relations: Journal of Applied Family & Child Studies*, Vol 38(2), pp. 215-219.

Keller, Heidi (Sep-Oct 2003). Moving towards consensus on how to characterize culture: Reply to the comments of Catherine Tamis-LeMonda and Kristin Neff. *Human Development*, Vol 46(5), pp. 328-330.

Kelly, G. (1955). The psychology of personal constructs. New York: Norton.

Kennedy, David Patrick Jr (2003). Gender, culture change, and fertility decline in honduras: An investigation in anthropological demography. *Dissertation Abstracts International Section A: Humanities & Social Sciences*, Vol 64(3-A), pp. 968.

Kennerley, Cati Marsh (Fal 2003). Cultural Negotiations: Puerto Rican Intellectuals in a State-Sponsored Community Education Project, 1948-1968. *Harvard Educational Review*, Vol 73(3), pp. 416-448.

Kent, Ian; Nicholls, William (1977). The psychodynamics of terrorism. Mental Health & Society. Vol 4(1-sup-2), pp. 1-8.

Kinzie, J. David, Sack, William H., Angell, Richard H., Manson, Spero M. et al. (May 1986). The psychiatric effects of massive trauma on Cambodian children: I. The children. *Journal of the American Academy of Child Psychiatry*, Vol 25(3), pp. 370-376. Journal URL: http://www.jaacap.com/

Klass, D. & Heath, A. O. (1997). Grief and abortion: Mizuko Kuyo, the Japanese ritual resolution. Omega: Journal of Death and Dying; 34: 1-14.

Klass, D. (1996). Ancestor worship in Japan: Dependence and the resolution of grief. Omega: Journal of Death and Dying; 33: 279-302.

Kohn, R. & Levav, I. (1990). Bereavement in disaster: An overview of the research. International Journal of Mental Health, 19: 61-76.

Kopelman, M. D. (Oct 2000). Fear can interrupt the continuum of memory. *Journal of Neurology, Neurosurgery & Psychiatry*, Vol 69(4), pp. 431-432. Journal URL: http://jnnp.bmjjournals.com/

Koplewicz, Harold S., Vogel, Juliet M., Solanto, Mary V., Morrissey, Richard F., Alonso, Carmen M., Abikoff, Howard, Gallagher, Richard, Novick, Rona M. (Feb 2002). Child and parent response to the 1993 World Trade Center bombing. *Journal of Traumatic Stress*, Vol 15(1), pp. 77-85. Journal URL: http://www.wkap.nl/journalhome.htm/0894-9867

Korman, M. (1974). National conference on levels and patterns of professional training in psychology: Major themes. American Psychologist, 29, 441-449.

Kreidie, Lina Haddad (2001). Deciphering the construals of Islamic fundamentalists. *Dissertation Abstracts International Section A: Humanities & Social Sciences*, Vol 61(9-A). pp. 3753. University Microfilms International.

Kydd, Sally Anna (Oct 1999). A case study of program planning and evaluation in assisting Montserratian evacuees and British government officials in natural disaster planning. *Dissertation Abstracts International Section A: Humanities & Social Sciences*, Vol 60(4-A), pp. 1351.

La Greca, A.M., Silverman, W.K. & Wasserstein, S.B. (1998). Children's predisaster functioning as a predictor of posttraumatic stress following Hurricane Andrew. Journal of Consulting and Clinical Psychology, 66, 883-892.

La Greca, A.M., Silverman, W.K., Vernberg, E.M. & Prinstein, M. (1996). Symptoms of posttraumatic stress after Hurricane Andrew: A prospective study. Journal of Consulting and Clinical Psychology, 64, 712-723.

La Greca, Annette M., (Ed), Silverman, Wendy K., (Ed), Vernberg, Eric M.,(Ed), Roberts, Michael C., (Ed), (2002). *Helping children cope with disasters and terrorism.* Washington, DC, US: American Psychological Association. xvii, 446 pp.

La Greca, Annette M., Silverman, Wendy K., Vernberg, Eric M., Roberts, Michael C. (2002). Children and disasters: Future directions for research and public policy. In La

Greca, Annette M. (Ed); Silverman, Wendy K. (Ed); et al; . *Helping children cope with disasters and terrorism.* Washington, DC, US: American Psychological Association. pp. 405-423.

La Guardia, Anton and Gozani, Ohad (30 October 1995). Israel on Alert After Murder of Islamic Leader. *The Electronic Telegraph, World News.*

Ladd, Gary W. (Feb 1996). Chldren: Ethnic and political violence. *Child Development,* Vol 67(1), pp. 14-18. Journal URL: http://www.blackwellpublishers.co.uk/asp/journal.asp?ref=0009-3920

Ladrido-Ignacio, L. & Perlas, A.P. (1996). From victims to survivors: Psychosocial intervention in disaster management in the Philippines. International Journal of Mental Health, 24: 3-51.

Lahad, Shmuel and Abraham, Ada (Sep 1983). Preparing teachers and pupils for coping with stress situations: A multi-model program. *Israeli Journal of Psychology & Counseling in Education.* No 16, pp. 196-210.

Lahad, Shmuel, Abraham, Ada (Sep 1983). Preparing teachers and pupils for coping with stress situations: A multi-model program. *Israeli Journal of Psychology & Counseling in Education,* No 16, pp. 196-210.

Lamarche, Andre (1960). Rapport de la commission sur l'hygiene mentale du milieu rural. (Report of the commission on rural mental health). *Hygiene Mentale,* 49, pp. 52-74.

Lazarus, Arnold (1976). *Multimodal behavior therapy.* Springer Publishing Co.

Lazarus, Arnold A. (1989). The practice of multimodal therapy: Systematic, comprehensive, and effective psychotherapy. Johns Hopkins University Press.

Lazarus, Arnold A. (2000). Multimodal replenishment. Professional Psychology Research and Practice, Vol 31(1) 93-94.

Leach, J. (Jul 1995). Psychological first-aid: A practical aide-memoire. *Aviation, Space, & Environmental Medicine,* Vol 66(7), pp. 668-674.

Lebowitz, Michael (Jan-Mar 1983). Generalization from natural language text. *Cognitive Science.* Vol 7(1), pp. 1-40.

Lindemann, E. (1944). Symptomology and management of acute grief. American Journal of Psychiatry, 101, 141-148.

Lindner, Wulf-Volker (Jan 1982). Existential and neurotic anxiety/Existentielle und neurotische Angst. *Praxis der Psychotherapie und Psychosomatik.* Vol 27(1), pp. 33-40. literature. International Journal of Mental Health, 19: 77-90.

Lobao, Linda & Meyer, Katherine (Dec 1995). Economic decline, gender, and labor flexibility in family-based enterprises: Midwestern farming in the 1980s. *Social Forces,* Vol 74(2), pp. 575-608.

Loeb, Elizabeth & Dvorak, Joanne (1987). Farm families. *Family Therapy Collections,* Vol 22, pp. 97-109.

Lombas, Tiffany Marie (Jun 2002). A naturalistic exploration of stress and coping among rural law enforcement officers: Implications for the counseling profession. *Dissertation Abstracts International Section A: Humanities & Social Sciences,* Vol 62(11-A), pp. 3701.

Lonigan, C.J., Shannon, M.P., Finch, A.J., Daugherty, T.K. & Taylor, C.M. (1991). Children's reactions to a natural disaster: Symptom severity and degree of exposure. *Advances in Behaviour Research and Therapy,* 13, 135-154.

Lystad, M. (1990). United States programs in disaster mental health. *International Journal of Mental Health,* 19: 80-88.

Ma, H.; Lu, Q.; Liu, P.; A-Er-Ken; et al. (1995). Acute stress reactions of fire-disaster victims' family members: A clinical analysis. *Chinese Mental Health Journal,* 9: 107-109.

MacMullin, Colin & Odeh, Jumana (Fal 1999). What is worrying children in the Gaza Strip? *Child Psychiatry & Human Development,* Vol 30(1), pp. 55-70. Journal URL: http://www.wkap.nl/journalhome.htm/0009-398X

Mak, F.L. & Nadelson, C.C. (Ed.) (1996). International review of psychiatry, Vol 2. Washington, DC, USA: American Psychiatric Press, Inc.

Mandic, Nikola & Mihaljevic, Zeljka Vuksic (Dec 1993). Psychologic state of displaced persons from East Slavonia. *Socijalna Psihijatrija,* Vol 21(3-4), pp. 121-135.

Marsella, A.J., Friedman, M.J. & Gerrity, E.T. (1996). Ethnocultural aspects of post-traumatic stress disorder: Issues, research, and clinical applications. Washington, DC, USA: American Psychological Association.

Marshall, Randall D. & Suh, Eun Jung (Win 2003). Contextualizing Trauma: Using Evidence-Based Treatments in a Multicultural Community After 9/11. *Psychiatric Quarterly,* Vol 74(4). *Special Issue: The Fifteenth Annual New York State Office of Mental Health Research Conference.* pp. 401-420.

Martel, C. (1999). Quebec's psychosocial interventions in an emergency measures situation. TRAUMATOLOGYe http://www.fsu.edu/~trauma/contv5i3.html Vol 5, Issue 3, Art. 5 Retrieved May 1999.

Martinez-Brawley, Emilia E. & Blundall, Joan (Jul 1991). Whom shall we help? Farm families' beliefs and attitudes about need and services. *Social Work,* Vol 36(4), pp. 315-321.

Mateczun, John M., Holmes, Elizabeth K. (1996). Return, readjustment, and reintegration: The three R's of family reunion. In Ursano, Robert J. (Ed); Norwood, Ann E. (Ed); *Emotional aftermath of the Persian Gulf War: Veterans, families, communities, and nations.* pp. 369-392.

Mazur, Allan (Jun 1982). Bomb threats and the mass media: Evidence for a theory of suggestion. *American Sociological Review.* Vol 47(3), pp. 407-411.

McAdams, Dan P. (1993). *The stories we live by: Personal myths and the making of the self.* New York, NY, US: William Morrow & Co, Inc. 336 pp.

McFarlane, A.C. (1990). An Australian disaster: The 1983 bushfires. International Journal of Mental Health, 19: 36-47.

McInnes, Rita (Dec 2000). Landed gender: Rural couples caught between traditional and contemporary roles. *Australian & New Zealand Journal of Family Therapy*, Vol 21(4), *Special Issue: Innovative and contextual approaches to human problems.* pp. 191-200.

Melville, Margarita B., Lykes, M. Brinton (Mar 1992). Guatemalan Indian children and the sociocultural effects of government-sponsored terrorism. *Social Science & Medicine*, Vol 34(5), pp. 533-548. Journal URL: http://www.elsevier.com/inca/publications/store/3/1/5/

Mermelstein, Joanne & Sundet, Paul (Win 1988). Factors influencing the decision to innovate: The future of community responsive programming. *Journal of Rural Community Psychology*, Vol 9(2), *Special Issue: Mental health and the crisis of rural America.* pp. 61-75.

Michael, Donald N. and Anderson, Walter T. (1989). Norms in conflict and confusion: Six stories in search of an author. < Humanistic of>, Vol 29(2). pp. 145-166.

Mileti, Dennis S. & Darlington, Joanne Derouen (Feb 1997). The role of searching in shaping reactions to earthquake risk information. *Social Problems*, Vol 44(1), pp. 89-103.

Miller, Kenneth E. (Feb 1996). The effects of state terrorism and exile on indigenous Guatemalan refugee children: A mental health assessment and an analysis of children's narratives. *Child Development*, Vol 67(1), pp. 89-106. Journal URL: http://www.blackwellpublishers.co.uk/asp/journal.asp?ref=0009-3920

Miller, Thomas W. & Veltkamp, Lane J. (1988). Child sexual abuse: The abusing family in rural America. *International Journal of Family Psychiatry*, Vol 9(3), pp. 259-275.

Mitchell, J. T. (1993). When disaster strikes...The critical incident stress debriefing process. Journal of Emergency Medical Services, 8 (1), 36-39.

Mitchell, J.T. & Everly, G.S. (1997). Critical incident stress management: The basic course workbook. Ellicott City, MD: International Critical Incident Stress Foundation, Inc.

Miura, M. & Usa, S. (1970). A psychotherapy of neurosis: Morita therapy. Psychologia, 13, 18-34.

Monroe, Kristen Renwick and Kreidie, Lina Haddad (1997). The perspective of Islamic fundamentalists and the limits of rational choice theory. *Political Psychology*, Vol 18(1), pp. 19-43. http://www.blackwellpublishers.co.uk/asp/journal.asp?ref=0162-895X Blackwell Publishers.

Mosse, Hilde L.(Dec 1977). Terrorism and mass media. *New York State Journal of Medicine*, Vol 77(14), pp. 2294-2296.

Murphy, Ronald T., Wismar, Keith & Freeman, Kassie (Feb 2003). Stress symptoms among African-American college students after the September 11, 2001 terrorist attacks. *Journal of Nervous & Mental Disease*, Vol 191(2), pp. 108-114. Journal URL: http://www.jonmd.com/

Murray, Shoon Kathleen & Meyers, Jason (Oct 1999). Do people need foreign enemies? American leaders' beliefs after the Soviet demise. *Journal of Conflict Resolution*, Vol 43(5), pp. 555-569. Publisher URL:

Musacchio, John M. and Rozen, Amon (1988). Fundamentalist Fervor: Islamic Terrorism in the '80s. *Security Management* p. 56.

National Institute of Mental Health. (2002). *Mental health and mass violence.* Washington, D.C.: US Government Printing Office.

National Institute of Mental Health. (2002). Mental health and mass violence. Washington, D.C.: US Government Printing Office..

Neff, Kristin (Sep-Oct 2003). Understanding how universal goals of independence and interdependence are manifested within particular cultural contexts. *Human Development*, Vol 46(5), pp. 312-318.

Neki, J.S. (1973). Guru-chepa relationship: The possibility of a therapeutic paradigm. American Journal of Orthopsychiatry, 43, 755-766.

Newcomer, Hale A; Adkins, John W (Nov 1980). Terrorism and the business executive. Personnel Journal. Vol 59(11), pp. 913-915.

Newell, P. B. (1998). A cross-cultural comparison of privacy definitions and functions: A systems approach. Journal of Environmental Psychology, 18: 357-371.

Newnes, C. (Ed) (1991). Death, dying, and society. Changes: An International Journal of psychology and psychotherapy. Hove, England UK: Lawrence Erlbaum Associates, Inc. (1991). vi, 177 pp.

Norris, F.H.; Phifer, J.F. & Kaniasty, K. (1994). Individual and community reactions to the Kentucky floods: Findings from a longitudinal study of older adults. In: Ursano, Robert J. (Ed) & McCaughey, Brian G. (Ed); *Individual and community responses to trauma and disaster: The structure of human chaos.* New York, NY, US: Cambridge University Press. pp. 378-400.

Norris, F.H., Byrne, C.M., Diaz, E., & Kaniasty, K. (2001). *50,000 Disaster victims speak: An empirical review of the empirical literature, 1981-2001.* Report for The National Center for PTSD and The Center for Mental Health Services (SAMHSA).

Norris, F.H., Friedman, M., Watson, P., Byrne, C. M., Diaz, E., & Kaniasty, K. (2002). 60,000 disaster victims speak: Part I. A review of the empirical literature, 1981-2001. *Psychiatry,* 65, 207-239.

Oakes, Margaret Grace (Dec 1998). Emotional reactions to the trauma of war: A field study of rural El Salvador. *Dissertation Abstracts International Section A: Humanities & Social Sciences*, Vol 59(6-A), pp. 2188.

Oclander Goldie, Silvia S. (Dec 1999). The impact of a war experience on the inner world of a young child. *International Journal of Psycho-Analysis*, Vol 80(6), pp. 1147-1164.

Olson, Kenneth R. & Schellenberg, Richard P. (Oct 1986). Farm stressors. *American Journal of Community Psychology*, Vol 14(5), *Special Issue: Rural mental health.* pp. 555-569.

Papageorgiou, V., Frangou-Garunovic, A., Iordanidou, R., Yule, W., Smith, P. & Vostanis, P. (Jun 2000). War trauma and psychopathology in Bosnian refugee children. *European Child & Adolescent Psychiatry*, Vol 9(2), pp. 84-90. Journal URL: http://link.springer.de/link/service/journals/00787/index.htm

Parkes, C.M. (1997). A typology of disasters. In Black, Dora (Ed); Newman, Martin (Ed); et al. Psychological trauma: A developmental approach. (pp. 81-93). London, England UK: Gaskell/Royal College of Psychiatrists. Xii, 412 pp.

Paton, D. (1996). Responding to international needs: Critical occupations as disaster relief agencies. In D. Paton and J.M. Violanti (Eds). Traumatic stress in critical occupations: Recognition, consequences and treatment. (pp. 139-172). Springfield, IL, USA: Charles C. Thomas, Publisher. Xiv, 245 pp.

Paulsen, Julie (Sum 1988). A service response to a culture in crisis. *Journal of Rural Community Psychology*, Vol 9(1), pp. 16-22.

Paynter, Robert (Aug-Oct 2002). Time in the valley: Narratives about rural New England. *Current Anthropology*, Vol 43(Suppl), *Special Issue: Repertoires of timekeeping in anthropology.* pp. S85-S101.

Peak, Kimberly S.(Apr 2000). Oklahoma City: Posttraumatic stress disorder and gender differences. *Dissertation Abstracts International: Section B: The Sciences & Engineering*, Vol 60(9-B), pp. 4901.

Pedersen, P. (1976). The cultural inclusiveness of counseling. In Pedersen, P., Draguns, J.G., Lonner, W.J. & Trimble, J. (Eds.), Counseling across cultures. 2nd ed Honolulu: University Press of Hawaii.

Pedersen, P., Lonner, W.J. & Draguns, J.G. (Eds.) (1976). Counseling across cultures. Honolulu: University Press of Hawaii.

Peeks, Barbara (Dec 1989). School-based intervention for farm families in transition. *Elementary School Guidance & Counseling*, Vol 24(2), pp 128-134.

Peeks, Barbara (May 1989). Farm families in crisis: The school counselor's role. *School Counselor*, Vol 36(5), pp. 384-388.

Peltzer, Karl (Oct 1999). Posttraumatic stress symptoms in a population of rural children in South Africa. *Psychological Reports*, Vol 85(2), pp. 646-650.

Perilla, Julia L.; Norris, Fran H. Lavizzo Evelyn A. (Spr 2002). Ethnicity, culture, and disaster response: Identifying and explaining ethnic differences in PTSD six months after Hurricane Andrew. *Journal of Social & Clinical Psychology* Vol 21(1), pp. 20-45.

Perry, S., Cooper, A. & Michels, R. (1987). The psychodynamic formulation: Its purpose, structure, and clinical application. *American Journal of Psychiatry,* 144, 543-550.

Pfefferbaum, Betty, (Dec 2001). The impact of the Oklahoma City bombing on children in the community. *Military Medicine*, Vol 166(12,Suppl 2), pp. 49-50.

Pfefferbaum, Betty, Call, John A., Sconzo, Guy M. (Jul 1999). Mental health services for children in the first two years after the 1995 Oklahoma City terrorist bombing.

Psychiatric Services, Vol 50(7), pp. 956-958. Journal URL: http://psychservices.psychiatryonline.org/

Pfefferbaum, Betty, Gurwitch, Robin H., McDonald, Nicholas B., Leftwich, Michael J. T., Sconzo, Guy M., Messenbaugh, Anne K., Schultz, Rosemary A. (Mar 2000). Posttraumatic stress among young children after the death of a friend or acquaintance in a terrorist bombing. *Psychiatric Services*, Vol 51(3), . pp. 386-388. Journal URL: http://psychservices.psychiatryonline.org/

Pfefferbaum, Betty, Nixon, Sara Jo, Tivis, Rick D., Doughty, Debby E., Pynoos, Robert S., Gurwitch, Robin H., Foy, David W., Pfefferbaum, Betty (Fal 2001). Television exposure in children after a terrorist incident. *Psychiatry: Interpersonal & Biological Processes*, Vol 64(3), pp. 202-211. Journal URL: http://www.guilford.com/cartscript.cgi?page=periodicals/jnps.htm&cart_id=5472 16.21319

Pfefferbaum, Betty, Seale, Thomas W., McDonald, Nicholas B., Brandt, Edward N. Jr., Rainwater, Scott M., Maynard, Brian T., Meierhoefer, Barbara, Miller, Peteryne D. (Win 2000). Posttraumatic stress two years after the Oklahoma City bombing in youths geographically distant from the explosion. *Psychiatry: Interpersonal & Biological Processes*, Vol 63(4), pp. 358-370. Journal URL: http://www.guilford.com/cartscript.cgi?page=periodicals/jnps.htm&cart_id=5472 16.21319

Phillips, Michael R.; Li, Xianyun & Zhang, Yanping (Jul 2002). "Suicide rates in China, 1995-99": Erratum. *Lancet*, Vol 360(9329), pp. 344.

Pine, Daniel S., Cohen, Judith A. (Apr 2002). Trauma in children and adolescents: Risk and treatment of psychiatric sequelae. *Biological Psychiatry*, Vol 51(7), pp. 519-531. Journal URL: http://www.elsevier.com/inca/publications/store/5/0/5/7/5/0/

Pinter, E. (1969). Wohlstandfluchtlinge. Eine sozialpsychiatrische studie an ungarischen Fluchtlingen in der Schweiz. Bibliotheca Psychiatrica et Neurologica, No. 138.

Pinter, E. (1978). Immigrant status and psychic disturbances. Schweizer Archiv fuer Neurologie, Neurochirurgie und Psychiatrie; 122: 75-82.

Plante, Thomas G., Simicic, Azra, Andersen, Erin N. & Manuel, Gerdenio (Jan 2002). Stress and coping among displaced Bosnian refugees: An exploratory study. *International Journal of Stress Management*, Vol 9(1). pp. 31-41.

Plunkett, Scott W.; Henry, Carolyn S. & Knaub, Patricia K. (Spr 1999). Family stressor events, family coping, and adolescent adaptation in farm and ranch families. *Adolescence*, Vol 34(133), pp. 147-168.

Presty, Sharon Katharine (Jul 1996). Psychological sequelae of battered women residing in rural community shelters. *Dissertation Abstracts International: Section B: The Sciences & Engineering*, Vol 57(1-B), pp. 0707.

Prince, R.H. (1976). Psychotherapy as the manipulation of endogenous healing mechanisms: A transcultural survey. Transcultural Psychiatric Research Review, 13, 115-134.

Prince, R.H. (1980). Variations in psychotherapeutic experience. In H.C. Triandis & J.G. Draguns (Eds.), Handbook of cross-cultural psychology. Vol. 6. Psychopathology. Boston: Allyn & Bacon.

Priya, Kumar Ravi (Jan, Jul,& Nov 2002). Suffering and healing among the survivors of Bhuj earthquake. *Psychological Studies*, Vol 47(1-3), pp. 106-112.

Psychology, Vol 41(4), pp. 297-306. Journal URL:

Rabalais, Aline E.; Ruggiero, Kenneth J.; Scotti, Joseph R. (2002). Multicultural issues in the response of children to disasters. In: La Greca, Annette M. (Ed); Silverman, Wendy K. (Ed). *Helping children cope with disasters and terrorism.* Washington, DC, US: American Psychological Association. pp. 73-99.

Ragland, John D. & Berman, Alan L. (1990-1991). Farm crisis and suicide: Dying on the vine? *Omega: Journal of Death & Dying*, Vol 22(3), pp. 173-185.

Rajouria, Sunita (Jan 2002). The natural context of mother-toddler play interactions in a rural Nepali community. *Dissertation Abstracts International Section A: Humanities & Social Sciences*, Vol 63(6-A), pp. 2124 .

Ramirez-Ferrero, Eric Ernesto (Apr 2002). Troubled fields: Men, emotions and the Oklahoma farm crisis, 1992-1994. *Dissertation Abstracts International Section A: Humanities & Social Sciences*, Vol 62(9-A), pp. 3097.

Raphael, B. (1986). When disaster strikes. NewYork: Basic Books.

Raphael, B. (2003). *Early intervention and the debriefing debate.* In: *Terrorism and disaster: Individual and community mental health interventions.* Ursano, Robert J. ; Uniformed Services U of the Health Sciences; Dept of Psychiatry; Ctr f or the Study of Traumatic Stress; New York, NY, US: Cambridge University Press, pp. 146-161.

Rapoport, David C. (1990). Sacred Terror: A Contemporary Example from Islam. In *Origins of Terrorism: Psychologies, Ideologies, Theologies, States of Mind*, ed. Walter Reich. New York: Woodrow Wilson International Center for Scholars and Cambridge University Press, pp. 117-118.

Reardon, David C. (Jun 2002). "Suicide rates in China, 1995-99": Comment. *Lancet*, Vol 359(9325), pp. 2274.

Reeves, N. C.& Boersma, F. J. (1989,1990). The therapeutic use of ritual in maladaptive grieving. Omega: Journal of Death and Dying; 20: 281-291.

Reik, T. (1924). Some remarks on the study of resistances. Indian Journal of Psychology, 9, pp. 141-154. Retrieved May 1999.

Rettig, Kathryn D.; Danes, Sharon M. & Bauer, Jean W. (May 1991). Family life quality: Theory and assessment in economically stressed farm families. *Social Indicators Research*, Vol 24(3), pp. 269-299.

Reynolds, D.K. (1976). Morita psychotherapy. Berkeley: University of California Press.

Ricci, Michael A.; Caputo, Michael & Amour, Judith (Spr 2003). Telemedicine Reduces Discrepancies in Rural Trauma Care. *Telemedicine Journal & e-Health*, Vol 9(1), *Special Issue: Success Stories in Telemedicine: Some Empirical Evidence.* pp. 3-11.

Ridha, Hadi; Orlin, Malinda (Dec 1996). Dealing with disaster victims: A Kuwaiti model. *Journal of the Social Sciences*, Vol 24(4), pp. 229-238.

Rigamer, Elmore F. (May 1986). Psychological management of children in a national crisis. *Journal of the American Academy of Child Psychiatry*, Vol 25(3), pp. 364-369. Journal URL: http://www.jaacap.com/

Ritchie, E. C., Friedman, M., Watson, P., Ursano, R., Wessely, S., & Flynn, B. (2004). *Military Medicine, 169*, 575-579.

Robinson, R. & Mitchell, J. (1993). Evaluation of psychological debriefings. Journal of Traumatic Stress, 6, 367-382.

Rofe, Yacov; Lewin, Isaac (1982). The effect of war environment on dreams and sleep habits. *Series in Clinical & Community Psychology: Stress & Anxiety.* Vol 8, pp. 67-79.

Rogers, Kim Lacy (1994). Trauma redeemed: The narrative construction of social violence. In: McMahan, Eva M. (Ed) & Rogers, Kim Lacy (Ed); *Interactive oral history interviewing.* Hillsdale, NJ, England: Lawrence Erlbaum Associates, Inc. pp. 31-46.

Rogers, Rita (Sep 1980). On emotional responses to nuclear issues and terrorism. Psychiatric Journal of the University of Ottawa. Vol 5(3), pp. 147-152.

Ronen, Tammie & Rosenbaum, Michael (Mar 2003). Children's reactions to a war situation as a function of age and sex. *Anxiety, Stress & Coping: An International Journal*, Vol 16(1), pp. 59-69. Journal URL: http://www.tandf.co.uk/journals/gb/10615806.html

Rose, S. & Bisson, J. (1998). Brief early psychological interventions following trauma - A systematic review of the literature. Journal of Traumatic Stress 11, 4 697-710.

Rosenberg, Alfred (1982). The myth of the twentieth century: An evaluation of the spiritual-intellectual confrontations of our age. Noontide Press.

Rosenblatt, P. C. (1993). Cross-cultural variation in the experience, expression, and understanding of grief. In Irish, Donald P. (Ed); Lundquist, Kathleen F. (Ed); et-al. Ethnic variations in dying, death, and grief: Diversity in universality. Series in death education, aging, and health care. (pp. 13-19). Washington, DC, USA: Taylor & Francis. xxii, 226 pp.

Rosenblatt, Paul C. (1990). *Farming is in our blood: Farm families in economic crisis.* Ames, IA, US : Iowa State University Press . ix, 187 pp.

Rubin, N. (1990). Social networks and mourning: A comparative approach. *Omega: Journal of Death and Dying;* 21: 113-127.

Ryan-Wenger, Nancy A. (Apr 2001). Impact of the threat of war on children in military families. *American Journal of Orthopsychiatry*, Vol 71(2), pp. 236-244.

Sack, William H., Angell, Richard H., Kinzie, J. David, Rath, Ben (1986). The psychiatric effects of massive trauma on Cambodian children: II. The family, the home, and the school. *Journal of the American Academy of Child Psychiatry*, Vol 25(3), pp. 377-383. Journal URL: http://www.jaacap.com/

Salter, Charles A. (Dec 2001). Psychological effects of nuclear and radiological warfare. *Military Medicine*, Vol 166(12,Suppl 2), pp. 17-18. Publisher URL: http://www.amsus.org/

Sandoval, J. (1985). Crisis counseling: Conceptualizations and general principles. *School Psychology Review*, 14, 257-265.

Saraceno, Benedetto, Saxena, Shekhar, Maulik, Pallab K., Sartorius, Norman (Ed); Gaebel, Wolfgang (Ed); et al. (2002). Mental health problems in refugees. *Psychiatry in society.* New York, NY, US: John Wiley & Sons Ltd.. pp. 193-220

Saylor, C. F. (Ed) (1993). Children and disasters. New York, NY, USA: Plenum Press. xxii, 237 pp.

Schaafstal, Alma M.; Johnston, Joan H. & Oser, Randall L. (Sep-Nov 2001). Training teams for emergency management. *Computers in Human Behavior,* Vol 17(5-6), *Special Issue: Computer supported collaborative learning* pp. 615-626.

Schafer, Roy (1992). *Retelling a life: Narration and dialogue in psychoanalysis.* New York, NY, US : Basic Books, Inc . xvii, 328 pp.

Schiopu, Ursula (Jul-Dec 1983). Psychological mutations and peace problems *Revue Roumaine des Sciences Sociales - Serie de Psychologie.* Vol 27(2), pp. 101-103.

Schlenger, William E., Caddell, Juesta M., Ebert, Lori, Jordan, B. Kathleen, Rourke, Kathryn M., Wilson, David, Thalji, Lisa, Dennis, J. Michael, Fairbank, John A., Kulka, Richard A. (Aug 2002). Psychological reactions to terrorist attacks: Findings from the National Study of Americans' Reactions to September 11. *JAMA: Journal of the American Medical Association,* Vol 288(5), pp. 581-588. Journal URL: http://jama.ama-assn.org/

Schonfeld, David J. (Aug 2002). Almost one year later: Looking back and looking ahead. *Journal of Developmental & Behavioral Pediatrics,* Vol 23(4), pp. 292-294. Journal URL: http://www.jrnldbp.com/

Schreiber, M.D. (February 1999). School-based disaster mental health services in the Laguna Beach firestorm. Paper presented at the 1999 Rocky Mountain Region Disaster Mental Health Conference, Laramie, WY Feb 11-14, 1999.

Schulman, Michael D. & Armstrong, Paula S. (Aug 1989). The farm crisis: An analysis of social psychological distress among North Carolina farm operators. *American Journal of Community Psychology,* Vol 17(4), pp. 423-441.

Schulman, Michael D. & Armstrong, Paula S. (Sep 1990). Perceived stress, social support and survival: North Carolina farm operators and the farm crisis. *Journal of Sociology & Social Welfare,* Vol 17(3), pp. 3-22.

Schuster, Mark A., Stein, Bradley D., Jaycox, Lisa H., Collins, Rebecca L., Marshall, Grant N., Elliott, Marc N., Zhou, Annie J., Kanouse, David E., Morrison, Janina L., Berry, Sandra H. (Nov 2001). A national survey of stress reactions after the September 11, 2001, terrorist attacks. *New England Journal of Medicine,* Vol 345(20), pp. 1507-1512.

Seebold, Andrew (Sum 2003). Responding To A Murder/Suicide At A Rural Junior High School. *International Journal of Emergency Mental Health,* Vol 5(3), pp. 153-159 .

Shalif, Yishai, Leibler, Moshe (Oct 2002). Working with people experiencing terrorist attacks in Israel: A narrative perspective. *Journal of Systemic Therapies,* Vol 21(3), Special Issue: *Reflections in the aftermath of September 11.* pp. 60-70. Journal URL:
http://www.guilford.com/cartscript.cgi?page=periodicals/jnst.htm&cart_id=5472 16.21319

Shapiro, F. and Forrest, M. S. (2004). *EMDR: The breakthrough therapy for overcoming anxiety, stress, and trauma.* New York, NY, US: Basic Books xxv, 311 pp.

Shelly, Maynard W; Hoyle, Lawrence; Whitacre, Tamara (Aug 1981). The dynamics of learning with ILIA. *Psychological Reports.* Vol 49(1), pp. 91-102.

Shen, Yih-Jiun (2002). Short-term group play therapy with Chinese earthquake victims: Effects on anxiety, depression and adjustment. *International Journal of Play Therapy Vol 11(1), pp. 43-64.*

Simons, J. S.; Gaher, R. M.; Jacobs, G. A.; Meyer, D.; Johnson-Jimenez, E. (2005). Associations Between Alcohol Use and PTSD Symptoms among American Red Cross Disaster Relief Workers Responding to the 9/11/2001 Attacks. *American Journal of Drug and Alcohol Abuse.* Vol 31(2) 285-304.

Singer, T. J. (Mar 1982). An introduction to disaster: Some considerations of a psychological nature. *Aviation, Space, & Environmental Medicine,* Vol 53(3), pp. 245-250.

Slochower, Harry (Fal 1982). The bomb and terrorism: Their linkage. *American Imago.* Vol 39(3), pp. 269-272.

Slovak, Karen & Singer, Mark (Aug 2001). Gun violence exposure and trauma among rural youth. *Violence & Victims,* Vol 16(4), *Special Issue: Developmental Perspectives on Violence and Victimization.* pp. 389-400.

Slovak, Karen (May 2002). Gun violence and children: Factors related to exposure and trauma. *Health & Social Work,* Vol 27(2), pp. 104-112.

Slovak, Karen Lynne (Mar 2000). The mental health consequences of violence exposure: An exploration of youth in a rural setting. *Dissertation Abstracts International Section A: Humanities & Social Sciences,* Vol 60(8-A), pp. 3138.

Slovak, Karen; Singer, Mark I. (Feb 2002). Children and violence: Findings and implications from a rural community. *Child & Adolescent Social Work Journal,* Vol 19(1), pp. 35-56.

Smith, G. A.; Thompson, J. D. & Shields, B. J. (Apr 1997). Evaluation of a model for improving emergency medical and trauma services for children in rural areas. *Annals of Emergency Medicine,* Vol 29(4), pp. 504-510.

Smith, Patrick, Perrin, Sean, Yule, William & Rabe-Hesketh, Sophia (Mar 2001). War exposure and maternal reactions in the psychological adjustment of children from Bosnia-Hercegovina. *Journal of Child Psychology & Psychiatry & Allied Disciplines,* Vol 42(3), pp. 395-404. Journal URL: http://uk.cambridge.org/journals/cpp/

Smith, Patrick, Perrin, Sean, Yule, William, Hacam, Berima & Stuvland, Rune (Apr 2002). War exposure among children from Bosnia-Hercegovina: Psychological adjustment in a community sample. *Journal of Traumatic Stress,* Vol 15(2), pp. 147-156. Journal URL: http://www.wkap.nl/journalhome.htm/0894-9867

Solomon, S.D. & Canino, G.J. (1990). Appropriateness of DSM-III-R criteria for posttraumatic stress disorder. Comprehensive Psychiatry, 31: 227-237.

Solomon, S.D.; Bravo, M.; Rubio-Stipec, M.; & Canino, G.J. (1993). The effect of family role on response to disaster. Journal of Traumatic Stress, 6: 255-269.

Solomon, S.D.; Bravo, M.; Rubio-Stipec, M.; & Canino, G.J. (1993). The effect of family role on response to disaster. Journal of Traumatic Stress, 6: 255-269.

Starcevic, Vladan, Kolar, Dusan, Latas, Milan, Bogojevic, Goran & Kelin, Katarina (2002). Panic disorder patients at the time of air strikes. *Depression & Anxiety*, Vol 16(4), pp. 152-156. Publisher URL: http://www.interscience.wiley.com

Stein, B. (1997). Community reactions to disaster: An emerging role for the school psychologist. School Psychology International, 18: 99-118.

Stein, B. (1997). Community reactions to disaster: An emerging role for the school psychologist. School Psychology International, 18: 99-118.

Stein, B., Comer, D., Gardner, W. & Kelleher, K. (Sep 1999). Prospective study of displaced children's symptoms in wartime Bosnia. *Social Psychiatry & Psychiatric Epidemiology*, Vol 34(9), pp. 464-469. Journal URL: http://link.springer.de/link/service/journals/00127/index.htm

Stein, Howard F. (Spr 1984). Sittin' tight and bustin' loose: Contradiction and conflict in midwestern masculinity and the psychohistory of America. *Journal of Psychohistory*, Vol 11(4), pp. 501-512.

Stevan E. (Ed); deVries, Marten W. (Ed); *Extreme stress and communities: Impact and intervention.* New York, NY, US: Kluwer Academic/Plenum Publishers. pp. 489-497.

Stevenson, Thomas B. (1997). Migration, family, and household in highland Yemen: The impact of socio-economic and political change and cultural ideals on domestic organization. *Journal of Comparative Family Studies*, Vol 28(2), pp. 14-53.

Strauss, Anselm; Corbin, Juliet (1994). Grounded theory methodology: An overview. In: Denzin, Norman K. (Ed); Lincoln, Yvonna S. (Ed). Handbook of qualitative research. Thousand Oaks, CA, US: Sage Publications, Inc. pp. 273-285.

Stroebe, M. S. (1992,1993). Coping with bereavement: A review of the grief work hypothesis. Omega: *Journal of Death and Dying*; 26: 19-42.

Stuber, Jennifer, Fairbrother, Gerry, Galea, Sandro, Pfefferbaum, Betty, Wilson-Genderson, Vlahov, David (Jul 2002). Determinants of counseling for children in Manhattan after the September 11 attacks. *Psychiatric Services*, Vol 53(7), pp. 815-822. Journal URL: http://psychservices.psychiatryonline.org/

Sue, D.W. (1977). Counseling the culturally different: A conceptual analysis. Personnel and Guidance Journal, 55, 422-425.

Sutton, John M. Jr. & Pearson, Richard (Apr 2002). The practice of school counseling in rural and small town schools. *Professional School Counseling*, Vol 5(4), pp. 266-276.

Swisher, Raymond R.; Elder, Glen H. Jr. & Lorenz, Frederick O. (Mar 1998). The long arm of the farm: How an occupation structures exposure and vulnerability to stressors across role domains. *Journal of Health & Social Behavior*, Vol 39(1), pp. 72-89.

Szapocznik, J., Scopetta, M.A., Arandale, M.A. & Kurtines, W. (1978). Cuban value structure: Treatment implications. Journal of Consulting and Clinical Psychology, 46: 961-970.

Taft, R. (1977). Coping with unfamiliar environments. in Warren, N. (Ed.), Studies of cross-cultural psychology. Vol. 1. London: Academic Press.

Tanaka-Matsumi, J. (1979). Cultural factors and social influence techniques in Nai-kan therapy: A Japanese self-observation method. *Psychotherapy: Theory, Research and Practice* 16, 385-390.

Tang, Sharon S. & Fox, Steven H. (Aug 2001).Traumatic experiences and the mental health of Senegalese refugees. *Journal of Nervous & Mental Disease*, Vol 189(8). pp. 507-512. Journal URL: http://www.jonmd.com/

Taplitz-Levy, Beth Dana (Jan 2002). Phoenix falling: The collapse of a collaborative research project. *Dissertation Abstracts International: Section B: The Sciences & Engineering*, Vol 63(6-B), pp. 3071.

Taylor, A.J.W. & Frazer, A.G. (1981). Psychological sequelae of Operation Overdue following the DC 10 aircrash in Antarctica. Wellington, NZ: Victoria University. Pp. 72.

Taylor, A.J.W. & Frazer, A.G. (1982). The stress of post-disaster body handling and victim identification work. Journal of Human Stress, 8, 4, 4-12.

Taylor, A.J.W. (1984). Socioticism: A new concept to encompass one of the ultimate tragedies. Recent Developments in World Seismology, 1, 18-24.

Taylor, A.J.W. (1987). A taxonomy of disasters and their victims. Journal of Psychosomatic Research, 31, 4, 535-544.

Taylor, A.J.W. (1989). Disasters and disaster stress. New York: AMS Press.

Taylor, A.J.W. (1990). A pattern of disasters and victims. Disasters: The Journal of Disaster Studies & Management, 14, 4, 291-300.

Taylor, A.J.W. (1991). Individual and group behavior in extreme situations and environments. In R. Gal & A.D. Mangelsdorf (Eds.). Handbook of military psychology. (pp. 491-505). New York: Wiley.

Taylor, A.J.W. (1992). Research questions arising from the 1989 student protest in Beijing. In J. Westerink (Ed). Critical incident stress management across the lifespan. Conference Proceedings. (pp. 159-159). P.O. Box 79, Turramurra, NSW, AUSTRALIA.

Taylor, A.J.W. (1998). Observations from a cyclone stress/trauma assignment in the Cook Islands. TRAUMATOLOGYe, 4:1, Article 3 http://www.fsu.edu/~trauma/art3v4i1.html Retrieved May 1, 1999.

Tehrani, N. &Westlake, R. (1994). Debriefing individuals affected by violence. CounselingPsychology Quarterly, 7, 251-259.

Thabet, Abdel Aziz Mousa; Abed, Yehia & Vostanis, Panos (May 2002). Emotional problems in Palestinian children living in a war zone: A cross-sectional study. *Lancet*, Vol 359(9320), pp. 1801-1804.

Thackrey, M. (1987). Therapeutics for aggression: Psychological/physical crisis intervention. New York: Human Sciences Press. the literature. Group, 17, 70-83.

Torrey, E.F. (1972). What western psychotherapists can learn from witchdoctors. American Journal of Orthopsychiatry 42, 69-76b.

Toubiana, Y.H. and Milgram, N.A. (1988). Crisis intervention in a school community disaster: Principles and Practices. Journal of Community Psychology 16: 228-240.

U.S. Department of Health and Human Services. (3959). *Mental health response to mass violence and terrorism.* DHHS Pub. No. SMA. 3959. Rockville, MD: Center for Mental Health Services, Substance Abuse and Mental Health Services Administration, 2004.

U.S. Department of Health and Human Services. *Developing cultural competence in disaster mental health programs: Guiding principles and recommendations.* DHHS Pub. No. SMA 3828. Rockville, MD: Center for Mental Health Services, Substance Abuse and Mental Health Services Administration, 2003.

Valkenburg, Patti M., Cantor, Joanne & Peeters, Allerd L. (Feb 2000). Fright reactions to television: A child survey. *Communication Research*, Vol 27(1), pp. 82-97.

Van Hook, Mary P. (May 1987). Harvest of despair: Using the ABCX model for farm families in crisis. *Social Casework*, Vol 68(5), pp. 273-278.

Van Hook, Mary P. (Win 1990). The Iowa farm crisis: Perceptions, interpretations, and family patterns. *New Directions for Child Development*, No 46, pp. 71-86.

Van Ommeren M, Sharma B, Prasain D, Poudyal BN. *Helping torture survivors in Nepal: a public mental health perspective.* In: de Jong JTVM, ed. Trauma and War: A Public Mental Health Approach. New York, NY: Plenum Publishing Corp. In press."

Van Ommeren, Mark, de Jong, Joop T. V. M., Sharma, Bhogendra, Komproe, Ivan, Thapa, Suraj B., Cardena, Etzel (Jul 2001). "Psychiatric disorders among tortured Bhutanese refugees in Nepal": Erratum. *Archives of General Psychiatry*, Vol 58(7). pp. 707. Journal URL: http://archpsyc.ama-assn.org/

Vernberg, E. M. (2002). *Intervention approaches following disasters.* In: *Helping children cope with disasters and terrorism.* La Greca, A. M. and Silverman, W. K. Washington, DC, US: American Psychological Association, pp. 55-72.

Vila, G., Bertrand, C., Friedman, S., Porche, L. -M., Mouren-Simeoni, M. -C. (Nov 2000). Trauma par exposition indirecte, implication objective et subjective. Translated Title: Trauma by indirect exposure, objective and subjective implication. *Annales Medico-Psychologiques*, Vol 158(9), pp. 677-686. Journal URL: http://www.elsevier.com/inca/publications/store/6/2/2/2/8/8/

Vizek-Vidovic, Vlasta, Kuterovac-Jagodic, Gordana & Arambasic, Lidija (Dec 2000). Posttraumatic symptomatology in children exposed to war. *Scandinavian Journal of* Volume 5, No. 1, http://www.fsu.edu/~trauma/art1v5i1.htm Retrieved 2/1/99.

Volkman, V. (2006). *Critical incident stress management and traumatic incident reduction: a synergistic approach.* Ann Arbor, MI: Loving Healing Press.

Volkman, V. (2006). *Traumatic incident reduction: research and results, 2nd Ed..* Ann Arbor, MI: Loving Healing Press.

Wagenfeld, Morton O. (Win 1988). Rural mental health and community psychology in the post community mental health era: An overview and introduction to the special issue. *Journal of Rural Community Psychology*, Vol 9(2), *Special Issue: Mental health and the crisis of rural America.* pp. 5-12.

Walker, James L. & Walker, Lilly J. (Jan 1988). Self-reported stress symptoms in farmers. *Journal of Clinical Psychology*, Vol 44(1), pp. 10-16.

Wallace, Julia; O'Hara, Michael W. (Aug 1992). Increases in depressive symptomatology in the rural elderly: Results from a cross-sectional and longitudinal study. *Journal of Abnormal Psychology*, Vol 101(3), pp. 398-404.

Wardlaw, Grant (Jul 1983). Psychology and the resolution of terrorist incidents *Australian Psychologist.* Vol 18(2), pp. 179-190.

Webb, Nancy Boyd (2002). September 11, 2001. In Webb, Nancy Boyd (Ed) *Helping bereaved children: A handbook for practitioners* (2nd ed.). New York, NY, US: Guilford Press. pp. 365-384.

Webster, Jeffrey D. (1995). Adult age differences in reminiscence functions. In: Haight, Barbara K. (Ed); Webster, Jeffrey Dean (Ed). *The art and science of reminiscing: Theory, research, methods, and applications.* Philadelphia, PA, US: Taylor & Francis. pp. 89-102.

Webster, Jeffrey D. (Sep 1993). Construction and validation of the Reminiscence Functions Scale. *Journals of Gerontology*, Vol 48(5), pp. P256-P262.

Webster, Jeffrey Dean (Spr 1997). Attachment style and well-being in elderly adults: A preliminary investigation. *Canadian Journal on Aging*, Vol 16(1), pp. 101-111.

Webster, Jeffrey Dean (Spr 1999). World views and narrative gerontology: Situating reminiscence behavior within a lifespan perspective. *Journal of Aging Studies*, Vol 13(1). *Special Issue: Narrative gerontology.* pp. 29-42.

Webster, Jeffrey Dean; McCall, Mary E. (Jan 1999). Reminiscence functions across adulthood: A replication and extension. *Journal of Adult Development*, Vol 6(1). *Special Issue: Aging and autobiographical memory.* pp. 73-85.

Weidman, H. (1975). Concepts as strategies for change. *Psychiatric Annals*, 5, 312-314.

Weimann, Gabriel (Win 1983). The theater of terror: Effects of press coverage *Journal of Communication.* Vol 33(1), pp. 38-45.

Weiner, Tim (May 12, 1995). U.S. Lists Threats of Terrorism, Mainly from Iran. New York Times p. 3.

Wendt, Sarah & Cheers, Brian (Jun 2002). Impacts of rural culture on domestic violence. *Rural Social Work*, Vol 7(1), pp. 22-32.

Wendt, Sarah; Taylor, Judy & Kennedy, Marie (Dec 2002). Rural domestic violence: Moving towards feminist poststructural understandings. *Rural Social Work*, Vol 7(2), pp. 26-30.

Wessely, S., Rose, S. & Bisson, J. (1998). A systematic review of brief psychological interventions (debriefing) for the treatment of immediate trauma related symptoms and the prevention of posttraumatic stress disorder (Cochrane Review). In The Cochrane Library, Issue 2. Oxford Software, 1998. Updated quarterly.

Weyer, Sharon M.; Hustey, Victoria R. & Rathbun, Lesley (Apr 2003). A look into the Amish culture: What should we learn? *Journal of Transcultural Nursing*, Vol 14(2), pp. 139-145.

Whitsel, Bradley Christian (Mar 1999). Escape to the mountains: A case study of the Church Universal and Triumphant. *Dissertation Abstracts International Section A: Humanities & Social Sciences*, Vol 59(9-A), pp. 3634.

Wilkinson, Paul (1977). Terrorism and the liberal state. Halsted, New York, N.Y.

Williams, Christopher (Jul 2002). 'New security' risks and public educating: The significance of recent evolutionary brain science. *Journal of Risk Research*, Vol 5(3), pp. 225-248. Publisher URL: http://www.tandf.co.uk

Willson, E. A. (1928). Education and occupation of farm reared children. *Quarterly Journal of the University of North Dakota*, 18, pp. 361-373.

Wittkower, E.D. & Warnes, H. (1974). Cultural aspects of psychotherapy. American Journal of Psychotherapy, 28, 566-573.

Witty, Cathie J. (Oct 2002). The therapeutic potential of narrative therapy in conflict transformation. *Journal of Systemic Therapies*, Vol 21(3), *Special Issue: Reflections in the aftermath of September 11*. pp. 48-59. Journal URL: http://www.guilford.com/cartscript.cgi?page=periodicals/jnst.htm&cart_id =547216.21319

Woilman, D. (1993). *Critical Incident Stress Debriefing and crisis groups: A review of World Disaster Report 1998*. (1998). Oxford University Press: International Federation of Red Cross & Red Crescent Societies.

World Health Organization. (2003*). Mental health in emergencies*. Geneva: Author.

Wrenn, G.C (1962). The culturally encapsulated counselor. *Harvard Educational Review*, 32, 444-449.

Wright, Fred; Wright, Phyllis (Sum 1982). Violent groups. *Group*. Vol 6(2), pp. 25-34.

Wright, Robin (1986). *Sacred Rage*. New York: Simon & Schuster.

Wright, Robin (Summer 1992). Islam, Democracy, and the West. *Foreign Affairs*, p. 143).

Young, B.H., Ford, J.D., Ruzek, J.I., Friedman, M.J. & Gusman, F.D. (1999). Disaster mental health services - A guidebook for clinicians and administrators. Department of Social Work - Walter Reed Army Medical Center and the National Center for Post Traumatic Stress Disorder. http://www.wramc.amedd.army.mil/departments/socialwork/provider/DMHS.ht m Retrieved March 26, 1999.

Yule, William (1994). Posttraumatic stress disorder. Ollendick, Thomas H. (Ed); In King, Neville J. (Ed); et-al. International handbook of phobic and anxiety disorders in children and adolescents. Issues in clinical child psychology. (pp. 223-240). New York, NY, USA: Plenum Press. xiii, 496 pp.

Zafrir, Ada (1982). Community therapeutic intervention in treatment of civilian victims after a major terrorist attack. *Series in Clinical & Community Psychology: Stress & Anxiety*. Vol 8, pp. 303-315.

Zarowsky, Christina (Sep 2000). Trauma stories: Violence, emotion and politics in Somali Ethiopia. *Transcultural Psychiatry*, Vol 37(3), pp. 383-402.

Zimmerman, Toni Schindler (Apr 1994). Family ranching and farming: A consensus management model to improve family functioning and decrease work stress. *Family Relations: Interdisciplinary Journal of Applied Family Studies* Vol 43(2), pp. 125-131.

Zuckerman-Bareli, Chaya (1982). The effect of border tension on the adjustment of kibbutzim and moshavim on the northern border of Israel: A path analysis. *Series in Clinical & Community Psychology: Stress & Anxiety*. Vol 8, pp. 81-91.

Websites

Websites with information and links about disaster mental health, trauma, PTSD, and debriefing

Australasian Journal of Disaster and Trauma Studies
Provides online articles, book reviews, links to other sites. Published by the Department of Psychology, Massey University in Palmerston North, New Zealand. It is a peer-reviewed electronic journal which collates and distributes original material on disaster and trauma studies within Australia, New Zealand and the Pacific Rim. Provides a forum for publication of original research, reviews and commentaries which will consolidate and expand the theoretical and professional basis of the area.
http://www.massey.ac.nz/~trauma

The Cochrane Library: an electronic publication designed to supply high quality evidence to inform people providing and receiving care, and those responsible for research, teaching, funding and administration at all levels. It is published quarterly on CD-ROM and the Internet, and is distributed on a subscription basis. The Abstracts of Cochrane Reviews are available without charge and can be searched.
http://www.cochrane.co.uk

Debriefing References
http://www.geocities.com/eureka/3297/debrief.html

Disaster Mental Health Institute at the University of South Dakota.
http://www.usd.edu/dmhi

Disaster Mental Health Services - A Guidebook for Clinicians and Administrators: Produced by the Department of Social Work - Walter Reed Army Medical Center and the National Center for Post Traumatic Stress Disorder.
http://www.wramc.amedd.army.mil/departments/socialwork/provider/DMHS.htm

Gulf War Syndrome: annotated links to reports, history, medical and psychological information, research, resources and help information about the Gulf War and Gulf War Syndrome. It is presented in five sections: Introduction; Official Response; Medical Research; Conspiracy Theories; and Resources.

http://www.angelfire.com/biz/odoc/gulf.html

Health Canada's Emergency Services Division's Disaster Mental Health Manual

http://www.hc-sc.gc.ca/msb/emergency/index_e.htm

International Critical Incident Stress Foundation, Inc. (ICISF) is a non-profit, open membership foundation dedicated to the prevention and mitigation of disabling stress through the provision of: Education, training and support services for all Emergency Services professions; continuing education and training in Emergency Mental Health Services for Psychologists, Psychiatrists, Social Workers, and Licensed Professional Counselors; and consultation in the establishment of Crisis and Disaster Response Programs for varied organizations and communities worldwide.

http://www.icisf.org

Knowledge Exchange Network: Mental Health Also look on this site for information and publications available for free. You can order books and videos directly online through this site. Disaster Relief and Crisis Counseling Publications through Knowledge Exchange Network (CMHS).

http://www.mentalhealth.org

National Center for PTSD (NCPTSD): Research and Education on Post-traumatic Stress Disorder. The NCPTSD is a program of the U.S. Department of Veterans Affairs and carries out a broad range of activities in research, training, and public information.

http://www.ncptsd.org

State of Missouri Disaster Services Home Page - Links to information about services, calendar, publications, and Red Cross Disaster Mental Health Services Training.

http://modmh.state.mo.us/homeinfo/progs/disaster.html

O'Dochartaigh Bookstore: PTSD, Stress Management, Traumatology, Gulf War aftermath, Hurricane books for children, and Disaster Mental Health shelves. Emphasis on Children and Families, Workers and Victims too.

http://www.angelfire.com/biz/odochartaigh/books.html

Personal Services: Psychosocial Planning for Disasters.
http://www.phac-aspc.gc.ca/emergency-urgence/pdf/pers_e.pdf

PILOTS Database: Interdisciplinary index to the worldwide literature on PTSD and traumatic stress.
http://www.dartmouth.edu/dms/ptsd/PILOTS.html

Puppeteering For Mental Health - A Guidebook available to help state officials and mental health administrators establish a disaster recovery program for individuals, families and communities. Links to other sites and further related information.
http://modmh.state.mo.us/homeinfo/progs/disaster/publ.html

Rocky Mountain Region Disaster Mental Health Conference: Abstracts and summary of the proceedings of the February, 1999 conference held in Laramie, WY. Links to further information and other sources included.
http://www.angelfire.com/biz/odochartaigh/conference.html
Also available in Spanish at:
http://www.angelfire.com/biz3/odocspan/conferencia.html

"Traumatology" Journal
Volume 5, Issues Number 2 and 3 are Special Issues devoted to Disaster Mental Health articles and studies many of which were presented at the 1999 Rocky Mountain Region Disaster Mental Health Conference held in Laramie, WY.
http://www.fsu.edu/~trauma

White Death - Blizzard of '77
http://www.whitedeath.com

Disaster Scenario

1. Friday morning, 11:20 am. You are contacted about a school bus which has rolled off a cliff on I-80 east of Buford, WY and landed upside down, trapping all passengers inside. Passengers are 50 teenagers and two adults. What actions do you take?

2. You are on duty at the hospital when the call comes about the bus accident. The bus was headed toward Laramie, WY (a small mountain town, pop. 30,000). The call comes in that you will be receiving casualties and a disaster alert is sent throughout the hospital. Develop a disaster plan of action for physicians, nurses, and mental health teams.

3. Casualties begin arriving and only then do you realize how serious the accident has been. The teenagers are members of the school choir at Central Nebraska High School (approx. 6 hour drive). They had been heading for a weekend with their counterparts in Laramie. Their trip terminated about 15 miles short of its destination, with 28 people dead and 24 critically injured.

   Only 8 of the injured victims come to the hospital in Laramie. Others were sent to hospitals in Cheyenne (about 45 minutes away). The staff is well prepared to handle the situation, and supplies and equipment are ready. The immediate physical needs of the victims are met as expertly as possible. How are you going to deal with the families and friends who begin arriving looking for their loved ones? Consider the following problems:

   - Someone will have to identify the accident victims. None of them are able to speak and not everyone has identification on their person.

   - Where do families go to obtain information about the condition of family members, since victims were distributed to three hospitals and a morgue? Who will inform the parents of their child's condition? Who will help the family begin to make plans for the immediate future?

- There is a need for shelter and food for the families if they stay overnight.

- Emotional support for family members is needed. Someone will have to be with the family when they are told of the condition of their child, for it will be a time of extreme anxiety and grief.

- Acute crisis intervention is needed to manage shock and grief reactions.

Since all persons involved are either dead or in critical condition, none of the families will be receiving "good news". It is anticipated that 50 to 100 family members will be arriving in Laramie shortly and they will be asking, "How is my child?" "Where is my child?"

4. You receive word that families are being directed to a central disaster area located in Laramie where all information regarding the whereabouts and condition of their children is being centralized. Two Disaster Mental Health Professionals have gone to the disaster center to evaluate what arrangements have been made and what assistance the rest of our mental health personnel can provide. Several nurses from the county health department, clergymen, and many Red Cross workers have volunteered to assist families at the center. However, more manpower is needed so that each family member can have, if at all possible, at least one mental health professional to meet and stay with them throughout the ordeal, or at least until each family is settled for the night. What actions do you take to accomplish this?

5. When the families arrive at the disaster center, they register at the door giving their name, address, phone number, religious preference, name of their child, and whether they will require housing for the night. At this point, a mental health professional and/or clergyman introduces him/herself and remains with them.

The family is told by the deputy coroner if their child is dead or in the hospital. If the child is alive, the family is sent on to the appropriate hospital. Mental health professionals escort such families to the hospital where another mental health team is waiting to provide help.

Those families whose child—in one case children—is/are dead have to go through the painful process of answering questions, making funeral arrangements, and, in some instances, viewing the body and gathering their child's personal belongings. How do you help families get through this process?

6. The feelings of pain and grief are intense at the center. Local families offer their homes to the stricken families for the night, and bring homemade food for them and the volunteers. Telephones are installed to enable families to call relatives and friends.

Amidst the physical activity in the disaster center, the grief work for the families begins. Families arrive after driving 200 miles to the disaster center hoping that their child is alive, but with a gnawing fear that their child is one of the 28 dead. They answer questions, their body postures tense, eyes red from crying, and then they usually whisper "Is she…, is he…dead? And the answer is, all too often, "Your son…, your daughter is dead." Then the shock and pain.

Most people cry, holding each other as the anguish and realization goes deeper into their being. A few cry out in grief and begin to run until embraced and held tightly by their spouse or a friend or worker.

The mental health team works with the families, encouraging them to cry, to express the depth of their pain. Places are found for family members to sit together so that they can share their grief and support and lean on each other. Mental health professionals hold and touch grievers, which helps them. This simple gesture frees the family members who usually play a supportive role to cry and find comfort for themselves.

You listen to families talk of their dead children over and over again. They keep repeating comments such as "I just saw her this morning?" "We were saving our money to go skiing together." :"She was so good; she went to church every week." :He was going to be a lawyer." "I'll never see her again." How do you respond? How do you deal with this for yourself? How do you help your fellow workers deal with this?

7. In the midst of their shock and distress, the families have to answer questions for the coroner's office and make preliminary funeral arrangements. How do you help the families answer questions and guide them through various activities?

8. Families ask "Did he suffer?" "Is her face smashed?" It is important to answer these questions when they arise. Some parents may not be ready to deal with issues such as funeral arrangements and viewing the body. How do you intervene to assist the family with this?

9. Although the bodies have already been identified by the choir director, the families are asked if they want to view their child's body. Some

families are reluctant to do so, being afraid that the body is marred. Some say that they want to remember their child as he/she was last seen. When this happens, how do you respond? How do you assess the situation?

10. One family refuses to see their daughter's body. One mental health professional then tells the family that she is worried that they would later wonder if their child was really dead. The family agrees that this could happen. What do you as a mental health professional do next?

11. You assess the grief reactions of the families for potential complications. In some families there may be a single family member who shows little emotion. The danger for such a person is a delayed or repressed grief reaction which might later express itself through psychosomatic disease or depression. What do you do to help stimulate discussion by these families in order to encourage an accompanying emotional response?

12. You are concerned about those people who do not express grief directly, but spend time and energy helping others. A possibility is that these people are doing for others what they want done for themselves, and by focusing on others, they are not experiencing their own grief. What are some of the dangers in this reaction? How do you handle this with them?

13. Another reaction which concerns you is an extreme and profound expression of guilt. "I killed her—if I hadn't been gone, she would be alive! She wouldn't have been in the choir if I hadn't left. I killed her—it's all my fault." How would you intervene to deal with this?

14. Follow-up is provided for those families who appear to be at high risk in terms of having difficulty beginning grief work. How do you accomplish this?

15. Because of the tragic nature of the accident and the intensity of emotion involved, the staff at the disaster center has to deal with their own reactions as well. These reactions parallel those of the families, although they may be less intense. At times, staff had tears streaming down their faces as they comforted family members. Staff began comforting one another with a hand on a shoulder or an embrace. Most talk of feeling numb and describe feeling like a sponge that soaked up the pain and grief of others until a saturation was reached. How do you debrief the staff and help them deal with their feelings?

16. For the next couple of days, several staff members experience dreams and vivid visual images of the day's experiences. The staff are aware of feelings of inadequacy and helplessness. They find themselves thinking of their own children and loved ones. No one remains untouched. What follow-up do you provide for staff? How do you deal with your own personal reactions and feelings?

17. What do you do to respond to ongoing concerns over the ensuing months and even years following this tragedy? What about anniversaries?

Appendix **B**	# Disaster Victims' # Needs Assessment	

Personal Information

_____

Name Last / First / MI   Date of Birth

_____

Address   Sex

Living Situation

___Single ___Couple ___Family ___Other ___Dependent Children
___Other Dependents

Evacuation

How long did the evacuation last? _____

_____

Relocation? ___Yes ___No

If yes, where? _____

Losses

Did you lose persons or things which were important to you?___Yes ___No

If yes, who or what were they? _____

_____

_____

Natural Support Network	Yes	No
Have you received support from your family, friends, and people in your group?		
Was this support sufficient?		
Was this support helpful?		
Are you still receiving support?		
If so, is this support sufficient?		
If so, is this support helpful?		
Did this incident create difficulties?		
...in your daily life? If so, what are they?		
...in your relationships (couple, family...)? If so, what are they?		
...in regard to your children's behavior? If so, what are they?		
...in regard to your work? If so, what are they?		
...In regard to financial matters? If so, what are they?		
...on the social level? If so, what are they?		

Reactions Caused By the Incident

Do you have reactions that you did not have before the incident and which are persisting? If so, has there been an increase or a decrease in these symptoms during the last two weeks?

Reactions Caused By the Incident	Yes	No	Increase	Decrease
More nervous				
More worried				
More irritable				
More impatient				
More withdrawn				
Difficulty sleeping				
Nightmares				
Loss or increase in appetite				
Headaches				
Difficulty concentrating				
Increased alcohol consumption				
Other reactions If so, what are they?				

Do you have someone with whom it is easy for you to talk? ___Yes ___No

State of Health

1. How has your health been since the incident?

___Good ___Average ___Has deteriorated

2. Were you obliged to go to see a doctor?   ___Yes ___No

3. How is the health of your spouse and children?

___Good ___Average ___Has deteriorated

4. Did they have to visit a doctor?   ___Yes ___No

Degree of Intensity of the Effect on the Person

If we were to describe the moment you were emotionally affected by the incident as the number 10 on a scale of 0 to 10, what number would you apply to your state today? _____

Activities Offered By The Red Cross And Others	Yes	No
Have you participated in the activities offered by the Red Cross or by the community following the incident?		
Have these activities helped you? How? ___To experience the incident better ___To understand ___To manage the stress better ___Other (Please specify) _____ _____		
If you are still having difficulties, would you be interested in receiving assistance? If so, what type of assistance? ___Private interview ___Small group with professionals ___Other (Please specify) _____ _____		

What type of activities would you like us to organize?

___Incident Debriefing Session ___Conference on the cause of the disaster

___Relaxation Session ___Community Activity ___Other Suggestions:

_____

_____

_____

Crisis Intervention in Disasters: Training For Workers an Introduction

15 Contact Hours

In order to complete the course and receive your certificate indicating successful completion, you must do the following:

• Take the test. Multiple choice answers (Part 1) should be written on the Answer Sheet (p. 269). For questions requiring an essay response (Part 2), please use separate sheets of paper and be sure to indicate the number of each question you are answering.

• Send a copy of your test answers with your check or money-order for the course fee (US$95.00) to:

> Rocky Mountain Region
> Disaster Mental Health Institute
> P.O. Box 786
> Laramie, WY 82073-0786

Check or Money Order must be made out to: RMRDMHI

Upon receipt of your course fee and your completed answer sheet, the test will be graded. You must attain a score of at least 75% in order for a certificate to be issued. The certificate will indicate the number of Contact Hours for the course and any CEU approvals from other organizations that have approved the course for continuing education.

PART 1: Multiple Choice
Please use the Answer Sheet on p. 269 to record your answers

1. A Critical Incident is defined as
   a) The reactions that occur during or immediately after the actual incident or stressor.
   b) An on-scene opportunity for workers involved in a stressful incident to vent their feelings, and institute coping strategies which can reduce stress while they are still working in the assignment setting.
   c) Any situation faced by emergency responders or survivors that causes them to experience unusually strong emotional reactions which have the potential to interfere with their ability to function, either on the scene or later.
   d) A crisis situation that involves people in crisis who need medical attention due to injuries incurred.

2. Debriefing can be defined as
   a) Focusing on providing immediate emotional support at times when a person's own resources appear to have failed to adequately cope with a problem.
   b) An organized approach to supporting disaster workers who have been involved in emergency operations under conditions of extreme stress in order to assist in mitigating long-term emotional trauma. Usually done at the end of an assignment as part of exiting procedure to assist the worker in putting closure on the experience.
   c) An on-scene opportunity for workers involved in a stressful incident to vent their feelings, and institute coping strategies which can reduce stress while they are still working in the assignment setting.
   d) A chance for all involved to assess the job they have done and delineate the strengths and weaknesses of their approach with recommendations for improvement in performance.

3. In the aftermath of a disaster and loss of loved ones, friends, property, pets, etc. what stages of grieving do most people go through and, generally, in what order?
   a) Bargaining, Anger, Denial, Depression, Acceptance
   b) Denial, Anger, Bargaining, Depression, Return to Equilibrium

    c) Denial, Anger, Bargaining, Depression, Acceptance

    d) Denial, Depression, Equilibrium, Acceptance, Rebuilding

4. Individuals and communities usually go through a number of stages due to disaster. What are the stages of disaster?

    a) Heroic, Honeymoon, Disillusionment, Reconstruction

    b) Heroic, Honeymoon, Disillusionment, Return to Equilibrium

    c) Impact, Honeymoon, Reconstruction, Return to Equilibrium

    d) Impact, Honeymoon, Disillusionment, Reconstruction

5. During the Heroic Stage,

    a) There is a strong sense of having shared a catastrophe experience and lived through it.

    b) Lasts from 1 week to 3-6 months after the disaster.

    c) Victims clear out debris and wreckage.

    d) People use energy to save their own and others' lives and property.

6. Which of the following is/are symptoms of psychological trauma that could result from exposure to a disaster or critical incident?

    a) exaggerated startle response or hyper-vigilance

    b) difficulty with memory

    c) phobia about weather conditions

    d) all of the above

7. What is BASIC ID?

    a) Simple Freudian explanation of disaster personalities.

    b) An acronym for studying the basic responses of the Id to disasters.

    c) An acronym useful for assessing multi-modal behavior in stressful situations.

    d) An approach to behavior that is relatively simple and basic.

8. Which of the following somatic reactions in victims may be associated with disasters and critical incidents?

    a) sleep disturbances

    b) trouble breathing or "getting breath"

    c) fatigue or generalized weakness

d) all of the above

9. Three levels of anxiety in pre-school children following a disaster were discussed. They are

    a) Contagious Anxiety; Intense Anxiety; Profound Anxiety

    b) Contagious Anxiety; Subjective Anxiety; Profound Anxiety

    c) Contagious Anxiety; True or Objective Anxiety; Profound Anxiety

    d) Relative Anxiety; Stranger Anxiety; Phobic Anxiety

10. Children may react to a disaster with which following behaviors?

    a) regressive behaviors such as bedwetting, thumb sucking, clinging

    b) not wanting to attend school or athletic or social events

    c) increased playfulness with new friends

    d) both a and b

11. What is one of the most common problems for children following a disaster?

    a) difficulties getting along with school friends

    b) sleep disturbances

    c) problems with obedience

    d) finding out what really happened

12. Some possible school activities for children to help them adjust following a disaster might include:

    a) field trips to disaster sites; use of puppets to re-enact disasters; coloring books about the disaster

    b) mandatory counseling sessions; teacher talks; religious explanation of why the disaster happened

    c) school rap groups; school newsletters; chat rooms on the internet

    d) both a and c

13. Magical thinking is more prevalent in children than in adults. Very young children may believe that wishing for, or thinking about something can make it happen. For example, children may believe that fighting with a sibling can cause a parent's death and that ceasing to fight will prevent the other parent from dying. How do you handle this?

a) Give them reassurance that the parent's death was not their fault, that it was caused by an accident or illness.

b) Let them know that the dead parent wants them to stop fighting.

c) Encourage the children to fight it out in order to get the anger out of their system while making sure they do not hurt each other.

d) Tell the child that he/she will have to see a counselor if they continue fighting.

14. What children will require more intensive attention in a disaster situation?

a) Unruly ones who have a history of acting out to gain attention.

b) Exceptional children who have developmental disabilities or physical limitations and those who have been injured or became ill due to the disaster.

c) Those who are not being supervised properly by their parents and/or teachers.

d) Younger children who have not been socialized enough to be able to understand the seriousness of their situation.

15. Studies have shown that the difficulties experienced by adolescents after a disaster are boredom and loneliness resulting from isolation from peers due to disturbance of their activities and rehousing of their families.

a) False

b) True

16. What are some of the feelings and behavior symptoms experienced by many older adults following a disaster?

a) depression, withdrawal, apathy, agitation, anger, irritability, suspicion, confusion, disorientation, memory loss, increased somatic complaints

b) clinging behaviors, increased anger, spousal abuse, attention-seeking, lack of understanding

c) depression, withdrawal, clinging, increased abuse, attention seeking, long-term memory loss

d) Suspicion, confrontational behaviors, increased abuse, decreased somatic complaints, depression, anxiety

17. What are some other groups to consider when working with disaster victims?

a) Socioeconomic classes, political groups, religious groups

b) Socioeconomic classes, cultural and racial differences, institutionalized persons, people in emotional crises, people requiring medical care, relief workers and first responders, cultural and ethnic minorities

c) cultural groups, political groups, first responders, medically indigent, peers

d) First responders, cultural and ethnic minorities, institutionalized persons, politicians, religious groups, labor unions, sports teams

18. What are some of the cognitive signs of Acute Stress?
   a) Mental slowness, inability to make decisions, loss of objectivity in evaluating own functioning, loss of ability to conceptualize thoughts and prioritize tasks

   b) Mental slowness, inability to make decisions, decreased computational skills, hyperactivity, excessive fatigue, headaches

   c) Mental slowness, irritability, headaches, chest pain, anxiety, decreased memory and attention span

   d) Mental slowness, confusion, inability to express self verbally or in writing, isolation

19. A disaster worker is exhibiting excessive fatigue, irritability, anxiety, impatience and similar behaviors. This worker is likely showing beginning symptoms of
   a) fatigue

   b) burn-out

   c) over-extension

   d) disaster worker syndrome

20. When is the ideal time for a debriefing?
   a) 12 weeks after the traumatic event

   b) a few weeks following the traumatic event

   c) 24-72 hours following the traumatic event

   d) within 24 hours of the traumatic event

21. What is the objective of a debriefing?
   e) a rational way of dealing with stress reactions

    f) to help individuals understand their emotional reactions and behaviors

    g) to encourage the return to dynamic equilibrium

    h) both b and c

22. Crisis intervention
    a) Refers to the reactions that occur during or immediately after the actual incident, disaster or stressor.

    b) Focuses on providing immediate emotional support (psychological first aid) at times when a person's own resources appear to have failed to adequately cope with a problem.

    c) Is any situation faced by emergency responders or survivors that causes them to experience unusually strong emotional reactions which have the potential to interfere with their ability to function, either on the scene or later.

    d) Is an on-scene opportunity for responders involved in a stressful incident to vent their feelings, and institute coping strategies which can reduce stress while they are still working in the assignment setting.

23. Crisis Intervention Teams are important resources in responding to disasters and critical incidents. In order to fully understand the necessity for them and their functions, it is important
    a) to understand that grief is the process of working through all the thoughts, memories and emotions associated with that loss.

    b) to develop an awareness of the relationship between the event and the sensations of stress experienced by victims and workers.

    c) to understand that all survivors of a disaster suffer loss.

    d) to have a basic understanding of the psychological factors which influence the emotional responses of disaster victims and responders.

24. The strengths or weaknesses of certain factors may be directly related to the initiation or resolution of a crisis. Such factors can help promote a Return to Equilibrium. These include:
    a) The situational reports which are available; levels of grief experienced; presence or absence of stress.

b) Perception of the event by the individual; presence of severe stress; internal changes that occur.

c) Perception of the event by the individual; the situational reports which are available; mechanisms of adaptation.

d) Mechanisms of adaptation; levels of stress experienced; how the event will affect one's future.

25. Why do some people reach a state of crisis while others do not?
a) Internal changes occur.

b) They are more prone to stress.

c) They are not as well informed.

d) Events are larger.

26. In which stage of disaster recovery do people demonstrate a strong sense of having shared a catastrophe experience and lived through it?
a) Heroic

b) Reconstruction

c) Honeymoon

d) Disillusionment

27. The disaster stage in which victims come to the realization that the rebuilding of homes and businesses is primarily their responsibility is
a) Disillusionment stage

b) Reconstruction stage

c) Honeymoon stage

d) Realization stage

28. Symptoms of disaster caused stress vary greatly based on one's prior history of personal trauma, age and ethnic background. A typical symptom experienced by both victims and responders is
a) They may experience phobias about weather conditions (e.g., responses to wind noises following a tornado or hurricane) or other reminders that the accident or situation could happen again.

b) Concern over the increased costs of goods and services following an event.

c) Anger at the lack of response by the federal government.

d) Difficulty deciding where to spend their vacation this year.

29. A basic principle in working with children who have experienced a disaster is relating to them as essentially normal children who have experienced a great deal of stress. Relief from stress and the passage of time will help re-establish equilibrium and functioning for most children without outside help.

    a) True

    b) False

30. Sleep disturbances are very common for children following a disaster. Associated behaviors are likely to take the form of

    a) Resistance to bedtime

    b) Unwillingness to sleep in their own rooms or beds

    c) Refusal to sleep by themselves

    d) all of the above

31. Following a disaster, when children (ages 6-12) show excessive clinging and unwillingness to let their parents out of their sight,

    a) They need to be disciplined in order to effectively eliminate such inappropriate behaviors.

    b) The parents should sneak away in order for the child to learn that they are ok without their presence.

    c) They are actually expressing and handling their fears and anxieties of separation or loss most appropriately.

    d) They need to be referred to a psychiatrist for medication.

32. In dealing with children's fears and anxieties following a disaster or critical incident,

    a) They should be confronted with the real information and told that they need to behave better.

    b) It is generally best to accept them as being very real to the children.

    c) They should be referred to a psychiatrist for anti-anxiety medication.

    d) Routine rules need to be enforced to re-direct their concerns.

33. When a mother or father dies, most children are fearful of what will happen to them if the remaining parent dies as well. Explanations dealing

with heaven and hell, or afterlife, or the flat statement that after death there is nothing are reassuring to a child.

    a) True

    b) False

34. Following a disaster or critical incident, confusion among teens generally refers to

    a) Possible suicidal ideation.

    b) Inability to perform tasks or complete school assignments.

    c) A disorientation in which the teen has lost the ability to sort out incoming stimuli, whether sensory or cognitive.

    d) Display of feelings inappropriate for the situation.

35. A basic principle in working with problems children encounter following disasters or critical incidents is

    a) That they are essentially normal children who have experienced great stress.

    b) That they are not strong enough to handle events due to disabilities they may have.

    c) To encourage them to work things out on their own.

    d) To evaluate the need for medication to control behavior.

36. The following is an example of a group technique with children following a disaster

    a) Ask all the children what happened to them and their families in the disaster.

    b) Provide the children with paper, plastic materials, clay, or paints, and ask them to depict the disaster. The less verbal children will find this helpful.

    c) Ask member of the group to take turns being helpers. The children are paired and then take turns, first asking for help with a problem and then acting as helpers with the others' problems.

    d) All of the above

Course Test: Multiple Choice Answer Sheet (Part 1)

Name:_____ Date_____

Address:_____

_____

_____

1.	19.
2.	20.
3.	21.
4.	22.
5.	23.
6.	24.
7.	25.
8.	26.
9.	27.
10.	28.
11.	29.
12.	30..
13.	31.
14.	32.
15.	33.
16.	34.
17.	35.
18.	36.

Course Test: Scenario (Part 2)

To complete this section, respond to each question below and return your comments with the test above. Please number each item as you answer it. Refer to the Disaster Scenario in Appendix A to address these items.

1. What actions do you initially take?

2. Develop a disaster plan of action for physicians, nurses, and mental health teams.

3. How are you going to deal with the families and friends who begin arriving looking for their loved ones?

4. More manpower is needed so that each family member can have, if at all possible, at least one mental health professional to meet and stay with them throughout the ordeal, or at least until each family is settled for the night. What actions do you take to accomplish this?

5. Those families whose child (in one case, multiple children) is/are dead have to go through the painful process of answering questions, making funeral arrangements, and, in some instances, viewing the body and gathering their child's personal belongings. How do you help families get through this process?

6. You listen to families' talk of their dead children over and over again. They keep repeating comments such as "I just saw her this morning?" "We were saving our money to go skiing together." "She was so good; she went to church every week." "He was going to be a lawyer." "I'll never see her again." How do you respond? How do you deal with this for yourself? How do you help your fellow workers deal with this?

7. In the midst of their shock and distress, the families have to answer questions for the coroner's office and make preliminary funeral arrangements. How do you help the families answer questions and guide them through various activities?

8. Families ask "Did he suffer?" "Is her face smashed?" It is important to answer these questions when they arise. Some parents may not be ready to deal with issues such as funeral arrangements and viewing the body. How do you intervene to assist the family with this?

9. One family refuses to see their daughter's body. One mental health professional then tells the family that she is worried that they would later wonder if their child was really dead. The family agrees that this could happen. What do you as a mental health professional do next?

10. You assess the grief reactions of the families for potential complications. In some families, there may be a single family member who shows little emotion. The danger for such a person is a delayed or repressed grief reaction which might later express itself through psychosomatic disease or depression. What do you do to help stimulate discussion by these families in order to encourage an accompanying emotional response?

11. You are concerned about those people who do not express grief directly, but spend time and energy helping others. A possibility is that these people are doing for others what they want done for themselves, and by focusing on others, they are not experiencing their own grief. What are some of the dangers in this reaction? How do you handle this with them?

12. Another reaction which concerns you is an extreme and profound expression of guilt. "I killed her—if I hadn't been gone, she would be alive! She wouldn't have been in the choir if I hadn't left. I killed her—it's all my fault." How would you intervene to deal with this?

13. Follow-up is provided for those families who appear to be at high risk in terms of having difficulty beginning grief work. How do you accomplish this?

14. Because of the tragic nature of the accident and the intensity of emotion involved, the staff at the disaster center has to deal with their own reactions as well. These reactions parallel those of the families, although they may be less intense. At times, staff had tears streaming down their faces as they comforted family members. Staff began comforting one another with a hand on a shoulder or an embrace. Most talk of feeling numb and describe feeling like a sponge that soaked up the pain and grief of others until a saturation was reached. How do you debrief the staff and help them deal with their feelings?

15. For the next couple of days, several staff members experience dreams and vivid visual images of the day's experiences. The staff are aware of feelings of inadequacy and helplessness. They find themselves thinking of their own children and loved ones. No one remains untouched. What follow-up do you provide for staff? How do you deal with your own personal reactions and feelings?

16. What do you do to respond to ongoing concerns over the ensuing months and even years following this tragedy? What about anniversaries?

* * * * * * * * * * * * * * * * *

About the Author

George Doherty has held positions as counselor/therapist, Masters Level psychologist, consultant, educator, disaster mental health specialist and is a former U.S. Air Force Officer. President of O`Dochartaigh Associates since 1985. President & CEO: Rocky Mountain Region Disaster Mental Health Institute.

Past Adjunct instructor - University of Wyoming. Psychologist for Rural Clinics Community Counseling Center (State of Nevada) Ely, NV, Adjunct Instructor Northern Nevada Community College. Current Adjunct Faculty member Warren National University; Certified Instructor - International Critical Incident Stress Foundation (ICISF); Wyoming Peace Officers Standards and Training (POST) Certified Instructor.

Associate Member - American Psychological Association; Member: American Counseling Association, American Academy of Experts in Traumatic Stress, Association of Traumatic Stress Specialists, Traumatic Incident Reduction Association (TIRA). Life Member - Air Force Association, Life Member - Military Officers Association of America, Life Member - Penn State Alumni Association;

Alumni Admissions Volunteer - The Pennsylvania State University. Served as USAF Officer (Connally Navigator). Eleven years with Civil Air Patrol (an Air Force Auxiliary) as Squadron Commander, Deputy Wing Commander, Air Operations Officer & Master Observer. Level II Member - International Critical Incident Stress Foundation; Research Advisor & Research Fellow American Biographical Institute; Book Reviewer & Editorial Advisory Board Member - PsychCritiques (APA Journal). Member: Albany County Suicide Prevention Task Force; Member: Wyoming Department of Health Emergency Preparedness Advisory Committee. ICISF Certificate of Specialized Training in the field of Mass Disaster and Terrorism.

Publications include: "Responders to September 11, 2001: Counseling: Innovative Responses to 9/11 Firefighters, Families, and Communities"; "Understanding Oslo in Troubled Times" (2006) - A Review of "The Oslo Syndrome: Delusions of a People Under Siege"; "Stress Management, Wellness, and Organizational Health" (2006) - A Review of "Research Companion to Organizational Health Psychology"; "The Environmental Crisis, Globalization, and the Changing Culture" (2005) - A Review of "Rethinking Freire: Globalization and the Environmental Crisis"; "Mental Health and the New Technologies" (2005) - A Review of "The Mental Health Professional and the New Technologies: A Handbook for Practice Today"; "Leadership Competency and Conflict" (2007)- A Review of "Becoming a conflict competent leader: How you and your organization can manage conflict effectively for us"; "Leadership: Lessons from the Ancient World" (2007) - A Review of "Leadership lessons from the ancient world: How learning from the past can win you the future";. "Crisis Intervention Training for Disaster Workers," online course for continuing education through PsychCeu, "The Trauma of Cultural Diversity", 2003; "A Review of: American Hazardscapes", Population and Environmental Psychology Bulletin, (Winter) 2003; "A Review of: Problems and Issues of Diversity in the United States," Population and Environmental Psychology Bulletin, 2001; "Cross-Cultural Counseling in Disaster Settings," Australasian Journal of Disaster and Trauma Studies, 1999; "Towards the Next Millennium: Disaster Mental Health-Learning from the Past and Planning for the Future," Traumatology-e, 1999. Edited publications include: "Proceedings of the 5th Rocky Mountain Region Disaster Mental Health Conference" (2007); "Conference Proceedings: Disaster Mental Health Conference: Estes Park, CO" (2005); Special Issues of Traumatology-e on "Disaster Mental Health" (1999); Special Issue of Traumatology-e on "Crisis in Rural America" (2004).

Index